ANDERSONS' SUPERSONIC CENTURIES

The Retrofuture Worlds of Gerry and Sylvia Anderson

ANDERSONS' SUPERSONIC CENTURIES

The Retrofuture Worlds of Gerry and Sylvia Anderson

FRED McNAMARA

First published in the UK in 2022 by
Telos Publishing Ltd
www.telos.co.uk

Telos Publishing Ltd values feedback. Please e-mail us with any comments you may have about this book to: feedback@telos.co.uk

ISBN: 978-1-84583-197-4

Andersons' Supersonic Centuries © 2022 Fred McNamara

The moral right of the author has been asserted.

British Library Cataloguing in Publication Data.
A catalogue record for this book is available from the British Library.

This book is sold subject to the condition that it shall not by way of trade or otherwise, be lent, resold, hired out or otherwise circulated without the publisher's prior written consent in any form of binding or cover other than that in which it is published and without a similar condition including this condition being imposed on the subsequent purchaser.

CONTENTS

Foreword by Ayshea Brough	7
Introduction: Stand By For Critical Analysis	9
Series Guide: Supersonic Productions	12
Main Mission: 21st Century Ideologies	**19**
Cold Underwater War: How *Stingray* Transformed Supermarionation	21
Days of Disaster: The Necessary Destruction of *Thunderbirds*	27
The Posthuman Heart of *Captain Scarlet*	35
Cold War Games: The Perverse Innocence of *Joe 90*	39
Journey to the Far Side of Spy-Fi: *Doppelgänger*'s Espionage Soul	45
A Question of Survival: Paranoia's Meaning in *UFO*	52
The Bringers of Fear: The Horror of *Space: 1999*'s Year 1 and Year 2	57
Power, Family & Authority in Century 21	62
Tracys, Ladies and Manservants: Gender and Class Structure in *Thunderbirds*	69
Marine Morals: *Stingray*'s Aquatic Antagonists	75
Stumble in the Darkness: Isolation and Alienation in Century 21's Live-action Worlds	78
Straker's Office: 21st Century Episodes	**87**
Fireball XL5: 'The Granatoid Tanks'	89
Stingray: 'Subterranean Sea'	94
Joe 90: 'See You Down There'	99
UFO: 'A Question of Priorities'	104
Space: 1999: 'The Troubled Spirit'	109
Terrahawks: 'The Ultimate Menace'	114
New Captain Scarlet: 'Dominion'	119
Thunderbirds Are Go: 'The Long Reach'	124
Brains' Lab: *Thunderbirds*' Definitive Episodes	**131**
5: 'Sun Probe'	133
4: 'Terror in New York City'	139
3: '30 Minutes After Noon'	146
2: 'The Cham-Cham'	151
1: 'Atlantic Inferno'	156

CONTENTS

The Amber Room: *Captain Scarlet*'s Characters	**161**
'Fate Will Make Him Indestructible': Captain Scarlet	163
'Initiative Should Never Clash With Discipline': The Spectrum Men	169
'Launch All Angels': The Angels	177
'You Know What You Must Do': Captain Black	181
'Beyond the Comprehension of Man': The Mysterons	187
Marineville Control Tower: 21st Century Structures	**195**
Stand By for Stardust: *Stingray*'s Blossoming from *Fireball XL5*	197
Failure To Launch: Why the *Thunderbirds* Movies Misunderstood Their Audiences	205
Life As We Don't Know It: *Zero-X* on the Small Screen	214
Spectrum is Canon: Continuity in *Captain Scarlet*	222
Supersonic Fantasies: Celebrating the Mecha of Supermarionation	228
Ironmongery vs. Agony: When Was *UFO* At Its Best?	232
The Unsolvable Mystery of *The Investigator*	238
Cubed Humour: Tracking *Terrahawks'* Comedic Evolution	243
Instruments of Destruction: How *New Captain Scarlet* Evolved its Characters	250
Recreating the Future: How *Thunderbirds: The Anniversary Episodes* Collides Past, Present and Future	256
Nebula-75's 33 Million-Mile Adventure	262
Atomic Tomorrows: The Blast Off, Crash-land & Relaunch of Supermarionation	266
Publishing History	278
About the Author	279

FOREWORD

Back in 1969, I had just started a singing career and had released some records, with a big break in 1968 when I got the job as presenter of the TV show *Discotheque*. However, I wanted to continue with acting which I had done as a child in the sixties.

My role in *UFO* came about because Sylvia Anderson had seen a photograph of me in the newspapers, and asked the casting director Rose Tobias Shaw to call me in as she liked the look of me. It transpired that she was looking for tall, Amazonian women, and the photograph in the newspaper had me pictured with a statue. Unbeknown to Sylvia, it was a very small statue and I was only five foot three tall! However, when I arrived for the audition, they liked me, and offered me the role of Lt Johnson, SHADO Operative!

I was booked for one episode. But Sylvia came down to the set while I was filming and told me that they wanted to keep me on for the whole series, which was just wonderful!

UFO was an incredible opportunity, and I relished working with such amazing actors as Ed Bishop, George Sewell and Wanda Ventham (who is Benedict Cumberbath's mother). It was very fortuitous that I had just started *Lift Off* on ITV, and Gerry and Sylvia brought me in as that show literally took off – they had taken a chance with me, as a virtual unknown, but ended with me in their show at the same time as *Lift Off* became successful!

George Sewell was the comedian on the show! He made us laugh so much. The night before my wedding to Christopher, the crew thought it would be funny to hand me a call sheet and tell me that I had to be on set at seven the next morning – when I had already asked permission not to work for a couple of days as I was getting married! They were all in on the joke and insisted that I had to be there, and left me not knowing what I was supposed to do as, of course, I was under contract to work on the show. They let me panic for about an hour and then took pity on me and told me it was a joke! On the same day, Ed, in the middle of a scene, did a big dip and kissed me on the lips in front of everyone! I thought Commander Straker had gone insane! Being a professional, I just carried on and delivered my lines as if nothing had happened, much to the amusement of the entire crew.

Sylvia and Gerry Anderson were a truly memorable creative couple. I was lucky to have been chosen by Sylvia to appear in the show. And the

FOREWORD

care Sylvia took personally over my hair, makeup and costume were above and beyond. They both took me under their wing and made sure that I was looked after. Gerry was kind and instructive to a young girl at the beginning of her career. They took such care of me, as though I was one of the stars, and I was privileged to have worked with these creative giants.

Gerry and Sylvia worked so hard on all their shows, creating inventive ideas and scenarios and making sure that all the details were right, and in this book, Fred McNamara looks at all their work, and tries to unpick all the information and themes which made their programmes so compelling.

I was honoured, privileged and so happy to have been a part of it.

Ayshea Brough

STAND BY FOR CRITICAL ANALYSIS

Are the television works of Gerry and Sylvia Anderson among the greatest in science fiction entertainment? Quite possibly, but there's no guarantee of a definitive answer that can be deemed to be 'correct' for such a loaded, subjective question. However, a question with a more resoundingly affirmative answer to ask would be the following: are the television works of Gerry and Sylvia Anderson the most *exciting* in science fiction entertainment?

The symphonic build-up of Steve Zodiac and Venus boarding *Fireball XL5* before it's catapulted into space; Commander Shore alerting viewers before an eruption at sea engulfs the TV screen; the magnificent countdown of the five Thunderbird craft; the electrifying horror of a vast ascending and descending orchestral surge before a mystery assassin attempts to murder Captain Scarlet in a darkened alleyway – these and more are all opening moments that captured generations of audiences across the globe. Many have never let go of that excitement.

I am one of those people. From being casually entertained by *Stingray* from an age so early I can't quite recall how or when exactly the series entered my life, my world was shocked from black and white into videocolor when *Thunderbirds* and *Captain Scarlet and the Mysterons* received their regenerative viewings on BBC Two throughout the early 2000s. From there, my eyes were opened even wider to the vast breadth of Gerry and Sylvia's output, along with Gerry's further works after he and Sylvia ended their professional and personal relationship, as well as works that continue to be made born out of the Andersons' original visions. From Supermarionation to live-action, Supermacromation, Hypermarionation and Ultramarionation, we're getting our marionette hands dirty with this book.

I'm enthralled by Gerry and Sylvia's works across puppets, live-action and animation to such an extent that you're now reading a book that attempts to capture these shows in a similar manner to the way in which these productions captured me. It is not arrogant or misjudged to say that this is the first ever essay anthology devoted to critically exploring Gerry and Sylvia Anderson's output of television and film productions. Nevertheless, the arrogance prevails somewhat when reading that last sentence back. Has there really never been another book that unboxes the Andersons' work to such a degree as *Andersons' Supersonic Centuries* does?

STAND BY FOR CRITICAL ANALYSIS

In the world of cult television literature, books like these are ten for a penny. *Doctor Who*, *Blake's 7*, *The Prisoner* and *The Avengers* prove to be infinite mines full of analytical treasures that writers have an insatiable desire to unearth. By comparison, books covering Gerry and Sylvia's works barely exist. Where my previous book, *Spectrum Is Indestructible*, tasked itself with capturing (enveloping, even) as much *Captain Scarlet and the Mysterons* media as possible into a celebratory retrospective of the franchise, *Andersons' Supersonic Centuries* looks further afield.

This isn't a book that focuses squarely on the Supermarionation era of the 1960s, or the live action era of the 1970s, or what came after. We're targeting everything. Nearly all of Gerry and Sylvia's science fiction works are accounted for here. This book, quite purposefully and gleefully, tramples over plenty of terrain. I subject the widely divisive *Terrahawks* to the same critical style as *Space: 1999*. The primitive attitude of *Fireball XL5* is probed to the same degree as the more sophisticated *Captain Scarlet and the Mysterons*. Throughout **Main Mission: 21st Century Ideologies**, themes of class, gender, horror, paranoia, comedy, isolation, the Cold War and more are all vigorously applied to Gerry and Sylvia's worlds. I apply these concepts in a broad sense to many of Gerry and Sylvia's series and, throughout **Straker's Office: 21st Century Episodes**, individual episodes from various shows. We follow a similar path in **Brains' Lab: *Thunderbirds*' Definitive Episodes**, in which I target five of International Rescue's most noteworthy missions.

We also dive deep into the ensemble characters of *Captain Scarlet*, unboxing the mechanics of a series whose approach to characterisation continues to split opinion. This section of the book, **The Amber Room: *Captain Scarlet*'s Characters**, features original interviews that I conducted with those who worked on *Captain Scarlet* itself. Special effects model maker Alan Shubrook, model maker and designer Mike Trim, scriptwriter Shane Rimmer and writer/director Leo Eaton all lend their experiences in shaping this book's perspective into how *Captain Scarlet* portrayed its decidedly posthuman characters. Things become more speculative in the final section of the book, **Marineville Control Tower: 21st Century Structures**, as we examine how a *Zero-X* TV series may have developed, how exactly *Stingray* evolved out of the ashes of *Fireball XL5* and why the two 1960s *Thunderbirds* movies totally misunderstood their target demographic, amongst other avenues of exploration. From exaggerated sci-fi adventures to downbeat espionage thrillers, Gerry and Sylvia's worlds contain an atomic variety of thematic ingredients that enables each and every production to stand apart from the rest. If nothing else, I envision *Andersons' Supersonic Centuries* as celebrating that far-reaching diversity across their work.

Fashioning the book in this way is rooted in the experiences that I've gained from writing about Gerry and Sylvia's work over the last eight years for a variety of print and digital publications. An essay anthology targeted at dissecting their television series and films had been on my creative bucket list for some time, it was just a case of working out how best to structure it. The idea eventually came to me that a book collating together my favourite articles that I've written, brought together into a single volume, would be the best way forward. Eventually, this concept blossomed into relying less on previously published pieces and me producing more original essays for this venture. The end result is a book that boasts a much more unified tone, with much of the essays originating from the same frame of mind.

I've been told that I have a conversational style of writing, which I feel summarises this book quite succinctly, because I do consider this book to be a conversation. Both *Spectrum Is Indestructible* and *Andersons' Supersonic Centuries* are united by their playfulness, their subjectivity, their investigative nature in exploring what makes these TV series and films tick. The majority of books that are about Gerry and Sylvia's works tend to lean towards being objective series guides and official production histories. Compared to those books, *Andersons' Supersonic Centuries* is far more interpretive and transformative. It doesn't passively repeat previously known historical information about these productions. It grapples with them to, hopefully, offer a new perspective on their functionality. Akin to how conversation flows indeterminately, I like to think that *Andersons' Supersonic Centuries* can perhaps encourage different perspectives being cast on Gerry and Sylvia's work, that the sheer volume of material to their name is matched by a diverse array of subtext that can be shaped into intriguing, enlightening and accessible criticism. This kind of discourse appears to be so barren for Anderson subjects, the implication therefore being that the likes of *Thunderbirds*, *Captain Scarlet* and *Stingray* aren't worthy of being critically discussed to the same level as *The Prisoner* or *Doctor Who*. If I may be allowed one lofty ambition for *Andersons' Supersonic Centuries*, it's that this is the book that puts those attitudes to bed.

Writing this book has aided in reminded me of my atomic-powered passion for these productions. Their wide-eyed sense of adventure kept me immensely entertained as a child and now their deeper meanings and ideas continue to prove thoroughly fascinating to pore over, to celebrate in an investigative manner and, ultimately, to present to you in a book that I sincerely hope does these productions justice.

Let's blast off then into Gerry and Sylvia's supersonic centuries.

Fred McNamara
December 2021

SERIES GUIDE: SUPERSONIC PRODUCTIONS

Supercar
(Original TX: January 1961 – April 1962, 39 episodes)

Stationed at Black Rock Laboratory, test pilot Mike Mercury, Doctor Horatio Beaker, Professor Popkiss, their young accomplice Jimmy and Mitch the Monkey fly into adventure in the marvel of the age – Supercar, an experimental machine that can venture into the skies, on land, under the sea and beyond. The multi-function nature of Supercar enables the series to accumulate an eclectic array of adventures, even if the vaguely defined nature of the premise doesn't hold up to scrutiny. Whilst *Supercar* undoubtedly pales in comparison to what would come before, all the strongest aspects of *Stingray*, *Thunderbirds*, *Captain Scarlet and the Mysterons* and more find their roots here.

Fireball XL5
(October 1962 – October 1963, 39 episodes)

Colonel Steve Zodiac pilots the fantastic *Fireball XL5*, patrolling Sector 25 of outer space as part of the World Space Patrol's mission in keeping the peace for humanity and aliens alike. Accompanied by Doctor Venus, Professor Matthew Matic, Venus' pet Lazoon Zoonie and the mechanically minded Robert the Robot, the crew of *Fireball XL5* regularly encounter strange cosmic characters when defending deep space. *Fireball XL5* isn't the strongest of the Supermarionation era and may be juvenile in many of its elements, but it's also prime analogue space-punk that captured many young minds during the Space Race.

Stingray
(Original TX: October 1964 – June 1965, 39 episodes)

In the mid-2060s, the world's oceans are safeguarded by the World Aquanaut Security Patrol, spearheaded by the fantastic submarine *Stingray* and its crew: Captain Troy Tempest, navigator Phones and Marina, the girl from the sea. The primary antagonist of WASP is the villainous undersea dictator Titan, who wages an aquatic Cold War against the Terranians. However, the *Stingray* crew also encounter a myriad of other undersea races, some evil, some friendly, along with extraordinary oceanic anomalies beyond imagination. *Stingray* was the first Supermarionation series to be filmed in colour, and its focus on visually dazzling spectacle combined with warm and witty characterisation and storytelling make it a highlight of Gerry and Sylvia's filmography.

Thunderbirds
(Original TX: September 1965 – December 1966, 32 episodes)

The technologically-advanced world of 2065 is prone to disaster on an enormous scale and only one organisation can regularly be relied upon to save the day – International Rescue. *Thunderbirds* tells the adventures of the heroic Tracy family's worldwide rescue service in diving into the danger zone armed with their incredible Thunderbird machines. From the farthest reaches of space to the darkest depths of the world's oceans, no mission is too small for International Rescue. Undoubtedly Gerry and Sylvia's best-known work, *Thunderbirds* champions selfless heroism against a backdrop of imaginative, disaster-driven adventure, coupled with an emphasis on visually breath-taking science fiction machinery.

Thunderbirds Are Go
(Released: December 1966, feature film)

The gargantuan spacecraft *Zero-X* is leading the first manned mission to Mars, but its maiden flight is beset by catastrophic interference from International Rescue's nemesis, The Hood. International Rescue is called upon to provide security for the craft following its rebuild and second attempt. Whilst the take-off is a success, despite another attempt of sabotage from the Hood, Alan Tracy must prove himself to his family when *Zero-X*'s eventual return from Mars is thrown into chaos. The first of two cinematic adventures for International Rescue, *Thunderbirds Are Go*'s lack of quality control over its muddled story and characterisation results in the dependably wondrous special effects of Supermarionation forced to do the heavy lifting.

Captain Scarlet and the Mysterons
(Original TX: September 1967 – May 1968, 32 episodes)

In the year 2068, worldwide global security outfit Spectrum battles a galactic Cold War against the Mysterons, invisible aliens armed with the power of retrometabolism. This war of nerves is the accidental result of one of Spectrum's own men – Captain Black, who becomes the Mysterons' primary Earth-based agent. Also captured by the Mysterons is Captain Scarlet, who eventually succeeds in breaking free of the aliens' murderous control, but retains their indestructible qualities, becoming Spectrum's top agent in the fight against the Mysterons. *Captain Scarlet and the Mysterons* took Supermarionation into significantly darker territory, with violence and death featured more prominently than before, a primary theme of the stupidity of war and a greater emphasis on serialised storytelling.

Thunderbird 6
(Released: July 1968, feature film)

Various members of International Rescue take to the skies aboard Brains' latest invention for its maiden voyage – the luxury airship *Skyship One*. However, the villainous Black Phantom lays a cunning trap for Lady Penelope and her cohorts that results in catastrophe for everyone on board. None of International Rescue's major craft can perform the inevitable rescue, prompting an unusual expansion of the Thunderbird fleet to save the day. Edge-of-your-seat adventure is swapped out for an oddly low-key spy-fi caper that places Lady Penelope and Brains as the film's central characters. However, this unusual approach to which characters get the most screentime can't mask the distinct impressions that Century 21 Productions was already running low on ideas to prolong *Thunderbirds*.

Joe 90
(Original TX: September 1968 – April 1969, 30 episodes)

Professor McClaine invents a miraculous invention that can transfer brain patterns from one person to another. The Brain Impulse Galvanoscope Record and Transfer (BIG RAT) becomes utilised by McClaine's friend, Sam Loover, who works for the World Intelligence Network in their mission to maintain world peace. McClaine's adopted son, Joe, becomes WIN's most special agent, regularly given the brain patterns of a variety of professions – astronauts, doctors, fighter pilots and more, and regularly battles against a rogues gallery of international criminals. *Joe 90* returned to the smaller casts of earlier Supermarionation series and curiously succeeds in maintaining the bloodthirstiness of *Captain Scarlet*, but injecting it with a much warmer, character-driven dynamic.

The Secret Service
(Original TX: September – December 1969, 13 episodes)

Father Stanley Unwin hides a secretive nature beneath his clergyman collar. He is in fact an agent for British Intelligence Service Headquarters Operation Priest (BISHOP). Aided by faithful sidekick and vicarage gardener Matthew Harding, the pair are regularly assigned top secret missions in saving the world. To aid him in his missions, Father Unwin isn't armed with a multi-function spacecraft. Instead, he's verbally equipped with a form of gibberish to confound his enemies to novel effect. *The Secret Service* lasted only a mere 13 episodes. Some may say even that was too much. This eccentric twilight outing for Supermarionation is a far cry from the glory days of Century 21 but remains weirdly charming for its unconventional yet modest nature.

Doppelgänger
(aka *Journey to the Far Side of the Sun*, Released August 1969, feature film)

A joint mission between NASA and fellow space agency EUROSEC reveals the existence of a tenth planet in our solar system. Colonel Glenn Ross and Doctor John Kane are tasked with discovering the mysterious new world, only to crash-land dazed and confused back on Earth after weeks in space. Gradually, Ross discovers the surreal truth that he has indeed reached the tenth planet, and that all is not as it seems. Gerry and Sylvia's sole foray into live-action sci-fi cinema treads the line between the meditative and the mundane. With *Doppelgänger*, Gerry and Sylvia chose to announce themselves to older audiences with this subdued, unsettling exploration of duality, rather than the videocolor vibrancy of classic Supermarionation.

UFO
(Original TX: September 1970 – March 1973, 26 episodes)

The first live-action television series produced by the Andersons and the final work from Century 21 Productions finds a balance between stylish sci-fi action and aching human drama. *UFO* focuses on the efforts of the Supreme Headquarters Alien Defence Organisation (SHADO) in combating a nameless but antagonistic race of aliens, desperate to harvest human beings for their organs to ensure the survival of their own race. Dominated by a majestic performance from Ed Bishop as Commander Ed Straker, *UFO* is cool, sexy, weird, downbeat, action-packed, serious and witty – sometimes in the space of a single episode.

The Investigator
(Produced 1973, released 2015, pilot episode)

Siblings John and Julie are shrunk to miniature and marionette form to aid the cosmic being known only as the Investigator. In their first mission for the Investigator, John and Julie must prevent the theft of a priceless work of art, making use of their unique stature to foil the efforts of businessman Karanti. This surreal venture, doomed to failure based on its head-scratching premise and turmoil endured during its production, has never enjoyed a broadcast screening, but remains viewable through its release on DVD. Approach with caution.

Space: 1999
(Original TX: September 1975 – November 1977, 48 episodes)

The 311 inhabitants of Moonbase Alpha are accidentally catapulted across the stars when a nuclear explosion propels the moon out of orbit from the Earth and into the unknown depths of the universe. Led by Commander John Koenig, *Space: 1999* sees its characters endure mind-bending cosmic phenomena, often unexplainable, in an intellectual blend of action, sci-fi, drama and horror. The most ambitious sci-fi production Gerry and Sylvia produced together, *Space: 1999*'s marriage of bizarre yet mature cosmic adventure and philosophical musings on humanity's place in the universe make for compelling viewing. Then the second series happened.

Terrahawks
(Original TX: October 1983 – July 1986, 39 episodes)

The villainous alien android Zelda arrives in our galaxy from Alpha Centauri. Claiming Mars as her base of operations, she wages war against the Earth and its primary defence force – the Terrahawks. Led by Doctor 'Tiger' Ninestein, one of nine clones, the Terrahawks valiantly defend the Earth against Zelda and her unpredictable army of monsters. After nearly a decade away from our television screens, Gerry Anderson returned with a series that greatly emphasises humour and catering to a younger audience than his live-action work, causing it to endure a divisive reception amongst Anderson fans. *Terrahawks* nonetheless catapulted Gerry back into mainstream focus, and remains an energetic fusion of adventure, science fiction, comedy and horror.

New Captain Scarlet
(Original TX: February – November 2005, 26 episodes)

New Captain Scarlet updates the war of nerves into an entirely 21st century style. The premise remains much the same, but every conceivable detail has become fiercely modernised, resulting in a lost classic amongst Gerry's back catalogue that's well worth exploring. The paranoia-infused action remains intact, but there's a greater focus on the relationships and personalities of the characters. The CGI hasn't aged gracefully, but the strikingly modern aesthetic and consistent quality to its storylines and characters ensures that this final series made by Gerry before his passing was a high point to end his career on, albeit unintentionally.

Thunderbirds Are Go
(Original TX: April 2015 – February 2020)

In this remake of the original series, International Rescue are ever on hand to save those in disaster. However, in this reinterpretation, Jeff Tracy is missing, his fate undetermined after an attempt to stop the Hood from stealing *Zero-X* results in his apparent demise. The Tracy brothers must balance regularly responding to disasters on and off the Earth with slowly discovering the truth behind the fate of their father. With its eye-catching mixture of models and miniature sets with CGI characters, *Thunderbirds Are Go* succeeds in capturing the heroic spirit of the original series, even widening the imaginative reach of the original series by having a greater variety of rescue scenarios.

Nebula-75
(Original TX: April 2020 – present)

In the year 2120, Commander Ray Neptune and the civilian crew of the *Nebula-75* find themselves flung millions of miles from home and into the unchartered depths of space where they encounter everything from space scrap merchants to ghostly apparitions and upper-class confidence tricksters, all whilst trying to navigate their way back home. *Nebula-75* flies the flag in reviving the art form of Supermarionation. The series is produced by Century 21 Films and mostly utilises recycled Supermarionation props, sets and marionettes from past productions of theirs into a series that firmly plants itself in the spirit of *Supercar* and *Fireball XL5*.

MAIN MISSION:
21ST CENTURY IDEOLOGIES

COLD UNDERWATER WAR: HOW *STINGRAY* TRANSFORMED SUPERMARIONATION

To a child's eye, and perhaps even an adult one, one such everlasting appeal of Gerry and Sylvia Anderson's works is how nothing appears as it seems. Luxurious, tropical islands in the Pacific and bustling movie studios are, in fact, none of these things. They're elaborate façades, designed to trick the unsuspecting passer-by into believing that there's no way that atomic-powered rescue and complicated security organisations could possibly be housed behind these innocent architectural structures. In the worlds of Anderson, the secretive base of operations serves several functions – it houses a fantastic fleet of vehicles that can be launched in an instant, it's able to launch devastating missile attacks against invaders, but it's also characters' homes. A refuge from the dangers of the worlds they live to rescue, ironically surrounding themselves with the tools and means to perform such heroic efforts.

The enduring appeal of the incognito headquarters in Anderson shows can be traced back to 1964's *Stingray*, one of the most thematically colourful and visually robust creations they produced. Gerry found inspiration for *Stingray*'s aquatic setting by envisioning the undiscovered secrets the ocean may hold; 'I was always fascinated by trenches on the ocean that are as deep as mountains are high. There are features that man has never seen and pressures that are almost impossible to withstand. I began to wonder if there were any areas of the Earth which had been little explored and felt justified in writing some whacky stuff. I was drawn towards anything that involved exploration, the future or predictions.'[1] What Gerry is telling us then is that the hidden quality of under the oceans lends itself superbly well to the growing concept of the secretive headquarters, an area where *Stingray* has proved to be hugely imaginative in its execution.

Stingray began the trend of the hidden fortress in Anderson productions, for both the heroes and the antagonists. The lush, underwater landscapes seen throughout the series were fertile ground for imaginative locales of the aquatic civilisations the World Aquanaut Security Patrol often engaged with.

---

[1] Archer, S. Marcus, H. (2002) 'Stand By For Action' *What Made Thunderbirds Go! The Authorised Biography of Gerry Anderson*. p. 89. BBC Books. 2nd edition.

Beyond such visual stimulants however, which surely tapped into the minds of young viewers, such an aesthetic move also helps to establish *Stingray* as prime Cold War entertainment, full of transforming rock faces, electronic seaweed and mechanical fish. *Stingray*'s position as a fictional Cold War has been noted elsewhere, with Sarah Kurchak writing in 2016 for The AV Club website how 'a more classically Cold War-style villainous Other emerges in the pilot episode' when writing about Titan.[2]

By making these transformative headquarters a core part of the series, *Stingray* rewrote the rules on how Supermarionation could be an exciting thing to watch explode into action before your very eyes. The hidden base trope, with natural or inconspicuous locations hiding vast atomic-powered rescue machines may be most closely associated with Tracy Island from *Thunderbirds*, but it has its roots in the preceding *Stingray*, which gave viewers these more-than-meets-the-eye establishments in abundance. Evolving from past offerings, the metamorphic Marineville, Titanica and a host of lesser-seen, one-off alien bases were worlds away from the comparatively static Space City from *Fireball XL5* and Black Rock laboratory in *Supercar*. These secret bases are far more exposed than those seen in *Stingray*. Despite a clear evolution taking place between the drab, uninspired Black Rock lab and the towering, rotating, sword-like stature of Space City, *Stingray* fully embraces the secret base as a visual identity for the benefit of the series itself in its own right. The destruction of Space City near *Fireball XL5*'s end in the episode 'A Day in the Life of a Space General', albeit in a dream sequence, reads as a comment on demolishing the limited vision of the past and marching forward to new, more exciting approaches to making the heroes' base of operations as stimulating as possible.

Battle Stations

At the centre of *Stingray*'s sharp eye on the visual spectacle of the base of operations as a fresh source of Supermarionation enjoyment is Marineville, the nerve centre of the World Aquanaut Security Patrol. Elaborate in its expanse yet streamlined in its functionality, the larger budget *Stingray* was blessed with compared to past AP Films productions at that point allowed for grander permanent sets to be constructed, such as the Marineville base. Seen from multiple angles during its tenure and filmed in glorious Videocolor, Marineville is a far cry from the barren desert settings of Black Rock and Space City.

---

[2] Kurchak, S. (2016) 'Puppet state: The growing Cold War anxiety of Gerry Anderson's Supermarionation shows'. *The AV Club*. Available from - https://tv.avclub.com/puppet-state-the-growing-cold-war-anxiety-of-gerry-and-1798246195.

Marineville's most recognisable and celebrated feature is its capability to descend below ground in the event of an oncoming aerial or aquatic attack. On the command of 'battle stations', all of Marineville's various components roar into life. Marineville Control Tower, Marineville Power Plant and the accompanying living quarters adjacent to the Tower gradually lower into the bowels of the Earth, the headquarters' most ingenious function. As Marineville undergoes its battle station procedures, exterior lights bolted onto the core trio of buildings (the Control Tower and the two living quarters) flash in rapid pulsation whilst vehicles are seen cruising along the hollowed-out sub-level basements of Marineville, reflecting the constant busy state of electrified action each of these scenes communicates when in full flow, accompanied by Barry Gray's thundering soundtrack, the primal bongo drums of Marineville's alarm system blending effortlessly with Gray's music. It's worth noting that we almost always see Marineville descending, but rarely ascending back to the surface once the danger in question has subsided. After all, Marineville is always infinitely more exciting when there's a ballistic missile bearing down on the world's only substantial defence against the threat of Titan. The sight of Marineville rising triumphant after another attempted attack by Titan has been quelled would mean that the danger of that week's episode had been defeated, until the next time the bongo drums ring out.

Titanica, the grimy, harsh dictatorship of Titan, is less trans-dimensional than Marineville, yet exhibits its own distinct qualities. Titanica's rust-coloured buildings don't soar like Marineville Tower. They're stubby, jutting upwards, like unnatural growths erupting from the seabed. Titanica bears a suitably rugged, alien quality to the comparatively streamlined Marineville, distinguishing the hero and the villain's role in the series via their taste for aquatic architecture. Every aspect of Marineville is visibly well-defined, yet with Titanica, it's difficult to determine what forms part of Titanica and what isn't. Non-descript buildings blend into the seaweed-coated background, the only giveaway of Titanica's unnatural form is the travel tubes connecting numerous buildings together, with alien craft passing through the tube, like Aquaphibian blood circulating through the veins of Titan's empire. Titanica and Marineville are at opposite ends of the aesthetic spectrum, yet they command an arresting attention for the viewer in providing a sense of identity for the heroes and the villains, respectively. Another case of stock footage utilised quite often in the series places our perspective of Marineville Control Tower looking upward, as if in wonder at its stature, yet we never look up to Titanica. Quite the opposite in fact. We instead have to venture down into the murky, unknown waters where Titanica is based, unintentional symbolism perhaps of looking up to our heroes and looking down on our enemies.

Other permanent miniature sets help to reinforce *Stingray*'s renewed emphasis on the secretive headquarters. Surface Agent X20, the Mr Smithers to Titan's Mr Burns, operates from a house that would have James Bond salivating, then recoiling in disgust at the apparent lack of amenities to make a martini. A precursor to Lady Penelope's mansion and Professor McClaine's cottage, X20's home on the Island of Lemoy is a veritable paradise for the retro superspy. Seemingly dilapidated to all concerned, on X20's command, just about every table and chair swivels round to reveal advanced Aquaphibian technology, culminating in a huge chunk of wall rising to reveal a vast bank of permanently switched-on computers that bookend a video screen that enables instant communication with his master, Titan. The clash of this proto-digital technology, used to not only engage with Titan but monitor and track the activities of *Stingray* and Marineville, forced to exist behind such antiquated Terranean domestics, suggests that Titanica and its loyal forces hold a firm disdain for human life and its tastes in interior decoration. Titan will happily give X20 all the technological bells and whistles as a surface agent, but also ensures that X20 lives as he sees humanity – in decadent Terranean squalor. The clean mechanics of Marineville have no place here.

'Even deeper than the deepest ocean'

Whilst Marineville and Titanica dominate the screen whenever they appear, both literally in their size and thematically in their stature, a variety of smaller, guest secret bases sit comfortably alongside the two main headquarters. *Stingray* either battles or befriends the underwater civilisations it presents, but a shared aspect of the underwater bases is how fantastical their headquarters are. The detachment between the *Stingray* crew and the creatures they encounter is felt more so considering that even the friendlier races have more in common with Titanica than Marineville in how their respective headquarters are constructed. Throughout the series, nearly a third of *Stingray*'s 39 episodes feature a veritable feast of eccentrically fashioned undersea locales, hidden in plain sight. The opening episode (simply named '*Stingray*'), 'Plant of Doom', 'Sea of Oil', 'The Big Gun', 'The Ghost Ship', 'A Nut for Marineville', 'Tune of Danger', 'Treasure Down Below', 'Emergency Marineville', 'The Invaders', 'The Disappearing Ships', 'Deep Heat' and 'The Lighthouse Dwellers' burst with imaginative hideouts that shoot off into distinct subgroups that stretch beyond Titanica and enable *Stingray*'s distinctly aqua-punk mentality to shine. The conversion of natural underwater landscapes and man-made sea-faring technology to suit Aquaphibian life is a common feature scattered throughout these alien homes.

'Deep Heat' and 'Emergency Marineville' see their respective antagonistic aliens living within converted natural areas, one a volcano and the other an island. 'The Ghost Ship' and 'The Disappearing Ships' feature underwater aliens perverting ancient or damaged man-made galleons and freighters for their own usage. '*Stingray*', 'Plant of Doom' and 'Tune of Danger' include appearances from Pacifica, the peaceful civilisation where Marina originated from. Its primary feature is a towering, skyscraper-esque building in the shape of a gargantuan, upturned clam, speckled with lights that reflect different levels of accommodation. Underwater HQs modelled after nature reappear in Solarstar Base, the city of the Solarstar people from 'The Big Gun', a sprawling metropolis fashioned in the shape of a starfish. The remaining episodes portray their respective aquatic lifeforms making domestic use of imposing rock features. This varied approach imbues a vitality into *Stingray* – whilst some enemy locales may be similar, none are predictable. On first viewing of the series, there's no way of guessing what manner of creatures *Stingray* will face in any given episode, aided by their enjoyably quirky secret bases, which lends a kinetic energy to the series as a whole.

Stand By for Videcolor

A shared idea between the majority of these invisible headquarters, particularly Titanica and Marineville, is their location, or at least their capabilities, of being underground, hidden from each other as effectively as possible. Some blend into their surrounding seascapes, some repurpose outsider technology to suit their own demands, some convert their surrounding seascapes to accommodate their existences. All of them however operate under covert conditions, resulting in *Stingray* being not so much a Cold War, but an underwater Cold War.

As mentioned earlier, the transforming headquarters is more likely rooted in the increased visual excitement factor in making Supermarionation even more appealing to young audiences. Century 21 Productions were, after all, conscious of making each production more entertaining than the previous one. However, the ever-growing popularity of the spy-fi genre was spreading itself far and wide into children's and adult's TV, film, comics and novels alike. Spy-fi itself refashioned the grim, bitter realities of the Cold War into something visually vibrant, fun and commercial. Something perfected for mass consumption, which the merchandise-friendly empire of Supermarionation had going for it in spades.

Stingray's covert headquarters encapsulate an aquatic spy war being fought in Supermarionation. It's a war fought in the shadows of the ocean's murkiest depths. Its secret agents don't hide behind dark alleyways, instead, freakish, alien submarines dart above, around and underneath the jungle-like aura the oceans give off. Both sides retreat back into their respective safe havens once battle is over, ocean doors and mechanical rock faces yawning open in welcome to their respective craft and their intrepid pilots, who live to fight another day. It's also just huge fun to keep your eyes peeled to the screen, to that classic shot of an underwater world, serene and untouched by any sort of dominating force, and eventually witness a chunk of rock wall or seabed stretch open to reveal a complex base of operations or a craft emerge to prowl the oceans for its next Terranean victim.

Stingray's impact on Supermarionation in this way is immeasurable. Tracy Island may be the crowning jewel in the art form's line-up of disguised, opulent headquarters, but that line-up also includes the infinite arrays of smaller, hidden compartments from *Captain Scarlet and the Mysterons* that house SPVs. The Tracy Island mould would reappear in its most domesticated form via Professor McClaine's cottage from *Joe 90*, a quaint, English country cottage that rests on top of a literally mind-bending laboratory. *Stingray*'s influence in this regard would stretch still further. *UFO* would attempt to recapture the imaginations that had been swayed by Tracy Island by making SHADO's HQ a bunker base lying in stealth beneath a fake movie studio, whilst *Terrahawks*' White House revived the concept of the base as not just a disguised piece of architecture but one that transforms entirely to allow for the starring craft to take flight. It's as if these secret operative outlets are subservient to the incredible vehicles so closely associated with Gerry and Sylvia Anderson shows, yet *Stingray* ensured that the secret headquarters was its own art form.

DAYS OF DISASTER: THE NECESSARY DESTRUCTION OF *THUNDERBIRDS*

Since its original broadcast, *Thunderbirds* has come to be defined by its heroic sense of optimism. It's a television series that prioritises the idea that life is there to be saved for no other reason than it needs saving whenever struck by disaster. International Rescue operate their services for no monetary gain or no clamour of fame. Jeff Tracy founds the organisation on the ideal of being able to perform rescues that no pedestrian rescue techniques can perform. In summary, it's a very positive series. In contrast to these upbeat ideas, the world of *Thunderbirds* is at odds with the atomic-fuelled heroism that blasts off from Tracy Island on a regular basis. The world of *Thunderbirds* is one that emphasises destruction, human failings and death. *Thunderbirds* is populated by morally repugnant villains, technological incompetence and a routinely angered mother nature. Ironically, these darker aspects give International Rescue purpose. Death and destruction necessitates International Rescue to act. It enables them and justifies their existence.

When writing about American cinema's obsessions with producing films that incorporate disaster in a global, all-consuming scale, feeding a demand from audiences to witness captivating spectacles, Wheeler Winston Dixon suggests that the World Trade Centre attacks on 11 September, 2001 were a defining moment for America, creating what he describes as 'for all intents and purposes, the United States is now in a state of perpetual emergency readiness, braced for the next terrorist attack against a nuclear power plant, a major metropolitan area, or another corporate skyscraper.'[3] Published back in 2003, the world Dixon had described had already been created in Supermarionation form some 40 years earlier with *Thunderbirds*. It's oddly coincidental that Dixon should describe a trio of scenarios that *Thunderbirds* had already explored (or should that be exploded?) throughout the series. See 'The Mighty Atom' for a nuclear power plant, 'City of Fire' for a major metropolitan area (if a city housed within a building is allowed to still count as a city) and 'Terror in New York City' for a corporate skyscraper.

---

[3] Winston Dixon, W. (2003) 'Invasion U.S.A.' *Visions of the Apocalypse: Spectacles of Destruction in American Cinema.* p. 59. Wallflower. 1st edition.

Throughout Gerry and Sylvia Anderson's output, and particularly the Supermarionation era, technology is presented as being the great advancer of humankind, its ultimate saviour, and nowhere is this more apparent than *Thunderbirds*. 'The Mighty Atom' sees barren deserts being converted into oceans. 'Sun Probe' sees a literal fragment of the sun successfully captured for human use. 'Attack of the Alligators!' introduces a food additive that could reduce world hunger. However, in order to justify International Rescue's heroic endeavours, the miraculous advances made in technology in *Thunderbirds'* world is terminally prone to disaster, whether it's through genuine mishap or enemy interference. The majority of *Thunderbirds'* stories are driven by a malfunctioning piece of technology that's initially presented as being some great triumph in the field of scientific advancement, but is easily scuppered by unforeseen forces.

'If only I knew their secrets ...'

To begin with, the optimistic world of *Thunderbirds* is strewn with villainous individuals. Some work individually, some are part of larger organisations and some are entire civilisations unto themselves detached from mainstream society. The most obvious person in this category then is the Hood, the nefarious master criminal of a thousand faces who continually eludes those who wish to bring him to justice, and who himself regularly fails to steal the secrets of the International Rescue machines. His efforts to scupper International Rescue gain a tragic undercurrent thanks to his brotherly connection to the Tracy's faithful manservant, Kyrano. The Hood's telepathic abilities allow him to cast Kyrano under his forceful spell on multiple occasions, aiding him in sabotaging various factors of the Thunderbirds (although at no point does the Hood ever think to simply ask Kyrano where Tracy Island is or to dispatch blueprints for the Thunderbirds himself). Kyrano doesn't even appear to know he has a half-brother, never mind that it just so happens to be International Rescue's mortal enemy. This then is how evil the Hood is. He's willing to exploit and abuse his family to gain the riches International Rescue's technology would surely bring to him.

In one episode, the Hood's villainous actions gives way to a curious combination of enemy motives and accidental techno-carnage combined together to deliver one of the most frightening moments in all of *Thunderbirds*. 'The Mighty Atom' sees the Hood accidentally destroy an atomic irrigation plant in Australia. Initially trespassing the plant in order to gain its secrets, an unexpected gun battle with the plant's security forces sees the Hood unwittingly trigger the plant's destruction, detonating in an atomic, billowing mushroom cloud and resulting in a radioactive cloud which swallows every piece of landscape it glides over, creeping towards cities and towns, only to be averted by strong winds. Speaking about this episode in particular on her archived website, *Thunderbirds* co-creator Sylvia Anderson vividly notes the apocalyptic atomic imagery, saying 'this Dennis Spooner adventure contains a weirdly horrific reference to an atomic accident that has echoes of the nuclear nightmare of Chernobyl in 1986'[4]. Atomic dangers were commonplace in Gerry and Sylvia's worlds by the time *Thunderbirds* arrived, but no episode had actually shown the tense horror such dangers could actually bring. For all of the Hood's villainy, even he didn't genuinely intend to cause an atomic holocaust. After all, how would he be able to own the world if there isn't a world left?

Would it therefore surprise you to realise that out of *Thunderbirds*' 32 episode run, he only appears in six episodes? In the space of those six episodes, his actions outweigh any room for character exploration or motives. He is evil for the sake of evil, constantly trying to capture other technological secrets of the world of 2065 beyond the Thunderbirds. He brings an antagonistic presence to *Thunderbirds* that's ready-made, compared to the other villains who come and go in the space of a single episode and who require their actions to be established within that episode itself. The Hood doesn't require such formalities. After 'Trapped in the Sky', he makes his presence felt. And yet, the darkest action relating to the Hood isn't found within the character himself. It's found within the actions of International Rescue. During the events of the film *Thunderbirds Are Go*, the Hood makes two attempts to sabotage the take-off of *Zero-X* Mk I and II, respectively. He escapes during his failed attack on Mk I, but during his attempted getaway when the attack on Mk II also fails, Lady Penelope and Parker are hot on his trail whilst the Thunderbirds guide *Zero-X* into deep space.

Instead of capturing the Hood and bringing him to justice for his crimes against International Rescue and the rest of the world, Lady Penelope and Parker seemingly kill the Hood in his craft. There's no on-screen confirmation that the Hood is dead, no acknowledgement from International Rescue themselves that their greatest enemy has been vanquished in the most violent way possible, yet Parker placing his cap on his chest in a solemn salute is the most obvious indicator that the Hood has met his end. The second sign is the fact that he doesn't make any further appearances, either in *Thunderbird 6* or the six episodes that make up the series' second season. The Hood-esque character Black Phantom can be taken as less of a new guise for the Hood and more a simple case of puppet recycling, a common tool Century 21 Productions would use (some of the *Zero-X* crew gain new roles as henchmen in *Thunderbird 6*). When quizzed as to the

---

[4] Anderson, S. (2008) 'Thunderbirds Episode Guide' *Sylvia Anderson*. Available from – https://web.archive.org/web/20080503080402/http://www.sylviaanderson.org.uk/html/episode_guide.html.

similarity between the Hood and Black Phantom, on the director's commentary to *Thunderbird 6*, Sylvia Anderson, half-seriously, suggests that the pair are cousins. Another half-brother might have been more convincing. Comparing *Thunderbirds* to other Cold War-influenced sci-fi/spy-fi media of the times, *Thunderbirds* doesn't actually put much of a foot wrong here. Shoot first and ask questions never was the go-to mentality for many of those fictional heroes that have come to define much of the 1960s' contribution to pop culture icons. Yet in the context of *Thunderbirds*, that series that values the preservation of life above all else, murdering your enemies seems like a step too far.

As we'll explore later in this book in the chapter **Power, Family & Authority in Century 21**, such a move from International Rescue casts a dark shadow over their efforts in maintaining peace, for the world and themselves. Is this the price they pay to maintain their secrecy? How many other potential security hazards have suffered similar fates? The positive morals of International Rescue are shot through the middle by a deadly determination to keep themselves defended from those who would harm them, at any cost.

Within the world of *Thunderbirds*, the Hood's villainous stance doesn't occur in a vacuum. Enemies of 2065 come from all walks of life: thieves, murderers, aircraft hijackers, spies, businessmen, military forces. It speaks volumes that *Thunderbirds'* world can be so accommodating to such a diverse platter of antagonistic outfits, all of whom are attempting various means of destruction. Warren Grafton, the scheming president of the Pacific-Atlantic Monorail Corporation, is intent on sacrificing human safety for corporate wealth. 'The Perils of Penelope' sees Dr Godber come close to triggering a world war with the secretive rocket formula that powers the Sun Probe. With characters like these, would International Rescue think twice about just who it is they're saving? Nevertheless, the inclusion of morally repugnant individuals such as the Hood routinely enabled International Rescue to blast off into action and to have their vast operations validated.

'Our equipment is way ahead of its time'

Returning to the idea of technology's representation in *Thunderbirds* as being a force for good, most evidently highlighted in the technologically advanced Thunderbird craft framed as the only ones who can save the day, the only other force capable of interfering with that miraculous technology beyond enemies is nature itself. Throughout *Thunderbirds*, several rescue operations are thrown into action, and sometimes further jeopardy once International Rescue arrive on the scene, by nature overpowering humankind. Technology in *Thunderbirds* is symbolised as humanity taking control of its surrounding world and beyond, such as the aforementioned 'Sun Probe' and 'The Mighty Atom'. Throughout the series however, nature fights back. The collapse of the Martian Space Probe in 'Day of Disaster' over the aged Allington Suspension Bridge due to the ancient structure unable to withstand the weight of the rocket confirms that technological miracles don't always pan out in *Thunderbirds*' world.

'End of the Road', 'Path of Destruction' and 'Pit of Peril' sees various path-making machines clearing all manners of dense, lush mountain terrain, woodland and jungles, all to enable various means of more human transportation possible. The Gray and Houseman Construction Corporation are on a time-sensitive mission to construct a road through the South-East Asia territories before the monsoon season hits. The Sidewinder's test run sees the animal-like military vehicle, dragging itself through the African jungle, Godzilla-like, sending creatures scurrying for safety as their homes are trampled. The Crablogger sees forests as something to not just be removed, but be destroyed, all in favour of humankind's technological domination.

As if in reaction, nature finds a way to retaliate against these marvellous machines. The Crablogger crew, struck with food poisoning from the night before, collapse at the controls of the craft as it surges through the South American forest and becomes locked on course for the San Martino Dam. If the Crablogger can't be stopped and its atomic reactor detonates within range of the dam, it will burst, sending cascades of water to wash over Crablogger, reclaiming the nature that the machine stole. Barely has the Sidewinder left the jungle which it has permanently scarred that the ground collapses beneath it, swallowing the creature-like vehicle and trapping its crew. When the mountain range begins to collapse into the freshly detonated roadway Gray and Houseman have blasted through, Eddie Houseman tasks himself to recklessly drive up into dangerous, unstable mountain territory in an attempt to blast the mountain away from the road. Setting off the charges succeeds, but endangers Eddie, as more of the mountain collapses around him. It's as if nature is constantly punishing humankind for its gluttonous reliance on technology. *Thunderbirds*' preoccupation with destruction hasn't gone unnoticed by its creators. In another reflective review on her former website, Sylvia noted 'Path of Destruction' as a key episode of the series in which '… the hazards of atomic energy are highlighted, as far back as the sixties'.

This schism lends an added sense of furious, unforeseeable danger to *Thunderbirds*. For all of International Rescue's bespoke capabilities and resources, nature is the one adversary that remains unpredictable and difficult to subdue. It's a power so immense that it's beyond humankind's abilities to stop it, an unthinkable problem in the otherwise advanced world of 2065. The most powerful natural force International Rescue has come up against is also the one that almost consumes them. 'Sun Probe' and 'Lord Parker's 'Oliday' sees the Thunderbirds up against the sun itself, with near-fatal results. When Scott, Alan and Tin-Tin manage to rescue the Sun Probe craft from flying into the sun, Thunderbird 3 also becomes locked on course, with Virgil and Brains in Thunderbird 2's Transmitter Truck forced to brave blizzard conditions in Mount Arkan to propel a powerful enough radio beam to steer TB3 back to Earth. Solar flares and arctic blizzards collide in overpowering fashion to give International Rescue one of its most gruelling missions – to save someone else, but then only to save themselves.

'Lord Parker's 'Oliday' sees a second and equally disastrous attempt on humanity's part to capture the power of the sun, though the commentary is far more on the nose than in 'Sun Probe'. Where a subplot of International Rescue having to save International Rescue was a result of having to provide extended material to stretch the episode out to 50 minutes in length ('Sun Probe' was one of the first eleven episodes of *Thunderbirds* produced under its initial half-hour format), 'Lord Parker's 'Oliday' sees its characters acknowledge the destructive consequences of going toe-to-toe with nature. When Lady Penelope and Parker journey to the Mediterranean hotspot of Monte Bianco, a town to be used as an experiment by Professor Lungren in being powered by a solar generator that captures the heat of the sun, it's the superstitious hotel waiter Bruno who warns anyone within earshot how the solar generator will be a great disaster, and that the sun will 'take its revenge'. Sure enough, this warning comes to fruition. With the aid of a freakish electrical storm that tears into the solar generator's tower during its inaugural night-time usage, the generator is sent careering down its mountainside, placed in such a position that it will burn Monte Bianco to a cinder once dawn rises.

What began as an artificially generated giver of life has now been perverted into doing the exact opposite. International Rescue's attempts to prevent the now-murderous power of the dish prove hazardous. Their attempts to tilt the dish upwards, away from the town, are scuppered as the dish eventually collapses entirely, slipping off from its precarious position and roaring downward to the ground below. The final statement the episode makes is that salvaging the invention meant to benefit people at the expense of exploiting nature isn't allowed. This particular achievement isn't to be rescued or repeated.

'Boys, I think we're in business'

Time after time, *Thunderbirds* shows us that humankind doesn't learn from its mistakes. Technological disasters occur seemingly without consequence from one episode to the next. Humankind continues to push the boundaries of technological innovation without reflection. Scientists, the military and commercial enterprises sees nature as something to be tamed, to be harnessed, to be controlled by brute force. Time after time, it backfires in such a way that the only people who can resolve the situation is a secretive rescue organisation who's resources aren't readily available to the masses when one could argue it feels like they really ought to be dispersed for general use. In terms of narrative momentum, the engulfing scale that natural disasters provide for *Thunderbirds* gives it a visual excitement and always works well for story-telling that prioritises exhaustive action. It's a go-to disaster tactic that never fails, because it's difficult to get wrong. However, a rare occasion where humanity holds nature within its grasp is seen within the series, one that lends a serene note for the original series to end on. The final episode of the original series, 'Give Or Take A Million', ends with the angelic view of Tracy Island experiencing its first ever white Christmas, enabled by Brains rigging up an artificial snow generator, enabling it to 'snow' on Tracy Island. It's an elegant afterthought that after nature should prove to be such a force to be reckoned with by International Rescue, the series should end with nature gently coerced into giving *Thunderbirds* a calm, low-key climax.

But how deep does *Thunderbirds*' fixation with disaster run? The answer lies in the era in which *Thunderbirds* was made, a time when paranoia surrounding cold war and nuclear warfare was influencing genre fiction TV directly and indirectly alike, but with elements cherry-picked from science fiction films of the 1950s. When discussing key tropes in this era of cinematic offerings, Steffen Hantke notes that one of the well-used types of characters in these films is that of the scientist; '1950s scientists perform heroic work as institutional employees'[5]. Quoting Andrew Tudor further, scientists 'were allowed to be heroes in ways almost unique to the period' (2016). This archetype of a character is very much reflected in Brains, the only man in the world capable of inventing the Thunderbird machines. Not only does he fit Hantke and Tudor's descriptions of the 1950s movie scientist in terms of being a mastermind, but his oft-seen involvement in rescue operations furthers this idea, equally placing him as the hero, too. 'Sun Probe' and 'Path of Destruction' see Brains join in with missions, yet 'Day of Disaster' and 'Alias Mr Hackenbacker' position Brains as the hero of the day.

Further on, Hantke describes another aspect of 1950s sci-fi cinema that *Thunderbirds* arguably adapts into its own identity. Hantke discusses how 'monsters and mutations are always and inevitably the product of technoscience' (2016), as if the price humanity pays for its reliance on technological advancement is its own freakish, biological destruction.

---

[5] Hantke, S. (2016) 'A Bright New Future, With Monsters' *Monsters in the Machine: Science Fiction Film and the Militarisation of America after World War II*. pp. 5-7. University Press of Mississippi. 1st edition.

Thunderbirds swaps out the monsters for the disasters. In those 1950s movies, turmoil escalates as the monsters arrive on the scene, but whilst the exact same tactic occurs with *Thunderbirds*, the series trades the mutations for spectacular disasters as the cataclysmic by-product of scientific and technological discovery.

Thinking back to Dixon's earlier encapsulation of an America that exists in a permanent state of preparation for technological emergency, this logic can be applied further to *Thunderbirds* that its focus on disaster is so paramount that International Rescue self-inflict themselves with atomic danger. The secretive nature of the outfit demands they operate as discreetly as possible. This is achieved by International Rescue existing on a covert state on a tropical island somewhere in the Pacific, disguised as the multi-millionaire bachelor Tracy family. Concealed behind the natural rock faces of Tracy Island are infinite manmade labyrinths of atomic machinery that powers Tracy Island, a mechanical labyrinth of atomic tension that ought to make the Tracy family live in a state of terminal fear – sleeping next to atomic technology that would surely only need the slightest kick to detonate. The image of an island littered with atomic weaponry brings to mind numerous island testing facilities used by American and British military forces for atomic weapons testing throughout the 1940s and 1950s, such as Operation Grapple and Operation Crossroads. The disaster-ready world of *Thunderbirds* is therefore a delicate balance between kinetic narrative spectacle and a hangover of nuclear paranoia. Making entertainment out of devastation was all in a day's work for Century 21 Productions, but such a characteristic trademark of the puppet pioneers gives *Thunderbirds'* celebrated humanitarian edge a grim underbelly from which the courageous Tracy brothers may launch into fearless action.

THE POSTHUMAN HEART OF *CAPTAIN SCARLET AND THE MYSTERONS*

Captain Scarlet and the Mysterons (1967-1968), the sixth television series produced by AP Films/Century 21 to be filmed in Supermarionation, is a blitzkrieg of old school science fiction action that touches upon moral and psychological ambiguity within the explosive, action-driven framework that was second nature to the production team at this point. Who the real enemy is in *Captain Scarlet* is a question the series dabbles in without directly asking it. Is it the Devil-like Mysterons, whose omnipotent and omnipresent capabilities threaten to turn the Earth inside out? Or is it Spectrum, whose trigger-happy agent Captain Black unwillingly kicks the 'war of nerves' into gear?

Captain Scarlet and the Mysterons tells the story of world security organization Spectrum's battle of wits against the Mysterons, a cryptic alien race that had been hibernating on the planet Mars until an accidental act of destruction on the part of key Spectrum agent Captain Black provokes them into declaring war on the Earth. Armed with the powers of retro-metabolism, their ability to destroy anyone and anything and replicate them/it for their own ends is gleefully and violently exploited throughout the show. Captain Scarlet becomes a Mysteron agent during the events of the first episode, but eventually both regains his human persona and retains the Mysterons' superpowers, becoming Spectrum's greatest weapon against the scheming aliens. *Captain Scarlet* slyly avoids exploring this rather human fallout of the war of nerves, a campaign of terror whereby the Mysterons routinely target important people, places or events throughout the world, placing their replicated agents into the heart of the action.

In a lesser show, this would be seen as a lazy cop-out, a senseless diversion from the show's larger themes that reward endless viewing and inspection on the part of the audience. Yet in the hands of series creators Gerry and Sylvia Anderson, it feels as if *Captain Scarlet* purposefully moves beyond the traditional expectations of incorporating such personal tragedies, and instead strives to deliver an experience that transcends our physical and cerebral definitions of what it means to be human. This philosophical attitude separates the show from the otherwise optimistic fare of previous Supermarionation sci-fi action.

THE POSTHUMAN HEART OF *CAPTAIN SCARLET AND THE MYSTERONS*

The largest case for *Captain Scarlet*'s posthuman identity is the insatiable bloodthirstiness of the Mysterons. As part of their campaign of terror, the Mysterons flex their muscles by routinely murdering and replicating human beings from all walks of life, transforming them into Mysteron agents—a metaphor that invokes, on purpose or not, the real-life workings of occupation and colonialism. These replicated beings act as alien sleeper terrorists, designed to slip in and out of situations disguised as their human counterparts, yet embedded with an innate loyalty to the Mysteron cause. More often than not, either through quick-witted thinking, Captain Scarlet's indestructible prowess, or sheer script convenience, Spectrum is able to prevent total catastrophe.

Captain Scarlet avoids diving into what effect Mysteron agents have on the people they actually replicate. Army generals, pilots, journalists, fashion models, doctors, garage workers—all fall under the Mysterons' spell, embodying a very literal definition of the posthuman as physical, alien-produced copies of human beings, armed with a wildly different functionality than 'regular' human beings. In the episodes 'The Mysterons' and 'Traitor', we see how Mysteron agents are capable of acting as living bombs, emitting gusts of smoke before detonating. But what becomes of the lives these people, subsumed by their malevolent replicas, unintentionally left behind? Do they have friends and families who would no doubt be scarred at the idea of invisible aliens killing and reconstructing their loved ones, perversely exploiting the image of the dead for their own ends?

We do see this idea bubble to the surface, on occasion. In 'The Launching', a Mysteron attempt to destroy the maiden voyage of the vessel President Roberts is foiled in heroic fashion by Captain Scarlet. The Mysteron agent-of-the-week, journalist Mervin Brand, is a close friend of the Vice President of Trans-Pacific Shipping, who's launching the vessel. Highlighting the covert nature of the Mysterons, the episode also marks a rare occasion in the series when humanity comes face to face with the Mysterons' capabilities. When Scarlet manages to shoot and kill the Mysteron replica, the Vice President can only stare over the body and stumble over the idea that it isn't that of his friend, but of an alien entity beyond his comprehension.

The idea is scaled up in 'Treble Cross', a well-constructed classic from the show's last few episodes that asks the endlessly intriguing question: what would happen if a Mysteron target who gets murdered and reconstructed was brought back to life? Experimental test pilot Major Gravener comes under the Mysteron knife early on in the episode, but the story's delightful subplot emerges when two passing doctors recover his body and manage to resuscitate him. Made aware of the Mysteron Gravener's villainous intentions to hijack a military jet armed with a nuclear warhead, Spectrum hatches a cunning plan to deceive the Mysterons into thinking the human

Gravener is their own. Major Gravener's reaction to being told he's been copied by an alien menace is: 'Well, apart from trying to assimilate all this, I'm fine.' The episode unfortunately doesn't allow the time for in-depth reflection of what Gravener might actually feel about having his body exploited by unseen hands and, to some degree, by Spectrum itself.

These precious few glances into the manipulative machinations of the Mysterons are kept at arm's length to avoid spoiling the overall otherworldly atmosphere of the series. By detaching the emotional entanglements that an event like the war of nerves produces, *Captain Scarlet and the Mysterons* absolves responsibility for any genuine depth in its characters. In the hands of any other show, this would be unforgivable; yet here it makes perfect sense. Scarlet himself reflects the show's somewhat cold-hearted mindset thanks to his transition from regular Spectrum agent to Mysteron tool of war to, finally, Spectrum's greatest asset in the fight against the Mysterons. In 'Winged Assassin', the consequences of Scarlet's Mysteron-occupied mind is cautiously explored without really being resolved. Save for the heat of the flames on the back of his neck in the aftermath of his own assassination at the hands of the Mysterons (an engrossingly tangible, and sadistic, bit of detail), he remembers nothing until his reversal from Mysteron agent back to Spectrum Captain. Bizarrely, everyone else on Cloudbase, Spectrum's airborne headquarters, appears to have undergone selective memory loss too.

When discharged from Cloudbase's medical bay, he receives a warning from Colonel White, the commander-in-chief of Spectrum, that the consequences of all of this may not be fully understood, yet he's placed back on duty, and everyone aboard Cloudbase promptly overlooks the fact that they have a failed Mysteron infiltrator working for them. Indeed, everyone proceeds to talk to Scarlet as if he's the original. 'It's great to have you back on duty, Captain Scarlet,' Captain Blue reflects joyfully. But *this* Captain Scarlet was never on duty. He ends up retaining the superhuman abilities that come with reconstruction, yet fails to recount any of his actions during his antagonistic, posthuman state. What wonders—and strategic advantages—those memories would have provided to Spectrum.

Why, then, does *Captain Scarlet and the Mysterons* not make more time for these concepts that lend themselves endlessly well to deep levels of introspection? Probably because the Supermarionation wonderland of Century 21 had already cemented its reputation for propulsive puppet programs defined by eye-popping action. There was commercial pressure to continue to do so. And yet, despite the surface-level antics being the chief draw into the dark-hearted world of *Captain Scarlet and the Mysterons*, it's the deeper ideas and concepts that resonate—even though they may not have been purposely planted there. When I interviewed *Captain Scarlet* writer/director Leo Eaton and asked about the overall darker edge of the show compared to *Thunderbirds*, he gave a disarmingly and unassumingly simple response: 'You know, it's weird, people read things into things after the event. We didn't think of it as particularly dark. It was fun, it was different.'

He may not have been talking about a specific idea or concept found in the show itself, yet his words encapsulate the working attitude towards the show. The fact that the series at least dips its toes in posthuman waters suggests a maturity and ambition on the part of its creators and writers that perhaps wasn't there in past shows. Gerry and Sylvia were keen advocate for giving each of his creations its own flavour, and was careful not to repeat too much of what had come before. Whether the edgier, philosophical undertones of the series were an intentional move or a happy accident, the result was a throbbing dread—who would be murdered and body-snatched in *this* episode—that elevated *Captain Scarlet and the Mysterons* above previous Supermarionation productions.

COLD WAR GAMES: THE PERVERSE INNOCENCE OF *JOE 90*

Despite the doe-eyed innocence the series insists on radiating through its youthful protagonist, *Joe 90* could very possibly hold the crown of being the most morally questionable of the Supermarionation series. When positioned alongside a humanitarian outfit that's willing to kill to maintain its secrecy and an intergalactic war of blood-thirsty aliens, this is quite an achievement. How the World Intelligence Network gathers its mental ammunition in defending the world from those who would subvert democracy and antagonise malicious geographical superpowers is prime speculative spy-fi, but the idea of WIN regularly recording brain patterns often without the person's consent comes with undeniable problematic morality.

The innocent simplicity with how Joe McClaine sees the world he saves from evil forces is at odds with the complex power struggles at work throughout *Joe 90*, as well as a relentless occurrence of death and destruction. From the snug safety of his and Professor McClaine's country cottage, away from the constant hubbub of the World Intelligence Network and all of its deadly spy tactics, Joe McClaine is a passing witness to the fraught power games at work in his world. Episodes often begin and end with scenes set in the McClaine's snug, welcoming home, the globe-trotting adventures Joe becomes embroiled in bookended by the comfortable familiarity of returning home in time for bed, ready for the next grand adventure to begin the following day.

Political Powers

The world of *Joe 90* is one that's not entirely in tune with Gerry and Sylvia Anderson's common vision for a utopian, near-future society. Throughout the Supermarionation era, harmonious coexistences between countries and cultures, so prevalently reflected in the multicultural set-up of Spectrum and the multi-faceted undersea civilisations of *Stingray*, were now out of the window, a possible reflection of Gerry and Sylvia's frustration at this point in their careers of still being forced to work with puppets over humans. Stepping away further from these idealised futures is the fact that *Joe 90* occurs within a much earlier timeframe compared to the fairly consistent

2060s in which *Stingray, Thunderbirds* and *Captain Scarlet* occur. In their place is a world that's permanently teetering on the brink of another World War, with the World Intelligence Network at the heart of a very open Cold War. Interestingly, all the steps *Joe 90* makes towards its world-building is straight out of the 1960s spy-fi tele-fantasy playbook, which by September 1968, the month and year in which *Joe 90* premiered, audiences were familiar with to the point of being desensitised. *The Man From U.N.C.L.E.* and *Danger Man* had come and gone. Sean Connery had returned his licence to kill. From an entertainment standpoint, audiences were perhaps finding the Cold War tepid.

Joe 90 positions its politics as powerful Western trouble-shooters versus underdog foreign troublemakers. Various non-USA centric governments, organisations and individuals are desperate to violently tip the balance of global power in their favour. The implication here then, whilst never overtly stated in the series itself, is that the world order is clearly determined by the West. Regions such as Russia, China and the Middle East are portrayed as being infinitely more susceptible to villainous influence than America. Corrupt politicians, war-mongering military men and civil unrest dominate these places. The all-white, all-American, all-male power of the World Intelligence Network is portrayed as being the only force capable of quelling these unruly activities. Sam Loover's nickname of Uncle Sam can be taken as a sign of familiarity on Joe's part, but also as the slang term for the US government, a further reflection of the authority WIN has on the world. One key example of this is the episode 'The Professional', where the American-based Kramer Foundation ceases giving a vaguely defined Eastern European country its regular funds following the country's anti-democratic hi-jacking. Money to be used in the building of hospitals is now ploughed into war machines. This enforces the grip that the Western powers have over the rest of the world, with the episode slyly avoiding any specifics as to what country this actually is, but also framing the country itself as dangerously easy to be overtaken by fascist rule and exploiting Western funds for military might.

This mentality rather flies in the face of the otherwise peaceful, multicultural set-up past Supermarionation series promoted, but in doing so helps to shape Joe 90's distinct world-building. The canonical distance Joe 90 puts between itself and the bulk of the Century 21 puppet shows is always worth remembering, too. Whilst the shared canonicity of these four series in particular are permanently debatable, it remains accepted that the four series take place during the 2060s. *Joe 90* takes place during a much earlier timeline, though the exact date is disputed between writer's guides and production histories as being anywhere between the late 1990s and 2013. There's therefore a wide gulf formed between these two sets of timelines, and actually works in the series' favour in granting *Joe 90* to have a more pessimistic worldview, where armies and spies compete for power, compared to the more optimistic fare of the 2060s.

Mentions of World Governments and a World President are still featured, and recognisable insignias for the World Army are scattered throughout the series, linking *Joe 90* with its Supermarionation brethren, though this could easily be written off as a simple and common case of prop reuse. Nevertheless, it remains striking that Joe 90's politics should be so on the nose. Politics is, of course, everywhere in every form of media we consume, whether we're conscious of it or not. Gerry and Sylvia Anderson's filmography is no exception, yet when you compare *Joe 90* to other works of theirs, the series stands out for how direct and integral politics is featured. In their other works, politics is less direct. In the *Stingray* episode 'Marineville Traitor', an enemy within Marineville ranks is passing secrets to enemies on the outside. Troy Tempest suspects Commander Shore of reaching out to the 'other side' in their underwater Cold War, for reasons unknown. As his suspicions grow, he innocently interrogates his commanding officer, asking him to explain what it could be that would make a man turn traitor. Shore suggests that, amongst several other reasons, politics could be a reason. He doesn't elaborate any further by defining what politics exactly may make a Marineville hero turn enemy, but this captures politics in the Supermarionation era – it's mentioned and therefore acknowledged by its characters, but only on occasion and lacking in specifics.

Fast forward to the Andersons' live action works *UFO* and *Space: 1999* and we have other instances of the impact that foreign politics plays in each series. Politics can be unravelled throughout *UFO*'s 26 episodes at great length, but in the interests of this chapter, I'd like to call upon an episode of *UFO* that actually didn't get produced. *UFO*'s first assistant director Leo Eaton, who had directed on *Captain Scarlet*, *Joe 90* and *The Secret Service*, wrote his sole script offering for the series with an episode named 'The Patriot', which ultimately went unmade. Speaking with the ufoseries.com website, which reproduced the script with Eaton's permission, Eaton suggests that the script was ultimately not filmed as it was deemed to be too political.[6] In the *Space: 1999* episode 'One Moment of Humanity', Commander Koenig acknowledges to a group of invading alien androids intent on discovering the meaning of hate so that they may learn how to kill (can you tell that such a premise comes from the infamous Year 2 rather than the more celebrated Year 1?) that Moonbase Alpha is a politically neutral community. In-between *Stingray*'s loose, in-universe acknowledgement of politics and *Space: 1999*'s in-universe dismissal of the concept entirely, there exists *Joe 90*, a series that wilfully and gleefully exploits real-world tensions

---

[6] Martin, M. (2005) 'The Script for the Unfilmed UFO Episode "The Patriot"'. *UFO Series*. Available from – http://ufoseries.com/scripts/patriot.html.

between global superpowers for the purposes of children's television entertainment. It's a far cry from the comparatively innocent days of *The Man From U.N.C.L.E.*, the official writer's guide saying that 'U.N.C.L.E. does not serve the interests that are peculiarly American. The Cold War or any of its ramifications do not exist for us.'[7]

The message being transmitted here is that *Joe 90* exists on a political spectrum beyond other Anderson productions, one that captures Cold War anxieties in a more apparent fashion than past ventures, unfiltered through aliens from outer space or under the oceans. *Stingray* and *Captain Scarlet* may have used alien invasions as a metaphor for Cold War attack, and *UFO* afterwards, but alien menaces have no place in *Joe 90*, furthering the distance felt between this series and the rest of the Supermarionation era. In the grand tradition of each series being an evolution of the previous one, perhaps there's the sense that the dwindling audience appeal of Supermarionation meant that there were less eyes watching to scrutinize depictions of foreign governments as needing to be whipped into an orderly state by their white neighbours. What softens the political blows that *Joe 90* punches is the fact that the series' direct politics is framed through models, miniatures and marionettes. Suddenly *Joe 90* becomes quaint and quirky by contemporary standards. But the politically-driven nature of the series has lost none of its momentum.

Sometimes, the series makes no illusions as to who the enemies are. Asian countries come off in particularly unforgiving fashions in *Joe 90*. 'Attack of the Tiger' and 'Mission X-41' are notable offenders of the type of racial portrayal *Joe 90* liked to give to its antagonists. Like the earlier episode 'The Professional' before them, neither episode specifically identifies their enemies, it's simply enough to categorise them as Asian, and have done with it. In the world of 1960s spy-fi, that's enough to set off imaginative alarm bells that alert the viewer in knowing that these are the bad guys that need to be defeated. In 'Attack of the Tiger', the military powers have constructed a transformable rocket base capable of disguising itself within its surrounding rocky regions and launching a spacecraft that will place a nuclear weapon in orbit around the Earth, holding the entire planet at ransom. 'Mission X-41' sees that episode's enemies develop a virus so potent it can consume any molecular structure within minutes of it being unleashed. At the centre of these political maelstroms, where enemy countries are equipped and standing by to launch immense global conflict, Joe prances into enemy territory with disarming innocence, his earnest exclamations that he's WIN's top agent sending his captors into disbelieving

---

[7] Walker, C, W. (2009) "Technology, Politics, and the Postmodern Setting". *Channelling the Future: Essays on Science Fiction and Fantasy Television* (eds. Geraghty, L.). p. 53. Scarecrow Press. 1st edition.

hysterics, letting their guard down, enabling Joe to eventually defeat them. It's a key tactic in how *Joe 90* not only maintains its innocence, but exploits it to good use.

'A nine-year-old boy? Have you been drinking?'

Joe McClaine himself, as a protagonist, appears unwilling or unable to understand the political complexities he's often parachuted into. For the benefit of his perspective, the boy hero on whose shoulders the fate of the world precariously balances, these scenarios are scaled down into a simple case of good versus evil. Good being the World Intelligence Network (in other words, his adult superiors) and evil being whichever covert enemy outfit or foreign manipulator happens to be residing within the files of Shane Weston. The command with which Joe's loosely-defined family of male guardians hold over him smothers any possibility for Joe to actually speak up himself on how he may think the fight between good and evil should be won, if he can even think of such a thing.

In my retrospective of *Joe 90*, published in issue #26 of the Gerry Anderson fanzine *Andersonic*, I wrote about how Joe lacks a genuine personality in comparison to his three male elders, to the point where right from the series' beginning, Joe rapidly disintegrates into becoming the least interesting character in his own show.[8] Professor McClaine, Sam Loover and Shane Weston are much more animated by comparison, their more concrete personalities and complimentary interactions with each other allow some distinct personality traits to naturally emerge. The fact that Joe, with no-one else his own age to engage with, spends much of the series mentally disguised as other people emphasizes his loneliness. Let's take the opportunity here to expand on this perspective. Joe stares upon the devastation he leaves in his wake with almost disposable innocence, quickly stepping away from one scenario into another with no real reflection on his actions. Then again, are they really his actions or the actions of the people whose impressive capabilities he's armed with? He can only interject casual, limp comments bolted onto the more adult conversations between Weston, Loover and Mac, the only adults in the room capable of managing and explaining the fraught geo-political manoeuvres WIN involves itself in. A simple question here, a passing remark there, his youthful mind-set is no match for his superiors in detailing the missions that he undertakes.

However, *Joe 90*'s rampant psychological implications lend themselves wonderfully well to unboxing more of the series than simply being a boy-in-a-man's-world action-adventure. Joe's seemingly doe-eyed, detached

---

[8] McNamara, F. (2020) 'The Child With the Man in his Eyes'. *Andersonic* (ed Farrell, R). No. 26, pp. 28-34.

engagement in his missions for WIN can be taken further as less of the innocence of a young child, but more that the World Intelligence Network make use of Joe as a vessel through which they're able to unleash their violent espionage. Joe's passive, unquestioning attitude towards WIN's actions make him little more than a blank reel of recording tape, ready to have information recorded on to it, transmitted, wiped and recorded again for further use. It's a hell of a way to live, but helps to give Joe's contributions some purpose and context. The permanently curious, morally finger-wagging antics of WIN, who routinely insist on involving themselves in situations no other world power can possibly resolve peacefully, is resolved through Joe's ability to baffle villains, ensuring victory. The series regularly frames your average episode of *Joe 90* as having almost a comical climax, as the villain-of-the-episode succumbs to the absurdity of a nine-year-old boy foiling their dastardly plans for world domination. It's witty. It's cute. It's bizarre. It's *Joe 90* at its best. The novelty of having a child hero manage to put right the political warfare so unstoppable in *Joe 90* is the series' greatest trick

Joe 90's core theme of kid-as-hero fantasy is a simple surface layer to its much more apparent theme of psychological spy-fi at its most indulgent, its kid hero's two-dimensional personality acting as a foil to mask any harsh political implications that come from how *Joe 90* portrays its clashing world powers. It's pure kid fantasy taken to its most morally repugnant extremes and thus makes *Joe 90* all the more a perverse and unique viewing experience. Joe McClaine is the eye of the storm that is the World Intelligence Network. The agent who is regularly dispatched to the most dangerous assignments is also the one who won't take acceptation to these assignments. Watching the series through the eyes of a child, as is intended, maintains the kid fantasy surface level, but experiencing *Joe 90* through a more mature lens brings these elements to the surface. As audiences, we're blessed to not be struck down by the same limitations of Joe. We're not trapped in our perspective. We see the show for what it really is, thanks to the evolution that takes place when viewing the same media through evolved generational lenses. *Joe 90* was already a quirky, memorable approach to 20th century spy-fi action and adventure, but the series becomes even more weirdly entertaining when you accept the clash of a childlike, innocent wonder and fascination collide with a grim, adult world where political turmoil and global war are just a brain pattern away.

JOURNEY TO THE FAR SIDE OF SPY-FI: *DOPPELGÄNGER'S* ESPIONAGE SOUL

Gerry and Sylvia Anderson must have witnessed the reaction to their solitary live-action feature film with a heart-sinking sense of *déjà vu* (the much earlier crime caper *Crossroads to Crime*, from 1960, was directed by Gerry prior to his and Sylvia's creative partnership fully blossoming). From its troubled conception to its fraught production, *Doppelgänger*'s eventual reception by audiences and critics alike would surely vindicate the hard work endured by all involved from a team desperate to escape the string and fibreglass confines of the previous, television-based works that had brought them recognition and success. However, that didn't quite happen. It would have been too easy for *Doppelgänger* to have been a total write-off at the box office and with critics alike. Instead, much like the two-man crew of the Dove shuttle craft, it tripped into a period of suspended animation, rather than failed to launch, much like the two *Thunderbirds* films that had preceded it. People didn't not like it. They just didn't know what to make of it. Contemporary reviews are mixed, whilst retrospective reviews praise the film's speculative story-telling, whilst both eras of criticism praise the special effects, but this *is* a Century 21 production we're talking about. By 1969, saying that a Century 21 film or TV show had great special effects almost had no value, given how dependably superb those special effects are.

A general consensus amongst past and present perspectives on *Doppelgänger* is how oddly inconspicuous it is. Low-key. Underwhelming. Not conforming to what people were expecting from a production company that specialised in explosive science-adventure. During a time when speculative science fiction cinema would veer wildly into absurd, extreme alternate realities to our own, Howard Thompson described *Doppelgänger* in *The New York Times* as 'civilised and restrained'[9], while Film4 claimed it stuck to 'the cheapest alternate Earth ever.'[10] Where the Andersons had perused dream-induced music videos and horrific monster aliens at the

---

[9] Thompson, Howard (12 November 1969). 'Journey to Far Side of Sun Opens'. *The New York Times*.
[10] 'Journey to the Far Side of the Sun. Film4 review'. (2011) Film4. Available from – https://web.archive.org/web/20110721174823/http://www.film4.com/reviews/1969/journey-to-the-far-side-of-the-sun.

expense of grounded story-telling in *Thunderbirds Are Go*, we have, quite suitably, the reversal in *Doppelgänger*, a barrage of exposition and story-telling tactics in place of visually arresting action. This summary is then suggesting that *Doppelgänger* isn't wild enough to be considered as genuine sci-fi. If it's not that, then what is it? Watching the film, it becomes clear that one substantial interpretation to put forward is that within the sci-fi mind of *Doppelgänger*, there's a spy-fi story trying to break out.

A Stumble in the Dark?

The premise of *Doppelgänger* is traditionally speculative sci-fi enough – a mystery planet on the exact opposite end of the sun to Earth is located by space exploratory outfit EUROSEC. Single-minded EUROSEC director Jason Webb tasks top American astronaut Glenn Ross and EUROSEC astrophysicist Dr John Kane to journey to this unknown planet and discover its secrets. A six-week trek in deep space descends into disaster when Kane and Webb's craft crash-lands on Earth three weeks earlier than expected, only for Ross to slowly discover that the planet he has arrived on is, in fact, not only the mystery planet, but that the planet itself is a parallel version of Earth. It's a plot that feels cherry-picked from *The Twilight Zone*, rather than big, blustering, blockbuster adventure designed to grip the imagination. The characteristics of *Doppelgänger*'s drawling story appear much closer to a spy drama than that of a full-blown sci-fi epic. The film's defining concept of two opposing Earths, concealed from each other between a solar curtain in place of an Iron Curtain, reads like spy-fi at its most cosmically exposed.

At this point then, it's worth defining just what we mean by sci-fi and spy-fi. The precise definitions of science fiction continue to generate debate amongst fans, academics and audiences alike, but certain mechanics of the genre are accepted as being futuristic and imaginative scale, as well as having technology and science at the forefront. Worlds, characters and concepts beyond our comprehension, generally driven by science and technology unlike our own, to summarise. Spy-fi has a more rigid explanation, rooted in Cold War tensions between the Soviet Union and the United States, which much fiction based on the subject tended to boil down as being the East versus the West. Gadgets capable of acquiring information and murdering your enemies are rife on both sides, the technological aspect of sci-fi rubbing shoulders with that of sci-fi. Spy-fi and sci-fi can perhaps be interpreted as two sides of the same coin and this was thoroughly apparent in throughout the 1960s. *Doppelgänger* exhibits elements from both genres then, but it was never marketed or intended to be a wielding of such styles. It was meant to be the sci-fi extravaganza that would be the big break for Century 21, but where the fantastical sci-fi concepts gave the film soaring ambition, its modest and grounded spy-fi leanings keeps its wings firmly in check.

The opening scene of Herbert Lom's briefly-seen character Dr Kurt Hassler photographing EUROSEC's findings from the Sun Probe operation that reveal the existence of the duplicate Earth is a tactic straight out of a James Bond film. This is taken a stage further when Hassler, arriving back at his laboratory, removes his right eye to reveal that it's, in truth, a secret camera made to look like a genuine eyeball, the first of several instances of spy-fi gadgetry seen in the film. Even Glenn's wife Sharon Ross' attempts at hiding contraceptive pills from her husband in an attempt to discourage him from having children has an air of hidden gadgetry about it. The subplot involving Glenn and Sharon's unhappy marriage is one cause for the film's criticism, with some arguing that such melodrama has little bearing or substance on the overall story, but it also helps to blur the sci-fi definitions that *Doppelgänger* shoots for. Hassler's sequence then gives way to the film's opening titles, a psychedelic montage of close-up shots of whirring machinery in pulsating life. It's a sequence that has far more in common with the opening titles of *Joe 90*, the Andersons' most blatant attempt at espionage, yet the multi-coloured swirls are more in *Doctor Who* territory. A sign that *Doppelgänger* is already treading the waters in trying to be two things at once.

Cold Star War

A position the film holds that it likely would rather not be remembered for when retroactively discussing the Andersons' work is that, essentially, it's the one before *UFO*, that downbeat sci-fi drama that was less of an intergalactic war and more of a Cold War with aliens. Obvious recycling's of props, models and music from the film's soundtrack resurface throughout *UFO*, but so too do several actors. A pre-Straker and pre-Freeman Ed Bishop and George Sewell have supporting roles, complimented by the more minor roles filled out by Vladek Sheybal, Norma Roland, Keith Alexander and Jeremy Wilkin. *Doppelgänger*'s proto-*UFO* status goes beyond the surface level details, however. Prior to EUROSEC being granted the financial backing by NASA to initiate operation Sun Probe, Webb must endure a bureaucratic response to his findings from a select committee, predating SHADO's own experiences of being put through interference in the name of scrutiny from higher powers. It's here that *Doppelgänger*'s sci-fi mask slips to reveal something of the Cold War face lurking beneath. When Webb's cosmic findings fall on deaf ears, his desperate attempts at convincing Bishop's NASA representative to grant his mission lift-off before another foreign power can seize the opportunity reads like a tense moment of paranoia between warring nations, made all the more apparent following EUROSEC's assassination of Hassler for stealing EUROSEC's secrets. Does EUROSEC have its own assassination division designed to quell security leaks like these, or is Jason Webb that desperate of a man? Webb's monumental desire to track this planet down before anyone else reads like a desire for Britain to maintain its standing as a superpower within the otherwise harmonious multi-nation set-up of EUROSEC, wanting to assert its dominance.

From here, *Doppelgänger* takes a firmer hold of the sci-fi premise that it promised its audience, delivering on the promise made by one such eye-catching poster which read 'Are you <u>two</u> people reading this poster?' Ross and Kane's journey to the Counter-Earth passes by without danger, even inducing an almost cosmic pastoral vibe, accompanied by Barry Gray's beautifully languid 'Sleeping Astronauts' piece (another form of music that would be reincarnated for *UFO*) and a non-violent burst of psychedelic colours to simulate the passage of time through the wonders of space. Even the film's most robust stab at being pure space-based science fiction is without thrills. It glides, rather than storms along, a world away from the frantically edited opening sequences to *Stingray* and *Thunderbirds*. The space this opens up for the film to explore its alternate espionage themes is readily apparent then, and all the more curious to watch. As if suddenly remembering that it's meant to be a sci-fi film, but in no rush to remind you of this.

A conscious choice perhaps, given the crash-bang-wallop of the *Dove*'s crash-landing on the Counter-Earth, as director Robert Parrish remembers he's making a sci-fi film. Ross and Kane's catastrophic arrival on the Counter-Earth is a vicious burst of much-needed energy for *Doppelgänger*. It's the closest the film comes to pure space horror as the *Dove* disconnects from the *Phoenix* craft to attempt a landing on the planet, still unknown in its alien qualities to Ross and Kane. Instead of a safe landing, the craft plummets from the thunderstruck skies like a pebble, crashing into mountainous region superbly made to look as alien as possible, shrouded in ever-changing night-time shadows as the accompanying storm whips up paranoia all around them. The only constant source of light proves to be the flames belching out of the wreckage of the *Dove* when it spirals into disaster. As Ross drags the unconscious and badly damaged body of Kane away from the burning remains of their only means of arrival and therefore escape from this new world, the thrashing soundscape of nature in full flow is disrupted by something more artificial, as the undefined outline of another craft floats down from above, piercing searchlights surveying the devastation. Hovering above Ross, a humanoid form descends, arms and legs outstretched in a non-human pose, protruding bodily forms barely distinguishable. Grabbing Ross, he's stunned and aggressive towards this humanoid creature as he's winched up into the unknown craft, only for the humanoid figure to tear back its face-like mask to reveal something even more unexpected for Ross – a perfectly normal, English-speaking human.

It's a superbly directed sequence that sets the tone for the gradual twist reveal of the existence of the Counter-Earth, during which the film swings back into more subdued, spy-fi tones. With this taut science fiction sequence over and done with, *Doppelgänger* continues to compartmentalise its components, rather than intertwine both of them, further evidence that the film isn't bold enough to mix its two genres that by this point are fighting for focus. With Kane reduced to being in a critical medical condition and eventually dying, the *Dove* destroyed and the *Phoenix* stranded in outer space, Ross is the sole link between the two Earths. His arrival on the Counter-Earth is much like an enemy spy crossing the Iron Curtain into dangerous territory, the unwelcoming tones from, what he thinks are, his colleagues immediate. The audience is clued into the fact that we're on the alternate planet early on, as we see the alternate Jason Webb with his suit's features placed on the opposite side of himself, as well as the EUROSEC logo seen from back to front, but Parrish's discrete direction ensures that not everyone may notice this on first viewing. As if in an espionage frame of mind, you may have to tune in to spot it on first glance, a film that's undercover.

Parrish goes to great yet subtle lengths to place us within Ross' perspective that not everything is right on this world, the world he seemingly left only three weeks ago and has unexpectedly returned to early. It's not until Ross himself starts to spot the growing discrepancies of this world's anomalies does Parrish engage the audience more fully with these events too. Driving on the wrong side of the road and his and Sharon's house being turned upside down, or rather, sideways, are noticeable enough, but it's the sharp, compressed close-ups of Ross realising that objects reflected in mirrors have their writing the correct way round instead of being traditionally reflected, as he knows it, that confirms we're not where we think we are. It adds a quiet speculative flavour to the film that reminds us this is science fiction, but his actions in matching the backwards writing to both Sharon at their home and to the alternate Webb at EUROSEC HQ can be interpreted as Ross attempting to crack some secret code that only another spy would understand. It's not precisely a foreign language to him, but he's now surrounded by encrypted messages that he must break. In turn, his own code is initially alien to those around him, both sides maintaining each other's secrets.

Once Ross determines that the answer must lie in the parallel relationship between this Earth and the other Earth, which rings harmoniously in Webb's speculative ears, it's decided by Ross and Webb that recovering the flight recorder from the abandoned Phoenix, still in stationary status, will prove both Ross' claims that this is, in fact, a parallel world, which in turn validates Webb's suspicions. A slight illogicality the film never quite recovers from is the passing acknowledgement that an autopsy on Kane shows his organs to be on the opposite side of his body, surely a more immediate and irrefutable confirmation that, from Webb's perspective, it's Ross and Kane that are the alternate versions of themselves. For *Doppelgänger*'s final gallop towards the finish line, the science fiction mentality swings the spy-fi personality out of the way, as a new *Dove* craft is constructed with opposite features to match the *Phoenix*'s own specifications. Disastrously, everything that could go wrong does go wrong. Blasting off from EUROSEC is successful enough, but Ross' attempts to dock with the *Phoenix* in the converted *Dove* malfunction, sending both craft spiralling back down to Earth and colliding with EUROSEC's space base. Ross, the *Phoenix* with its flight recorder and other key information relating to the confirmation of a parallel Earth are consumed by a roaring inferno, the secrets of either Earth dying within the vicious rage. It's very much the Anderson equivalent of a secret agent consuming their cyanide capsule to maintain their secrets from the enemy.

Ice Station EUROSEC

Comparisons to *2001: A Space Odyssey* are fraught when discussing *Doppelgänger*. That monolith of science fiction cinema, released well over a year before *Doppelgänger*, thus allowing the dust it kicked up to settle and for everyone to agree that a new standard of sci-fi had been set, impossibly hangs over the less experienced Andersons' own efforts. Ironic then that Stanley Kubrick should approach Century 21's special effects department to produce the model work for the film. However, if *Doppelgänger* has another cinematic parallel itself, one that's truly spy-fi to *Doppelgänger*'s sci-fi, then *Ice Station Zebra* is one such film that springs to mind. The similarities are distant but common – a star cast full of recognisable faces of Cold War era film and television, their directors had handled previous films with huge cult appeal (in Parrish's case, he was one of several directors on *Casino Royale*, whereas John Sterges directed the comparatively universally celebrated *The Magnificent Seven*), quality special effects and a divisive critical reception. Audiences and critics alike praise and disregard both films. Both films also could have been in close proximity right down to their release dates had Universal Pictures not delayed *Doppelgänger*'s release by a year. They both exude nail-biting climaxes that ultimately draw a line in the sand. In *Doppelgänger*'s case, its espionage heart beats louder due to the climax manifesting as a stalemate, both Earths keeping each other a secret from the other, like either side of the Iron Curtain's forces in *Ice Station Zebra*.

Doppelgänger gives the impression that it wants to be something more than many critics and other retrospective opinions on the film give it credit for. 'Thriller'[11] (Bentley, 2001), 'reportage'[12] (Cape Girardeau, 1970), 'speculative

---

[11] **Bentley, Chris** (2001). *The Complete Book of Captain Scarlet*. p. 114. Carlton Books. 1st edition.

[12] 'On the Rialto Screen'. *Southeast Missourian*. 65 (279). Cape Girardeau, Missouri: Naeter Bros. 4 September 1970. p. 9.

fantasy'[13] (Gerani, 2011), 'futuristic melodrama'[14] (Stoneham, 1972), 'science fiction yarn'[15] (Pittsburgh Press, 1969); many people summarised *Doppelgänger* as being many things, the most cohesive agreement to take away from the film's release is how people couldn't agree on what the film was trying to be, though it's quite telling that *Doppelgänger*'s espionage characteristics appeared to go unnoticed during the film's original reception. The strongest encapsulation one can make of *Doppelgänger* is how it veers between being science fiction in themes and spy-fiction in execution. Or the other way round, depending on which scenes we're watching. *Doppelgänger* swerves between its sci-fi and spy-fi mechanics, somehow trapped in both of them, unconfident enough to successfully merge the two together or attempt to break free from one or the other. The film's troubled genesis becomes an omen for its awkward fusion of genres. Producer Jay Kanter was unhappy with Gerry and Sylvia's near-200 page treatment, even after significant rewrites. Kanter only relented on the proposition that he would be allowed the final say on the film's director, eventually hiring Parrish. The Andersons unwilling to make further adjustments to a story they were already content with and Kanter was keen to assert his dominance.

Doppelgänger's efforts to find room for its espionage and science fiction themes have mostly gone unnoticed, even within the Gerry Anderson fandom itself. During Anderson Entertainment's 'The Gerry Anderson World Cup' event on Twitter in October of 2019, *Doppelgänger* found itself up against *UFO* and *Dick Spanner*, in an overall effort to determine the most popular Anderson productions, as voted for by the fans themselves. With *UFO* as its competitor, *Doppelgänger* didn't stand a chance, but its overall 4% of the votes, even compared to *Dick Spanner*'s 14% (with *UFO* stretching way out in front with 84%) is derisory. Time, otherwise a great healer to many misunderstood or skirted over works in television and film, hasn't been kind to this particular production, one that was planned as the great leap forward, but commands barely a passing acknowledgement even within Anderson circles. The one before *UFO*, as it's perhaps destined to remain, stands as a fascinating if unbalanced mixture of a science fiction heart with an espionage soul. *Doppelgänger* was designed to be the Andersons' giant leap, but winds up being a stumble in the dark. Like a secret agent, it mostly remains in the shadows.

---

[13] Gerani, Gary (2011). *Top 100 Sci-Fi Movies*. p. 29. IDW Publishing. 1st edition.
[14] Stoneham, Gordon (22 April 1972). 'Movie Week'. *The Montreal Gazette*. Network. p. 93.
[15] 'The Lively Arts'. *Pittsburgh Press*. E.W. Scripps Company. 28 December 1969. p. 50.

A QUESTION OF SURVIVAL: PARANOIA'S MEANING IN *UFO*

The climactic, claustrophobic moments of the episode 'Conflict' neatly summarise the genuine characteristics of *UFO*. Commander Ed Straker has ordered that all SHADO systems be shut down, including communication with SHADO Moonbase, their primary line of defence. This is done in stubborn defiance against his superior, General Henderson, who disbelieves Straker's seemingly wild theory that the aliens are using space debris dotted around Earth's orbit to cloak a fresh invasion. Straker demands that SHADO be rendered powerless in the hopes that he is proved right, that a UFO will slip through the net of SHADO, whilst all at SHADO and Moonbase freeze in desperate silence. Piercing out of the sky, a UFO plummets to Earth, inches away from attack. Reigniting SHADO into life, Straker orders a passing Sky-1 to quickly terminate the UFO's presence. Subdued, Henderson allows Straker's demands for all space junk to be cleared, a further weak link in Earth's defence exploited by the aliens is resolved.

Consider what it is that ignites the drama of this scene. It's not the oncoming attack of the UFO, a single craft that's easily and instantly destroyed by Sky-1. It's the clash of morals between Straker and Henderson, with the UFO attack a vital but background feature. Straker has his heart in his mouth and Henderson has blood in his eyes. Henderson and Straker's antagonistic relationship highlights the central idea of *UFO*: how humanity reacts to and survives this invisible alien war, one that's kept in the shadows, in the clouds, in the bucolic countryside. *UFO* isn't about humans versus aliens. It's about humans versus humans.

UFO is a series about the hows, not the whys. Minimal focus is given to the origin and purpose of the humanoid aliens of the series. They don't even have a name for their own species. They're just known as the aliens. The adventure doesn't occur on the alien's home world, it either occurs on Earth, the Moon or the space in-between the Earth and the Moon, all human locales. The capabilities, purpose, implications and emotional entanglements of SHADO are given much greater depth than their extra-terrestrial counterparts, and how those capabilities and purposes are shown gives *UFO* much of its narrative energy. In the world of *UFO*, the general reaction to the presence of alien life and the threat it presents is one of emotional paranoia, bureaucratic hysteria and militant exaggeration.

Survival Instincts

Based on little more than piecemeal evidence of unconfirmed sightings, SHADO is built from the ground up as an international military organisation with state of the art vehicles and personnel dotted across the globe. The construction of SHADO comes at great personal consequence to Straker. His newly formed marriage slowly deteriorates as his secretive and time-consuming work leading the formation of SHADO swallows him whole, whilst his once friendly relationship with Henderson becomes fractured as Henderson, of all people, is the one to recommend that Straker be SHADO's commander. All of this is seen within the events of the flashback episode 'Confetti Check A-OK'. Whilst it's not entirely explained why Henderson and Straker become increasingly bitter towards each other, several episodes down the line featuring appearances by Henderson suggest that SHADO's costly expense becomes a hindrance to him.

The paranoia in *UFO* ripples from episode to episode. In that same episode, Straker convinces the United Nations Special Committee to allow SHADO's birth by combining his factual, and skeletal, evidence with emotional speculation, suggesting that if the Earth is left unguarded, the aliens will attack more than humans, but families, loved ones, those who we can't live without including those of the committee who he's appealing to. It's emotionally exploitive on Straker's part, and encapsulates the runaway mental gymnastics humanity puts itself through to justify their line of work in defending the Earth against a civilisation who, as it eventually transpires, venture to Earth not out of hostility but out of avoiding their own extinction. 'Identified' establishes that the aliens in question come to Earth in an effort to harvest human organs for their own biological usage, but it's in 'ESP' that cements why the aliens are doing this. They come to Earth as a dying race, intent on consuming what they can of humanity's biological make-up in an effort to prolong their own existence. In *UFO*, survival goes both ways.

This is one layer of consequence to the paranoia of SHADO. The organisation's purpose is rooted in the suspicion that the aliens are hostile, driven by a desire to not simply murder humans but to decapitate them, when in fact the reason for their destructive means are not entirely antagonistic. Nowhere are the lines blurred better in the aptly named 'Survival', in which Captain Paul Foster and an alien find themselves marooned on the Moon's surface and forced to cooperate if either individual is to find help, resulting in a unspoken bond being formed. A tragic misunderstanding from a damaged radio communication on Foster's part results in the alien being killed by SHADO's Moon forces. Any hope at finding common ground is destroyed and the status quo of the alien menace resumes.

UFO's twilight episodes would scupper any chance for further reflection of the aliens' grey morals. Such episodes as 'Timelash', 'Mindbender', 'The Long Sleep' and 'Reflections in the Water' paint the aliens as destructive beyond reason, willing to manipulate human beings themselves to further their new-found aim of destroying SHADO itself, presumably as a result of SHADO's continued interference in the alien's plans. On a purely vehicular level, *UFO*'s trademark schizophrenia and emphasis on survival above all other factors is felt in SHADO's arsenal of machines. SHADO's core fleet of spacecraft, jets, submarines and tank-esque mecha recall a sense of thematically industrial scale in an Anderson production not felt since *Thunderbirds*. Again, fuelled by presumably precious few reasons beyond the personalised fear Straker was able to forcibly load into the United Nations Special Committee, SHADO is the very essence of undefined fear transformed into blatant, armoured, atomic danger, and all justified by the presence of a single UFO, two or three on a good day. The sight of a lone craft is enough to send SHADO into a scrambled frenzy of spacecraft launching, submarines charging and clipboards being passed around SHADO HQ. What keeps *UFO*'s paranoia intact and feeds its survival instincts is the distance maintained by SHADO in how much, or how little, it knows of the aliens it does battle against. Every strand of information SHADO has on the aliens is speculative, open-ended guesswork, determined by rigorous detective work. An entire military operation based on cosmic assumption. No wonder Henderson hates SHADO so much.

Humans as Cannon Fodder

UFO embraces its sense of the horrific unknown firmly with a curiously convoluted approach to the morals of the aliens. Throughout the series, episodes appear to clash on what kind of attitude the series wants to promote, in terms of how the aliens react and engage with SHADO and the Earth. On further inspection, the linear timeline portrayed a couple of paragraphs back in how the series cautiously portrayed the aliens as complex, desperate creatures before reducing them to fighting violently for the sake of violence perhaps isn't as linear.

Ironically, any sort of linear interpretation of *UFO*'s timeline can easily be argued against. Multiple viewing orders for the series distort which order you're supposed to view the series. Given *UFO*'s episodic nature, where episodes mostly exist on an independent basis from each other (with exceptions such as 'Exposed', which introduced Colonel Foster), this wouldn't normally be considered too much of an inconvenience. However, in the context of trying to pinpoint a straight forward sense of sensible progression for the aliens, *UFO* scrambles its intentions, perhaps deliberately, as the end result is the series' trademark paranoia remaining taut. Much like how SHADO engages with its human victims, you're refused an easy answer. In addition to 'ESP' and 'Timelash', 'Destruction', 'Flight Path', 'The Psychobombs', 'Kill Straker!' and 'The Man Who Came Back' all portray the aliens as boasting both telekinetic powers to connect with their human operatives and an in-depth understanding of human's emotional attachment. They torture their victims, rather than move in for a swift, easy kill. Mental and emotional manipulation characterise the method of attack used by the aliens in these episodes. It isn't readily apparent how, why or even who the aliens are targeting, shunting UFO into a cold war logic in which sleeper agents working for the other side slowly but surely manipulate the proceedings of SHADO in favour of the aliens.

SHADO continually operate in the dark with how little they come to know of the aliens over the course of the series, ensuring that SHADO's defences are left vulnerable to exploitation. The fear of the unknown drips in via not being able to know just how their vulnerable they are, given the rather omnipotent nature of the aliens, despite their seemingly weakened state of existence. From a story-telling perspective, such a move grants the series' writers the most offensive of excuses to wave away any tangible explanations for the aliens. The writers are granted to bestow any and all capabilities the aliens need, given whatever the story demanded, regardless of having to consider the consequences in how wildly juxtaposing one writer's characteristics from the next may be portraying the aliens. It's not the best move, but it does ensure some unpredictable scenarios for the organisation. The best example of SHADO's permanently weaned state and its unconsidered consequences in the scriptwriting department comes in the episode 'Reflections in the Water', in which Straker and Foster discover that the aliens have succeeded in creating exact replicas of SHADO's interior headquarters and its personnel, coupled with Straker fighting against Foster's replica, whom he first believes to be the real article. At no point does the episode attempt to divulge how the aliens were capable of performing such acts, when they remain portrayed as a race starved of resources. The episode is all about the forceful shock of alien-crafted doppelgängers, UFO's post-*Captain Scarlet* mentality coming to the boil. Nothing encapsulates the wild juxtaposition between UFO's on-the-nose paranoia and lack of well-defined world-building for its aliens than this episode. That very lack of explanations for the aliens grants UFO a relentless petrification. Once again, the focus isn't on the aliens, it's on the humans, and the state of permanent fear they're forced to exist in.

Paranoia Exposed

UFO goes for several tactics in ingraining a continual shock and fear onto its characters and its audience. 'Tiger' Ninestein may have regularly warned his colleagues, and *Terrahawks*' audiences, to expect the unexpected, but where

Terrahawks ensured that an all-ages approach was used to smoothed over the chaotic cracks of grotesque monsters and surreal story-telling, it was *UFO* that made the unexpected the driving force of maintaining its balance between angst-ridden human drama and explosive adventure, characteristic of both Gerry and Sylvia Anderson's output and of Lew Grade's commercially-driven television empire.

That reminder of the need for commerce in Andersons' productions, sometimes rubbing shoulders with artistic integrity and sometimes overpowering that integrity, points to a more tangible reason why the aliens are so loosely defined in *UFO* and why SHADO remains on perpetual red alert. The aliens' varying capabilities gives the series free reign to create diverse scenarios that kept an aesthetic freshness going, evidenced by the psychedelic nature of that final batch of episodes. SHADO's vehicular craft range from submarines, tanks, spacecraft, jet fighters and more, pointing to a renewed focus on the series' merchandise possibilities after *The Secret Service* and *Joe 90* had taken their eye off of the toy ball.

But *UFO*'s unrestrained paranoia is indisputable, whatever possible commercialised intentions may truly be giving the series its initial surface level appeal. Beneath that surface lurks a foreboding mentality in how to entertain audiences with science fiction adventure. *UFO*'s camp futurism can't help but date the series immensely and thus soften the impact the series attempts to make in how riddled with paranoia it is, often to terminal ends. Nevertheless, *UFO* showed on numerous occasions that it knew exactly what kind of series it wanted to be. With nearly a decade's worth of 'kidult' entertainment under their belt, the Andersons and Century 21 were intent on producing something that wasn't immediately accessible to kids. Something that casted a much more serious gaze upon the action-driven exploits of a super-secret security outfit defending the world from unseen, unknown aliens. Actions aren't easily resolved in the space of a single episode. Effects ripple from story to story. The responsibility seat is regularly shown to be a strenuous position that not everyone can stomach, its implications made all the more impossible to manage given the underlying, unspoken fear of when or how the next invasion may occur.

THE BRINGERS OF FEAR: THE HORROR OF *SPACE: 1999*'S YEAR 1 AND YEAR 2

Few have been able to recover from the thematic whiplash between *Space: 1999*'s first and second series, colloquially known as Year 1 and Year 2. The aesthetic makeover *Thunderbirds* experienced between its first and second series, cushioned by the necessary changes made to the styles of the marionettes for *Thunderbirds Are Go*, is whimsical by comparison. In *Space: 1999*'s Year 2, the sets have shrunk in size, established characters have vanished with no explanation, novice characters arrive without backstory and forced attempts at humour are made necessary to ensure that each episode ends on a note of cringe-inducing chummy pleasantness, all in an effort to appease the all-important American market. Where many elements that had made *Space: 1999*'s first series a standout production of 1970s science fiction were scrubbed clean and made to look as if they had never existed, one element managed to survive the culling. Far from intact, mind you. The driving, primal thrill of space horror is an essential tool in *Space: 1999*'s arsenal, but the manner in which Year 1 and Year 2 go about grappling with that horror clash to horrendous proportions.

Fear's Other Dominion

The philosophical stance of *Space: 1999*'s Year 1 has been widely documented and analysed elsewhere in other publications, as Moonbase Alpha's unexpected propulsion into deep space sends them on a journey that questions humanity's purpose, genesis, survival and even the idea that the nuclear accident responsible wasn't as random as first thought. A raw, animalistic nerve prowls itself around these chin-stroking ideas, ready to pounce on the viewer, an unending fear of the unknown the Alphans have been catapulted into. In Year 1 and Year 2, fear is presented as a consequence of Moonbase Alpha's perilous, unpredictable journey through the stars. The dangers the crew encounters on a regular basis are beyond their understanding of the universe. What distinguishes Year 1 and Year 2 is that in Year 1, fear is treated with a sincere seriousness, that this is something to be genuinely afraid of, whereas Year 2 strips away the fear factor and portrays something closer to horror as a gateway to inconsequential adventure that places Moonbase Alpha in danger but without any discernible sense of threat boiling over the surface. It's comparatively light-hearted.

Throughout Year 1, the fear ascends in its intensity, before shocking the audience in short, sharp bursts, with the episodes otherwise riddled in unease and suspense that's difficult to untangle. It leaves the Alphans in a mass. 'Death's Other Dominion' spends much of its runtime easing the audience into a state of distrust as the promise of an everlasting paradise from a human space exploration crew on the frozen planet Ultima Thule isn't all it's cracked up to be. The episode swells to one of the series' most memorable ends when, taken away from his self-made haven, Dr Cabot Rowland succumbs to an instant and gruesome death. The image of Rowland's decomposed corpse, flesh emitting air as if freshly dead, remains a superbly grim image for an episode of *Space: 1999* to end on. It is a startling, single summation of the price paid for immortality.

The events that spiral out of control in 'Earthbound' are equally grotesque, but reliant on the human form in a different way to 'Death's Other Dominion'. 'Earthbound' provides a conclusion to the character arc for Simmonds, senior commissioner of the International Lunar Commission, who has made no secret that his presence on Moonbase Alpha is as unwanted by Koenig as himself. A race of aliens slip into the Moon's view, asleep in a state of suspended animation as they journey from their barren world in search of a new, more fertile home. Simmonds seizes an opportunity to forcibly join their trip in the hopes of returning to Earth, safely encased in the same animation as the aliens. However, he demands that he join the aliens' mission before they have the required time and resources to adapt their animation technology to suit a human mind. Awakening inside his suspended animation chamber after take-off, Simmonds initially believes he has awoken from a long spell of deep sleep, but barely any time has passed. Unable to break free, he becomes doomed to drift through space in an alien tomb, his cries for help impenetrable to the other aliens. Like Doctor Helena Russell's screams at the end of 'Death's Other Dominion', it's an unfiltered, uncensored cry that brings the episode to an end. In Year 1, fear is treated with dignity in its delivery and economy in its amount.

But it's here that Year 2 rears its head, and … Oh boy. The good will built up throughout Year 1 is tossed out of the window in favour of sustaining the series for a new market. Ironically, some would argue that the series was no longer worth saving. Throughout Year 2, the build-up to these moments is removed entirely and replaced by episodes opening with a vast dump of expositional narration from Doctor Russell, spoken in-universe as a documentation of Moonbase Alpha's journey through space. It's something we never saw or heard her do in Year 1 and is just one of numerous minute details scattered throughout the second series that reminds us how desperate *Space: 1999* was now trying to be more like *Star Trek*, instead of *Space: 1999*.

Whilst this move comes in an effort to fill the gap left by that earlier sci-fi classic, it comes at the expense of how *Space: 1999* handled its fear motifs. These narrations serve to get introductory explanations as quickly and succinctly as possible, regardless of how tacked-on they feel, so that Alphans and viewers alike may be thrown into the action without the quiet build-up that Year 1 delighted in doing. *Space: 1999* is now fixated on telling us to be intrigued, rather than showing us.

One Moment of Fear

The things that Year 2 does show us is a kind of fear stretched away from the quieter philosophical learnings of Year 1. *Space: 1999*'s second series featured a greater reliance on aggressive and grotesque alien monsters. Year 1 wasn't entirely shorn of such a thing, but it was mostly content to veer between humanoid aliens and cosmic intelligences lacking a physical form. Year 2 plummets straight down the middle and opts for rubber-suited creatures terrorising the Alphans on a regular basis. How you react to such creatures can vary from one's personal phobias, but the message comes through loud and clear – *Space: 1999* was now trading in the gradual sense of unease for action-focused propulsion; the slow burn for the instant fix. On some level, it's disingenuous to regard the alien antagonists fought in Year 2 as being any more ridiculous than those in Year 1. It's all inherently ridiculous. That's the nature of cosmic sci-fi entertainment on the sort of scale that *Space: 1999* carves its identity out of. But throughout Year 2, the execution of these threats isn't shown to be as considered as those throughout Year 1.

Year 1 featured an array of unseen yet permanently felt cosmic intelligences. 'Black Sun', 'Ring Around the Moon', 'Space Brain' and 'Force of Life' all made use of these invasive forces making themselves known to the Alphans to disastrously cataclysmic effect. Consider that the one episode of Year 1 to feature a rubber costumed creature proudly stands as arguably the series' most successful stab at genuine horror. The creature in 'Dragon's Domain' is only ever partially seen, yet its presence, superbly executed, is more than felt. Bathed in undefined light and emanating steam, it's an incredible payoff to an episode filled with dread. Now consider that in Year 2, we have episodes such as 'The Rules of Luton' and 'All That Glisters', in which our antagonistic aliens consists of talking trees and gurgling rocks. The quality of these episodes overall, unsurprisingly, fail to reach the creative heights experienced in Year 1.

The Alphans do their best to react with the same shock and fear that they faced throughout Year 1, but rarely do things become as convincing as they did before. The engagement tactics from the audience become scuppered when, with Year 1's peaks still fresh in the rear view mirror, we can't help but be pulled out of the jeopardy when we witness how sub-par things become.

Even the dangers themselves can't be bothered to be sustained until the episode's end. Whereas many Year 1 episodes conclude on downcast moods in which the Alphans, reflective of the latest disaster they've been subjected to, acknowledge that there are aspects to the universe they will never fully comprehend, Year 2 episodes end on regularly annoying light-heartedness. Having all the characters so darn cheerful at the latest life-threatening attacks they've been forced to experience can be seen as providing a rare attempt at giving them a happy ending (so often absent in this series), but these chummy instances do much to render the episode's drama null and void.

Throughout Year 2, sandwiched between unnecessary info dumps and sickly larks, the petrifying thrills of *Space: 1999*'s first series give way to a rogues gallery of not entirely convincing rubber monster suits who terrorise Moonbase Alpha, which is where *Space: 1999*'s Year 2 attempts to find much of its own take on inducing fear. But as a rule, fear isn't totally reliant on a slow-burn approach. It can come in many different forms. In Year 1's case, it was often an internal experience but in Year 2, it was external, a physical sort of fear. The sight of numerous alien creatures, horrific in design, is a step further into grim body horror from Year 1's emphasis on humanoid aliens. In the series' only attempt at a genuine two-part adventure, 'The Bringers of Wonder' offers the most extreme variant on this method, featuring physically repulsive alien creatures disguising themselves as friends and loved ones of Moonbase Alpha, who convince the Alphans that, under their human disguises, they have managed to locate the Moonbase in an effort to rescue them. The aliens' true intentions and physical appearances are gradually revealed throughout the episodes. Where the Alphans initially embrace their human counterparts with welcoming friendliness, seeing the creatures in their undisguised forms results in cries of terror and utter rejection at their repulsive bodies.

Unfortunately, it's not as convincing as it wants to be. Once again, we have a scenario where the characters emit a sense of fear that struggles to be shared with the audience. The alien creatures remain an enthusiastic design – slime-covered with exposed bodily fluids oozing across their mountainous forms, glowing in a sickly alien colour, they're a far cry from the cerebrally-orientated horrors of Year 1, for better or worse, depending on how terrible you may find these particular creatures. Such is their mutated form that they don't walk, merely shuffle at a suitably sluggish pace, adding an unintentional whiff of comedy into the proceedings. There's little thematic and character-wise in Year 1 that felt compelled to be so oversaturated as the physical terrors 'The Bringers of Wonder' brings. With just their physical form to induce fear, there's not a great deal else that these aliens can do to petrify the audience. These unnamed jelly-like creatures have their lack of genuine danger they represent enhanced by the fact that only three alien costumes were ever produced, and life-sized photographic cut-outs of the creatures were utilised for crowd scenes. Terence Feely's script for this two-parter began life under the working title of 'The Globs', which sounds less like an alien menace hungry to attack and enslave human victims but more like something more suited to *The Trap Door*. This is Year 2's approach to infusing fear into *Space: 1999* in a cosmic nutshell – immediacy over substance.

Another Time, Another Fear

This isn't to say that a well-constructed alien enemy can't strike fear into the hearts and minds of those who watch it and will continue to be embraced by its lingering presence after watching it. Such cinematic classics as *Alien* and *The Quatermass Xperiment* are proof of this, their menacing other-worldly antagonists regarded as classics in the genre. The key to creative success comes in the execution. And curiously, *Alien* and one key episode from *Space: 1999*'s first year demonstrate how that physical horror can best be pulled off. *Alien* works so brilliantly in communicating its deadliness to the audience because the titular creature spends much of the film partially obscured. The audience become unable to place a grip on the creature before them, heightening a sense of dread. Almost four years before *Alien*'s May 1979 premier, *Space: 1999* had already pulled that same feat off with 'Dragon's Domain', another case of disguising your alien menace just enough to maintain a sense of gut-wrenching mystery, but showing enough to strike a very real terror into your audience. The aliens in 'The Bringers of Wonder', who are fully exposed all too early in the story when Commander John Koenig sees through their cover-up, somehow crystallises everything Year 2 couldn't do that Year 1 had already achieved.

Space: 1999's second series ultimately squanders the fear-drenched techniques established throughout the first series. The crash-bang-wallop approach Year 2 mostly sticks to feels camp in its execution and malnourished in its build-up. It's impossible to deny that all aspects of *Space: 1999* are ridiculous, which brings to mind how one distinguishes between the inherent ridiculousness of Year 1 and Year 2. The difference is that Year 1 is sincere and genuine in making you feel uncomfortable, in sharing the fear felt by the inhabitants of Moonbase Alpha as they pass through one horror to the next, without consent. Year 2 isn't concerned with such enriching viewing experiences. It's concerned with picking at tired horror-themed aesthetics and doing nothing cleverly scary with them. It's focused on action over substance, adventure over drama, disposability over being watchable. The deeper you slip into *Space: 1999*, the clearer it becomes that the real horror of Year 2 is, of course, having to endure watching it in the first place.

POWER, FAMILY & AUTHORITY IN CENTURY 21

Gerry and Sylvia Anderson's twenty first centuries salivate at the concepts of security, power and authority. Its heroes, whether marionette or live-action, can't get enough of it. A looming irony casts itself across these worlds, in that where much of these productions from *Supercar* to *Space: 1999* and beyond with Gerry's 'solo' works portray their worlds as being relatively peaceful, the abundance of security organisations that uphold that peace, with their various commanders' fingers on the atomic triggers, suggests otherwise. We've already explored how *Thunderbirds* positions its populace as being constantly on edge, ready for the next destruction. It becomes easy to stretch that mindset across many more of the Andersons' worlds, once you realise that the sheer gluttony of rescue, security and military outfits that are the focus of these productions implies a universe drunk in a quasi-fascist state of militant might, a worldview that's sometimes softened by the familiarity of family ties running these outfits.

Throughout the Supermarionation era in particular, the action and adventure so synonymous with an Anderson production arises from the multitude of organisations that maintain the security of the world the Supermarionation stories are set in. When we think of the adventures these heroes embark on, we envision such sights as Thunderbird 2 blasting off from Tracy Island, Marineville descending below ground as the cry for Battle Stations drums out, or some structural form collapsing to reveal an SPV, ready to hunt down the latest Mysteron agent. The prominence of these outfits, often independently run, free from scrutiny by governing powers, swells into a fetishizing of militant authority backed by technological power and with it a glamorisation of global conflict. The structure of regimented authority within Anderson worlds hasn't gone unnoticed elsewhere. Critic Mark Bould delivers a succinct summary that the Supermarionation era, from *Supercar* to *Joe 90*, celebrated 'patriarchal command structures' and 'inevitably sided with a global military.'[16] Let's take this opportunity then to expand and pinpoint on Bould's not entirely untrue encapsulation of how these productions portray power.

---

[16] Bould, M (2003). 'Film and television' *The Cambridge Companion to Science Fiction* (eds James, E. Mendlesohn, F). p. 90. Cambridge University Press. 12th edition.

International Bands of Heroes

Anderson productions aren't wholly unique in such portrayals of power. It's an inherent aspect of action-propelled science fiction. There are stories across all mediums of the genre that focus on semi-military organisations established to combat an evil force so monumental that it requires the assembly of a unique group of people and powers, a pure fantasy of adventure in its most explosive form. But the subtext remains readily visible, the consumption and abuse of authoritative power that the likes of Spectrum, WASP, the Terrahawks and more exhibit isn't so subtle. Speaking to Starlog Magazine, Ed Bishop gave quite an on-the-nose summary of how the Supreme Headquarters Alien Defence Organisation functions. 'I guess if you analyse the SHADO set-up, it's kind of a fascist organisation with a law unto itself ... answerable to practically no-one. Anarchic, despotic, but somehow, it was working for the total good.'[17] Bishop hits a key, unifying point in how many of the security and rescue outfits in the Andersons' worlds operate and their justification for doing so in such explosive manners – the idea of these outfits being a law unto themselves. Then again, *UFO* is one of the few Anderson productions where the security organisation in questions does have a higher power grinding them down in the form of General Henderson of the International Astrophysical Commission, a body seemingly designed to constantly question SHADO's actions and hold them to account.

The running theme of operating above traditionally established law and order grows in its portrayal of intensity from the World Space Patrol of *Fireball XL5* to the Hypermarionation reimagining of Spectrum. It even continues to have a ripple effect in *Thunderbirds Are Go* and *Firestorm*. Even in death it seems, the Andersons' themes remain unstoppable.

Fireball XL5 and *Stingray* share a more accountable aspect of their portrayal of authority, in that both the World Space Patrol and the World Aquanaut Security Patrol answer to something resembling a higher power. The presence of the World Security Patrol in *Stingray* implies, though it's never confirmed, that WASP is just one branch of a much larger outfit with high-tech security outfits designated a region of the Earth to maintain security. Throughout the series, we see how WASP and by extension *Stingray* act almost in an ambassadorial role to underwater aliens who may have their presence unwittingly discovered by the terraneans. Not everything in *Stingray* is as diplomatic, however. The lawless divide between human and alien results in *Stingray* having the power to unleash devastating retaliation against any underwater civilisation it so chooses.

---

[17] Hirsch, D. Bishop, E. (1982) 'Commander Straker Speaks! An Interview With Ed Bishop' *Starlog Magazine* (ed Zimmerman, H). No. 55, pp. 52-54.

Shoot first and ask questions later. The power WASP has therefore is summarised by the idea that WASP holds the underwater world in a much firmer grip than the mighty Titan could ever hope to achieve. Titan may have global domination in his sights, underwater and overland, but it's WASP that we see continually exercising their powerful presence over alien races who all too often fail to counter their explosive influence. If an alien race is deemed to be a threat, then *Stingray*'s eradication of them harks back to Bishop's perspective on fighting 'for the total good.'

One of the most explicit examples of this comes in 'The Big Gun', where Troy Tempest and crew succeed in demolishing an entire alien city when a single enemy craft belonging to that civilisation wreaks havoc. Judgement is delivered by the humans in the most extreme sense. It's both curious and chilling how despite Titan being portrayed as the one keen to overthrow civilisations and take his fascist empire to all of the underwater worlds, WASP are the ones who have just cause and the means to keep the underwater worlds in a state of fear.

Speaking of a world in fear, Spectrum and its live-action counterpart SHADO, match their petrifying antagonists with a colossal handling of authoritarian power framed as necessary security to keep their worlds functioning. Spectrum arguably represents science fiction's ultimate power fantasy, a gargantuan organisation with influence and resources across the world, seemingly left to function on its own terms, devoid of being held to account. Spectrum is such an enormous venture that it outstrips its main purpose of combating the Mysterons. During the series, Colonel White, commander-in-chief of Spectrum, clarifies that fighting against the Mysterons is Spectrum's calling. 'That is our basic function,' he explains. What he and the series overlook is that Spectrum were fully in existence prior to their accidental starting of the war of nerves. What exactly were Spectrum doing before the Mysterons declared their war? What power were they exercising on the world below Cloudbase? The series never divulges this.

Cloudbase itself hangs over the world like an ever-watchful eye, just as omniscient as the Mysterons themselves. Spectrum regularly leave a trail of destruction in their wake when countering the latest Mysteron threat, the London Car-Vu being a prime example at the expense the tax payer must endure for not being Mysteronised. Yet Spectrum justify their destructive expense by being the only organisation that has any hope of stopping the Mysterons in their slow-burning war against the Earth. This isn't strictly because Spectrum possess any unique capabilities, beyond the indestructible Captain Scarlet. It's simply because Spectrum are given free rein to perform any act they deem necessary to stop the Mysterons. However, it's worth still remembering that Spectrum was granted power in abundance long before the Mysterons were discovered, signalling that Spectrum do much to keep the world in check. No other Anderson series prior to *Captain Scarlet and the Mysterons* had portrayed unquestioned authority at such dizzying heights, and all in the name of worldwide peace.

Once the puppets had been dispensed with by Century 21 and a more adult audience became their targets, the Anderson worlds took on a darker edge. SHADO is disconnected from the world it defends, so much so that Commander Ed Straker runs the outfit like a dictator would run a totalitarian state. Straker's word even has the power to override his own superior in the form of General Henderson, even when Henderson is in full threatening mode. In the episode Conflict, Straker displays how effective and necessary his authoritarian stance is to Henderson during a UFO attack by switching off all of SHADO in an effort to prove to a disbelieving Henderson that the aliens are exploiting man-made space junk to pass through SHADO's defences. It's only seeing Straker at work, in full flow, does Henderson relent in his anger and allows the clearance of the space junk, effectively bowing to SHADO to continue running its morally judgemental mission of defending the Earth. Destruction employs a different approach by showing Straker's worldview coming into collision with real-world politics and how he's forced to navigate that. Any sense of subtly in how these themes would be delivered would be lost entirely with the 1980s TV pilot *Space Police*, the acorn from which Gerry's final live-action TV series *Space Precinct* grew, with its premise of intergalactic cops maintaining law and order amongst humans and aliens alike.

Family Ties

Other series employ a different spin on their showings of unquestioned authority in the name of security. Several Anderson productions give their semi-fascist states warmer portrayals thanks to family units forming the personnel of these organisations. *Thunderbirds* is the obvious contender here, but *Joe 90*, *Stingray* and even *Terrahawks* exhibit this tactic.

Following on from the likes of the World Security Patrol, *Thunderbirds* takes the plunge by positioning International Rescue as an outfit entirely freed from any sort of oversight whatsoever, but justifying this by framing the organisation as an entirely humanist one, in which vigilantism can be interpreted as do-gooder heroism. International Rescue are in possessions of vehicles and equipment that enable them to take high-scale disaster scenarios entirely into their own hands. Just as Spectrum are the only ones who can battle the Mysterons, International Rescue are the only ones who can combat against bombs strapped to atomic-powered passenger planes, collapsed skyscraper buildings and runaway space rockets. People place their lives entirely in International Rescue's hands, but never hold those hands to account, thanks to the organisation's life-saving efforts. That sense of power is at permanent risk of being exploited, however. In 'Trapped in the Sky', Jeff Tracy gives the alarming view that International Rescue's equipment could be used to destroy life, a deadly consequence of operating an outfit of this scale without checks and balances. The atomic arsenal housed within Tracy Island is under constant siege from the Hood, but never from the authorities.

If anything, we see that danger occur within the events of *Captain Scarlet*, as numerous Spectrum agents are Mysteronised over the course of the series, not only Captain Scarlet, but Captain Black, Captain Brown and Captain Indigo. 'Seek and Destroy' sees several Angel Interceptor jets hijacked by the Mysterons, whilst 'Attack on Cloudbase' sees Symphony Angel dream of the Mysteronised Captain Black quietly invading their headquarters amidst the devastation of Cloudbase being torn apart by the Mysterons, the ultimate image of the heroes' technology in enemy hands.

Despite International Rescue being one of the worst offenders for abuse of power, it's striking to think that it makes use of the semi-used family unit in Anderson productions to soften the image. The snug familiarity of a family-run rescue organisation somehow enhances the humanitarian aspect of International Rescue, but there remains the hierarchy of authority embedded within these organisations. Jeff Tracy isn't as temperamental as Commander Zero or Commander Shore, but as soon as John Tracy radios in from Thunderbird 5, he instantly becomes that same figure of authority, a human embodiment of the power commanded by International Rescue. Jeff's sons have a tendency to drop the father act whenever the Thunderbirds leap into action and refer to Jeff in 'sirs' during a rescue operation, the similar acknowledgement of authority that Troy Tempest would address to Commander Shore. It's an extension of the family atmosphere seen in *Stingray*, in which Shore and daughter Atlanta would casually maintain a strict commander-lieutenant relationship, only for that relationship to instantly melt into father-daughter recognition once Battle Stations were concluded.

Joe 90's World Intelligence Network may leave less destruction of property in their wake, but they arguably leave scarring of a more mental nature, yet this is made acceptable by the homely atmosphere of the series with its intimate group of characters, much of which are family. *Joe 90*'s world is one where one's identity is allowed to be copied and pasted into somebody else, all in the name of global security and freedom. WIN regularly resort to crude, morally questionable methods of capturing brain patterns for *Joe 90* to utilise, deciding that it's better to either not inform the unsuspecting captured person or to send up the ridiculous nature of their request, betting on the individual in question to jokingly go along with the gag. Brain transfers – whatever next! It's ludicrous, but it's a pleasant gag Joe, Professor Mac and Uncle Sam share between them. It's also utterly unnerving that these are the morals *Joe 90* decides to go with, made all the more apparent when the series refuses to divulge if WIN are held to account by a more neutral yet higher power. We're drip-fed minute chunks of confirmation that WIN functions in the interests of the free world, but it's a free world as conformed by totalitarian Western superpowers.

Fast forward some fifteen years and after a lengthily absence from our screens, Gerry Anderson, now divorced from Sylvia, focused back on entertaining a much younger audience with 1983's *Terrahawks*, rather than attempt to appeal to his now much older, original audience that had grown up on Supermarionation and live-action. *Terrahawks* harked back to the simpler, less sophisticated stance to world-building as seen in *Supercar* and *Fireball XL5*, yet it exhibited all the now stereotypical tropes of an independent, quasi-military outfit being the stars of the series. The Terrahawks organisation functions in much the same way as Spectrum or SHADO – independently run, tasked with a mission no other outfit could possibly endure, free to roam across the Earth and space causing as much havoc and destruction as the enemy for the sake of world peace. However, the handful of crew members who form the Terrahawks outfit lends the series an intimacy within the characters that echoes the family set-ups of *Thunderbirds* and *Joe 90*.

Post-puppet Power

Humour is maintained across the series through two distinct and dysfunctional family units – one involving android queen Zelda, her slovenly son Yung-Star, her self-absorbed sister Ci-Star and Ci-Star's malevolent, scheming child It-Star. Back on Earth, a less squabbling yet equally comical dynamic is found between Doctor 'Tiger' Ninestein, Captain Mary Falconer and the spherical robotic Sergeant Major Zero, who form a loose father-mother-child scenario. 'Tiger' acts as the overpowering authority figure, Mary the calming, humanist influence and Zero the eager, misunderstood, uncontrollable child. Both 'Tiger' and Zelda exert an iron-fisted rule over their respective outfits, but where 'Tiger''s might-makes-right mentality is a human embodiment of many of the authoritarian themes in Gerry and Sylvia's worlds (despite *Terrahawks* not featuring Sylvia's involvement), it's Zelda's ramshackle family that feels like a natural extension of *Stingray*, *Joe 90* and *Thunderbirds*' family values. Zelda's constant inability to defeat the Terrahawks and plunder the Earth is reflected in the instability of her family and her lack of control over it, the final comment seeming to be that family is the largest disruptive influence to authority in the Andersons' twenty first centuries.

The male-dominated, technologically enhanced future worlds of the Andersons' work would appear very much in tune with patriarchal attitudes that 20th century science fiction favoured. The influence of the family unit throughout these productions lends a curious and interesting spin on how power and authority is executed in how the Andersons decided the twenty first century should be portrayed. Linking the Supermarionation era with attitudes of its time still further, the distinct lack of mother figures in the Tracy and the McClaine families enhances the fact that authority in these marionette worlds is commanded by male figures. The likes of female authority figures of Zelda and Mary demonstrate widened view of how such an irrefutable element of the Andersons' output is represented. Power and authority, however problematic it may appear in its implications of abuse and world domination, is an inescapable aspect of the Andersons' work. It's a socio-political foundation from which the deafening roar of a Thunderbirds' blast off may be enabled and with it, the excitement of anything being able to happen within the next half hour, or longer.

TRACYS, LADIES AND MANSERVANTS: GENDER AND CLASS STRUCTURE IN *THUNDERBIRDS*

Thunderbirds has staying power for eclectic reasons. Its premise of a family-run rescue outfit provides an adrenaline-charged wholesomeness, with that premise is tied to cinematic-levels of techno-science adventure that hardwires an explosive sense of fun into the series. *Thunderbirds* is also celebrated for its memorable characters, the American Space Race captured in marionette form via Jeff Tracy and his five sons, but it's the characters outside of the Tracy family that command the most attention. Where the Tracy boys' interchangeable good looks and personalities blend together, the aristocratic secret agent Lady Penelope and her conman-turned-manservant Parker are the more iconic characters that the series has to offer, and with good reason. Daniel O'Brien goes so far as to say that these two are 'the only real *characters* in the show…'.[18] The culture clash between the upper class Penelope and the below-stairs Parker interjects some welcome bursts of comedy within *Thunderbirds*' action-heavy stories. But there are other reasons to pay attention to these two characters. Prizing their respective personas open more reveals that *Thunderbirds* offers up a distinctive perspective on the portrayal of women in science fiction, but Penelope and Parker also provide a gateway into how *Thunderbirds* delivers a purposefully composed approach to class structure.

Elegance, Charm and Deadly Gender

To start with, let's focus on the most obvious portrayal of class patriarchy and gender transgression that *Thunderbirds* offers – Lady Penelope and Parker. These two characters are *Thunderbirds*' greatest strengths in the series' definition of class and gender. For a series that's dominated by mecha-action, *Thunderbirds*' emphasis in exploring this avenue isn't wholly unique in the context of television science fiction. Explorations of gender and

---

[18] O'Brien, D (2000). 'Supermarionation, Superspies and Car Sickness' *SF:UK: How British Science Fiction Changed the World*. p. 83. Reynolds & Hearn Ltd. 1st edition.

sex have consistently proved fertile ground for sci-fi to explore in, whichever medium, as Rebecca Feasey notes; '... science fiction and fantasy television has a keen interest in exploring representations of sex and gender in society.'[19] A patriarchal command between the two classes, with the affluent upper class easily commanding the less privileged working class, is shown in Lady Penelope's employment of Parker and his unique, ie criminal, capabilities. Lady Penelope is the one in command of the situation, yet it's Parker who is often tasked, willingly or unwillingly, with getting his hands dirty, though Penelope will break out her own unique set of skills when dealing with enemy agents outside of International Rescue's danger zones. Where the Tracy boys exhibit a typical male dominance in science fiction by being the pilots of their own respective Thunderbird craft, Parker has a much greater claim to being the pilot of FAB 1, her ladyship's luxury Rolls Royce, than Penelope.

FAB 1 is capable of all manners of spy-fi combat techniques – machine guns hidden behind lightbulbs and grill plates, able to be deployed at the touch of a button. Yet it's always Parker who pushes those buttons and rarely Penelope, content to recline in the backseat and bark out her orders. There's a comment here on how despite Lady Penelope's presence as a central character within *Thunderbirds* pushing the envelope of male-centred sci-fi of the era, the tradition of male dominance at the controls of speculative future technology remains firmly in place. Early on in the series, *Thunderbirds* is keen to demonstrate why female characters aren't permitted within walking distance of the technology designed, built and flown by the male patriarchy. In 'Vault of Death', Lady Penelope's first on-screen experience of driving FAB 1 herself nearly results in the deaths of herself and her passengers when her utter inexperience and skill in driving the car quickly become apparent. Even earlier on, 'The Mighty Atom' sees Scott and Virgil engaged in stopping nuclear devastation in Australia, whilst Lady Penelope, who had begged to experience a genuine rescue in an effort to feel like part of the International Rescue team, remains on Thunderbird 2, offering no assistance. Her petrified reaction to the titular Mighty Atom itself, a robotic mouse capable of photographing enclosed spaces for the efforts of espionage, is the icing on a particularly sexist cake.

Fortunately, in the efforts of enabling the series to at least not continue being sexist instead of being genuinely progressive, Lady Penelope's immediate popularity with viewers ensured that her presence in *Thunderbirds* became a more positive one. More episodes began being composed with her as the capable, determined female spy and with it better

---

[19] Feasey, R (2008). 'Science fiction and fantasy television: challenging dominant gender roles' *Masculinity and Popular Television*. Edinburgh University Press. p. 58. 1st edition.

characterisation. By 'Brink of Disaster', her driving skills are shown to have improved tremendously, and with it her abilities to utilise FAB 1's arsenal. Being able to drive a road-going vehicle doesn't quite stand as the huge leap forward in positive depictions of female characters that *Thunderbirds* is often given credit for, particularly when in the world of *Thunderbirds*, a car is shown to be anticlimactic compared to the vast array of advanced air, land, space and sea vehicles. However, it also shows some sense of awareness on the show-makers to advance Penelope's character in positive directions and ultimately shows that she can now pilot her own vehicle as well as the boys, something ultimately pushed for by Sylvia Anderson herself.

If anything, slotting Penelope in the driver's seat is an everlasting image that further shows how the character was a world away from the male patriarchy of Tracy Island. O'Brien suggests that Jeff Tracy 'never thought to include a customised, fully armed pink Rolls-Royce, number plate FAB 1, in his fleet (probably not the kind of image Gerry Anderson wanted for the all-male, all-macho International Rescue).' Where O'Brien discusses FAB 1 disparagingly, the sheer success of Lady Penelope, first as a character and then proceeding to become a franchise within *Thunderbirds* herself, brings its own reward. It's a brief sequence and only happens in a single episode, but Lady Penelope in control of FAB 1 is a visual reminder of the power and influence the character was now having over the series, now finding it easier to command the screen within the male hierarchy. Even when Lady Penelope is introduced in the series as firmly part of the aristocracy and therefore high up the social ladder, *Thunderbirds* has always been more concerned with portraying a hierarchy of a more technological nature, one where International Rescue holds dominance over the rest of this futuristic world thanks to the whole point of the Thunderbird machines being that they're the most advanced craft of their kind. It takes a while for the series to elevate Lady Penelope to that same standard.

Below Atomic Stairs

Parker encapsulates the privilege of being male in a science fiction world. He isn't born into the upper class world of Penelope's. Instead, he opts for a life of crime prior to him becoming a part of International Rescue. The *TV21* comic book spin-off revealed the origins for how he and Penelope actually met, detailing how Penelope acquired his services in the middle of an attempted robbery, effectively blackmailing him to work for her in place of serving prison time. Despite not entering into the high society of Penelope or the technological decadence of the International Rescue, Parker is more than apt in piloting the futuristic vehicles bestowed upon him, shown in his lack of difficulty in driving FAB 1 or the even more sophisticated ocean-faring yacht FAB 2. In the mecha-defined world of *Thunderbirds*, the advantage of being male is not requiring any assistance in piloting the advanced super-mechs of this world. This reads like a comment on what really separates the genders of Penelope and Parker in the sci-fi context of *Thunderbirds*, ie where this series adheres to science fiction's trope of male hierarchy in technologically advanced worlds. This is something noted by Helen Merrick, commenting that science fiction 'has been considered a predominantly masculine field which, through its focus on science and technology, "naturally" excludes women and by implication, considerations of gender.'[20] In the context of *Thunderbirds*, this idea rings true, in that technology is in the hands of men and men alone. The Thunderbird machines are all piloted by men. The series' various 'guest' vehicles are piloted by men – Sun Probe, Fireflash, Crablogger, Sidewinder, Skythurst. Not even the more disguised and feminine coloured FAB 1 escapes this. Parker's working-class status puts him at odds with the more elevated, educated and experienced astronauts and pilots of Century 21, but his gender ensures that he isn't left behind in the same way that Lady Penelope is.

Equally, the series irregularly reminds us of Parker's working-class background. 'Vault of Death' shines a light on Parker's criminal background, whilst the likes of 'Danger at Ocean Deep', 'The Cham-Cham' and the more recent 'Introducing Thunderbirds' use Parker's below-stairs status as a source of physical comedy. This is embellished in *Thunderbird 6*. Parker is the only member of Skyship One's passengers who is not clued in on the fact that Alan Tracy has brought Tin-Tin along for the voyage, resulting in Parker being dumbstruck when the Tiger Moth which Alan and Tin-Tin arrive at Creighton-Ward Mansion appears to fly itself when Alan jumps out of the craft to greet Penelope. Alan, Tin-Tin and Penelope enjoy huge laughs later at keeping Parker in the dark, with Parker himself listening in on their boisterous laughter at his expense. This depiction of Parker as a source of comedy reaches its extreme during the movie's climax. When the passengers of Skyship One succeed in evacuating the craft on board the Tiger Moth, Parker is forced to clutch to the undercarriage of the biplane as Penelope struggles to pilot the craft. The film's penultimate parting shot before its ending scene of the Tracy family witnessing the newly christened Thunderbird 6 take-off is the image of Parker tangled up in a tree and plummeting *Looney Tunes*-style to the ground below. It's a strikingly raw usage of mean-spirited humour that highlights how class division is rife throughout *Thunderbirds*.

However, as Lady Penelope's presence in *Thunderbirds* grew stronger, so did her impact post-*Thunderbirds*. Such episodes as 'The Perils of Penelope',

---

[20] Merrick, H (2003). 'Gender in science fiction' *The Cambridge Companion to Science Fiction* (eds James, E. Mendlesohn, F). p. 241. Cambridge University Press. 12th edition.

'The Man From MI.5' and 'The Cham-Cham' are written with her as the starring heroine, alongside much of the brief second series and Thunderbird 6 placing herself and Parker in integral roles. Penelope's stature in *Thunderbirds*, and tele-fantasy science fiction, has grown over time, placing her as something of a cultural icon and a sign of marked progressiveness in the male fields of tele-fantasy. In 1965, what counts as being progressive can't help but feel antiquated by what contemporary audiences of today may define as progressive, but in 1965, Lady Penelope heralded that rare role of a positive female character in a science fiction production without being forced to be a mother/daughter figure, ie a character in need of rescuing. She was the rescuer.

The author Joanna Russ, when discussing the perceived lack of quality in American space opera literature, compartmentalised how females were depicted as belonging to several stock tropes found in American literature, including 'women are important as prizes or motives', 'women are supernaturally beautiful', 'women are weak and/or kept off stage' and 'active or ambitious women are evil.'[21] Lady Penelope stretches beyond the imaginations of the kind of writers Russ explains as being understandably frustrated. Penelope isn't portrayed as a plot device to enable males to be motivated into action. She isn't shown to be other-worldly or particularly weak. Granted, the series succumbed to reflections of these tropes early on, as mentioned, but by the time *Thunderbirds* blasted off into its last on-screen adventure with *Thunderbird 6*, Lady Penelope had advanced through the ranks. Sylvia Anderson herself appeared aware very early on that 'er Ladyship had to look, sound and act the part in the all-male world of *Thunderbirds.* '… by the time we got to *Thunderbirds*, the role of women was changing and I knew Lady Penelope had to be up there with the boys.'[22] It was Sylvia herself who insisted that the equally male-dominated writing team of Thunderbirds be encouraged to think beyond sexist storylines for Penelope; '… with Lady Penelope, we had an action girl who was a personality in her own right,' Sylvia comments.[23]

However, it's here in the case I'm making that I may have lost you, thanks to my rather purposeful choice of source material. American literature and British tele-fantasy may not be entirely compatible when making these sorts of arguments, but the tropes Russ describes can be found throughout a great many forms of science fiction. There's also a strange

---

[21] Russ, J. (2017). 'The image of women in science fiction' *Science Fiction Criticism* (ed Latham, R). p. 202. Bloomsbury Academic. 1st edition.
[22] Anderson, S. Scott, D. (2014). 'My favourite photograph by Sylvia Anderson' *Sunday Express Magazine*. p. 57.
[23] La Riviere, S. (2009). 'Calling International Rescue' *Filmed in Supermarionation: A History of the Future*. p. 109. Hermes Press. 1st edition.

linkage to be found via *Thunderbirds*, a British-made series, especially designed to appeal to the American market (Gerry Anderson himself felt that having the British characters of Penelope and Parker would be a key commercial tool to Americans themselves). There's also something to be said for how Russ chooses to elaborate on American science fiction in particular because, as she puts it, '... American science fiction and British science fiction have evolved very differently ...' and that 'In Britain science fiction not only was always respectable, it still is ...' and the idea of 'respectability' inherent in Lady Penelope's disguise as an individual of nobility, enticing an aristocratic sense of nationality, and respect from her male counterparts in International Rescue in being able to stand on her own efforts and merits as a secret agent.

'The finest man I have ever had the privilege to work for'

The intertwined motifs of class and gender stereotypes between Lady Penelope and Parker gives *Thunderbirds* a richly defined avenue of exploration away from its more easily definable elements. However, Penelope and Parker's discourse of structures in class and gender ripples from Lady Penelope's home to the far-off shores of Tracy Island. Where Penelope has Parker, International Rescue founder and leader Jeff Tracy has his faithful manservant Kyrano. The distance in class between the pair is amplified more than it is with Penelope and Parker. Kyrano's Malaysian ethnicity, working for a white American on an exotic island, has colonialist undertones, but Kyrano is a much more pleasant personality than the brash and easily swayed Parker.

Kyrano serves Jeff and his family out of his own desire, rather than being forcibly persuaded to. However, Kyrano is a much less developed character than Parker, the consequence being that the dynamic between him and Jeff is equally undeveloped when compared to the much more fleshed out relationship between Parker and Lady Penelope, which gives us significantly less source material to work with here. Kyrano's easy-going nature ensures that he has an interchangeable relationship with all others on Tracy Island, and lacks the comical capers Parker finds himself in, such as accidentally betting and losing the luxury yacht FAB 2 in a fit of gambling. Such a comparison highlights the surface level appeal in Kyrano's contribution to *Thunderbirds* and Parker's well-defined working class stereotypes as a source for humour in *Thunderbirds*. Alongside the sometimes transgressive, sometimes progressive characteristics of Lady Penelope, *Thunderbirds* approach to portraying gendered structures of class hierarchy displays how the subtext of *Thunderbirds* runs much deeper than marionette manufactured disaster action that is the series' speciality.

MARINE MORALS: *STINGRAY*'S AQUATIC ANTAGONISTS

For all of Gerry Anderson's protestations about being anti-war, *Stingray* leaves the initial impression of being a remarkably trigger-happy affair. It's odd to think that the concealed pacifism of Tracy Island is counteracted by its predecessor; the missile-ready Marineville. Whenever a life is in need of rescue, Tracy Island doesn't transform like Marineville. It remains static as its advanced craft blast off from beneath the rock faces and swimming pools into a world of adventure. Marineville has no patience for such neutrality. In the blink of an eye, it morphs from a secluded metropolis, housing supermarkets and hospitals for its staff, to a Cold War nirvana of never-ending rockets and launch pads. It's the Jekyll and Hyde of science fiction bases.

How fitting then, for this article, that it's the villains of *Stingray* that perhaps represent a more complex ideology rather than our heroes. Beyond the deliciously camp Titan, the vast, eclectic armada of undersea cultures the WASPs routinely invade, either purposefully or accidentally, present a variety of mentalities when reacting to the *Stingray* crew's interference.

Reprogramming the Ethics

We can split our underwater creatures into passive and aggressive categories. However, as if to legitimize their complex nature compared to the Terraneans, those who appear villainous sometimes turned into allies, while those who present themselves as friendly reveal their true nature as evil tricksters. Still, the majority of aliens adhere to the passive or aggressive categories, with some either sharing in Titan's goal for land-based supremacy or avoiding conflict all together. 'Hostages of the Deep', 'The Big Gun', 'The Ghost Ship', 'Emergency Marineville' and 'A Nut for Marineville' fall into the most straight-forward of villain-centric stories. These episodes all feature creatures who opt for a simplistic yet robust method of attack, either through human bargaining or technological might. 'Emergency Marineville' in particular sees Nucella and Chidora apply some methodical menace in their might by attacking Marineville's covert identity at its own game via specially-programmed missiles. 'Hostages of the Deep' and 'The

Ghost Ship' however boil their enemy's logic down to a sinking level by capturing key characters and bargaining for their lives, in exchange for either the capturing of *Stingray* or Troy Tempest himself.

The more subtle side of the aggressive races is when trickery is deployed to win the day. 'The Invaders' and 'Deep Heat' reflect these subversive attitudes with suitably weird, atmospheric episodes, including the takeover of the WASP Weather Station in 'The Invaders' and the venturing beneath the Earth's surface in 'Deep Heat'. 'Deep Heat' poses an oddity in the morale's of its villains. Turata and Fragil's luring of *Stingray* to their volcanic base may have alarm bells ringing, but it's only when Phones complicates their escape plan that they resort to violent methods, stealing *Stingray* whilst leaving Troy and Phones to drown in the spilling lava that erupts into their home. If Phones hadn't thrown a spanner into Turata and Fragil's plan, would they have gone along peacefully? The desperate nature of their plight suggests that the worst qualities of a character can be brought out when provoked, whether you're a human or a humanoid, marionette sea creature.

'The Invaders' uses similar tactics to create uneasy moods to reflect unclear motives, with the audience as much in the dark as the *Stingray* crew. The masterful eeriness of Epayus and Ilium's takeover of the WASP Weather Station is countered by their apparent neutrality in quizzing the *Stingray* crew over their presumed destructive capabilities. We're clued into the duo's real motives of invading Marineville quicker than the *Stingray* crew's, adding to the sense of unease that rests over the episode. However, one does wonder how Troy didn't crane his neck slightly and spot the gargantuan projection screen behind him during his interrogation that reveals his thoughts! In the ever-action-driven world of Supermarionation, it's no surprise that we saw more of the straight-forward aggressors rather than those who employed more deceptive means of attack. Despite this favouritism for one over the other, the fact that we got both kinds at all shows that the writers on *Stingray* were keen to explore different avenues in the struggle against good and evil where possible.

Misunderstood Victims

Taking this moral greyness to its next step, the more positively portrayed alien races, or at least the ones with a neutral relationship with the terraneans, displayed their own level of mild complexity. 'Sea of Oil' and 'The Disappearing Ships' flip the subversive nature of 'Deep Heat' and 'The Invaders' on its head by initially presenting their respective aliens as trigger-happy mercenaries, but in truth are simply misunderstood.

Their good guy nature generally shines through at the most inopportune of moments, usually whenever they've already initiated their final attack on Troy and co, and the episode makes use of *Thunderbirds*' favourite plot of a race-against-time-motif to resolve the situation. The action-heavy nature of *Stingray* traps these motifs somewhat, restricting them from any genuine levels of character-driven complexity, but it's intriguing to see that many layers of heroic and evil were utilised for narrative impact throughout *Stingray*.

Beyond these select episodes, there were others in which *Stingray* was content to resoundingly reinforce the idea that the might of WASP makes right. 'Pink Ice' and 'Invisible Enemy' are particularly culpable of this. Both of which feature villains attacking the land people, with 'Invisible Enemy' setting its sights squarely on infiltrating Marineville. However, neither episode is concerned with showing us the creature piloting these vehicles of destruction. This invisible depiction of the pilots ensures a lack of empathy on our part, and thus makes us root for the gallant WASP to win the day. It's not simply a case of making us, as an audience, side with the good guys, it's that the good guys are the only ones to side with.

This sting in the tail acts as another feather to *Stingray*'s cap when weaving its heroes and villains together. It's keen if understandably surface-level exploration of how the undersea communities the *Stingray* crew would either battle or protect gives the show a deeper substance than its first impression may give.

STUMBLE IN THE DARKNESS: ISOLATION AND ALIENATION IN CENTURY 21'S LIVE-ACTION WORLDS

Family units, surrogate and genuine, are commonplace within the Andersons' futuristic worlds. Beyond the obvious family bond of the Tracy clan, the World Aquanaut Security Patrol makes up a believable group of people caring and dependent of each other. Whilst the militant attitude of Spectrum ensured that characters kept their distance from each other emotionally, *Joe 90* brought the family appeal of *Thunderbirds* back firmly into the picture, with Joe McClaine essentially having one father and two uncles. *Captain Scarlet* may distinguish itself from this semi-running theme with its heroes and villains bearing mechanical personalities, not just in their literal form as advanced marionettes but as characters, but the series arguably helped to foreshadow the ideas seen in the Andersons' slew of live-action productions they undertook as Supermarionation faded into the twilight. Where these previous series depicted family-esque groups of individuals often working alongside other organisations to ensure the safety of planet Earth, less of this can be applied to the loose thematic trilogy of *Doppelgänger*, *UFO* and *Space: 1999*. If the Supermarionation era found harmony for its heroes in unity, then this trio of later, live-action works can be tied together by their shared motif of terminal isolation experienced by their characters.

The Andersons' various forays into live action from 1969 to 1975, including *The Protectors* and Gerry and Johnny Byrne's *The Day After Tomorrow*/'Into Infinity' pilot, display a universe's worth of ideas that Supermarionation built the foundations for, yet consciously stretches away from the perceived limitations of that previous medium. It's overly two-dimensional to separate these live-action works from the marionette era as being 'darker', especially when you consider the adventures Spectrum found themselves subjected to by the Mysterons on a regular basis. When pressed about the perceived darkness that was influencing his post-Supermarionation works, Gerry remained nonplussed saying that 'I don't think I ever considered whether something was dark or not dark.'[24] 'Darker' still maintains a degree of applicability here, since what we define as a story being 'dark' is often used as an uncomplicated, succinct term for something that's mature, adult in nature, not meant to be enjoyed or understood by younger audiences. In this context, it's understandable that *Doppelgänger*, *UFO* and *Space: 1999* should be defined as being darker, yet that does them a disservice. To be more accurate, these stories are isolated, lonely, loaded with moments of despondent reflection for the seemingly unsolvable situation these characters are in, an emotional aspect impossible to produce with puppets. Even the crew of the *Altares* in *The Day After Tomorrow* find some comfort in them being made up of two family groups when the ship's photon drive accelerates them into a series of continual threats from supernovas and black holes.

Doppelgänger

Throughout *Doppelgänger*, *UFO* and *Space: 1999*, characters are unable to connect and communicate with one another and the world around them, for a variety of reasons. Quiet, understated dramas of the human capacity to engage with one another, or to be specific a lack of that capacity, is rooted throughout these works, but those roots rarely become entangled, as the separation between them is maintained. It's often given an exaggerated, cosmic flavour thanks to encounters with life as these humans don't know it, but so much of the character relationships in these productions are fixated on how these intrepid space explorers and defenders of Earth react to inhuman situations. Where *UFO* and *Space: 1999* give us a universe of tangents to spiral out of as rapidly as Moonbase Alpha itself, 1969's *Doppelgänger* presents a comparatively smaller world of ideas. In the second and last of Century 21's excursions into live-action film-making, astronaut Colonel Glenn Ross and astrophysicist Doctor John Kane's investigations of a newly discovered planet in our Solar System takes a dive into the unknown when they unexpectedly appear to land back on Earth. The film gradually reveals that this is not their Earth, but a duplicate of their home world, with communicative aspects delivered backwards and that the new planet is a mirror image of Earth, exact in every detail.

Glenn Ross spends much of *Doppelgänger*'s second half stranded on this parallel planet, a world seemingly familiar at first glance, yet impenetrable to him on close inspection. He is an anomaly, human yet alien, unable to engage with the backward writing of this world or unable to convince those around him of the perilous mission that brought him there, with Kane

---

[24] (2008) 'The Den Of Geek interview: Gerry Anderson' Den of Geek. Available from – https://www.denofgeek.com/tv/the-den-of-geek-interview-gerry-anderson/.

sustaining more serious injuries than him during their chaotic crash-land and eventually dying, emphasising Ross' isolated position. The only other person who believes in Ross' wild claims of a doppelgänger of Earth is Jason Webb (or rather, the 'other' Jason Webb), the tenacious director of EUROSEC and the man responsible for this curiously-fated mission to explore the new world. In *Doppelgänger*, the characters must endure barriers placed before them, whether it's Ross and his wife's breakdown of their marriage (which now spreads between two worlds), Kane's death and Webb's lofty disdain of his colleagues in EUROSEC and NASA culminating in the failed attempt to dock a reconfigured *Dove* craft, piloted by Ross, with the abandoned *Phoenix* craft that Ross and Kane had initially journeyed in. The attempts to prove the existence of a duplicate Earth by retrieving the *Phoenix*'s black box, thus proving that the craft embarked on its six-week mission from one planet to the next, ends in a cataclysm of traditionally explosive Anderson pyrotechnics.

The docking fails and the *Dove* plummets back to Earth, colliding with EUROSEC's Space Centre. Ross dies carrying his knowledge of the parallel Earth with him. Much of EUROSEC's other evidence is destroyed in the ensuing inferno. The doppelgänger Webb is forced to succumb to the same sense of being stranded and abandoned that Ross felt, amplified across the stars to the other Earth too, if Ross' earlier suggestions that the doppelgänger Ross and Kane embarked on their own mission to the 'real' Earth at the same time are true. Two sets of disasters have therefore taken place as the events on the two Earths occur simultaneously. Two Webbs, both unanchored from the world around them, cut loose and impossible to re-join their respective flocks. The film's parting shot of an aged Webb confined to a wheelchair in some undisclosed care home confirms that his once merciless attitude has faded into a state of permanent abandonment. Foreshadowing *UFO* and *Space: 1999*, *Doppelgänger* is resolute in giving none of its characters a happy ending, one where it's suggested the happiness comes in the form of unity between duplicate Earths.

UFO

UFO carries its morose ideology of paranoid survival from the series' beginning to its end, but thinking back to **Power, Family & Authority in Century 21**, the consequence of what Ed Bishop defined as living within a semi-fascist set-up for a security organisation is a self-inflicted alienation from the world which SHADO exists to protect. If the core theme of *UFO* is survival, then it's the episode 'Confetti Check A-OK' that demonstrates the isolating effects that SHADO has on its members. That episode works in tandem with series favourite 'A Question of Priorities' in showing how and why Ed Straker's marriage is gradually yet severely chipped away as

SHADO begins to form and his duties command his attentions at the expense of his newfound loving union with Mary. It's worth remembering that despite Straker's position as commander-in-chief of SHADO, SHADO's demands cast no prejudice on the hierarchy of command within the organisation. Everyone in SHADO leads a life of total secrecy from the outside world, meaning that every character has had to endure their own 'Confetti Check A-OK'.

'A Question of Priorities' strips itself of the hardware that's responsible, trusted even, in propelling the action along to an exciting finale to any Anderson production and demonstrates how the series was capable of crafting something equally engrossing with its fraught character dramas. The erosion of Straker and Mary's relationship is one thing, but the death of their son John is kicker. Straker isn't even allowed to say goodbye to his child as the demands of SHADO forbid him from doing so. But if the overall message of this episode is that the hardware wasn't capable of delivering quality emotional drama for its characters, then 'Sub-Smash' counters this logic with its compressed atmosphere and uncontrollable side effects of literal isolation and abandonment at their most extreme. Trapped in a Skydiver sub with the only way out for Straker and the crew being one by one and oxygen supplies running dangerously low, Straker guides the painfully slow evacuation of his crew, saving himself for last. Encased alive in their vehicular underwater coffin, their stranded nature emits very primal actions and emotions.

Here, mental agony is shown to collapse out of isolated states. Cut off from the outside world, madness slowly engulfs the crew, one by one. First is Lieutenant Chinn's psychotic death, driven mentally imbalanced from injury when the submarine is attacked by a passing UFO. Lieutenant Barry's primal scream echoes throughout Skydiver's missile launch tube, the only other alternative exit, when her escape fails and she's unable to get out. It's less of a scream for help and more of a scream as a release of frustration and despair. Insisting that he be the last to escape in an effort to give his crew a chance for survival, Straker is affected the most by oxygen starvation, his isolation manifesting into flashbacks of the sacrifices he's made to keep SHADO a reliable, functioning unit. Images of John's death and Mary ending their marriage, taken from 'A Question of Priorities', ties these two episodes together even more. Barry's piercing cries from within Skydiver as she retraces her steps are what breaks Straker's spell, the pair collapsing into each other's arms as Straker musters what energy he can to free Barry before they're eventually rescued. The exhausted sobs from the pair feel like a raw resolution to how isolation is resolved.

A further consequence of the concealed war fought between SHADO and the unnamed aliens is that neither side can reveal themselves to the world. They are cut off due to circumstance and choice alike. SHADO consists of a covert set-up, its headquarters disguised as a movie studio and even then it's found underneath the studio itself, where civilian eyes cannot possibly bear witness to it. It's a determined choice for SHADO to remain in the shadows. In the case of the aliens, their isolated state arises from the circumstances they place themselves in. Travelling across the dangers of space in the hopes of harvesting human organs for their own survival, it's rare for more than three UFOs to make such a perilous journey to Earth at any one time, and even rarer for one UFO to make it to Earth itself. It raises that good ole' chestnut so common in action-focused science fiction media of why doesn't the enemy simply launch all their forces against the Earth at once instead of drip-feeding single enemies one after the other, but in this context, it makes perfect sense. The aliens are as emotionally remote as SHADO is.

Space: 1999

As if rising in a sense of scale, *Space: 1999* takes this idea of isolation to exaggerated extremes by having Moonbase Alpha blasted out of Earth's orbit, a galactic umbilical cord cut that was never meant to be so. Unmoored from its position of safe proximity to the Earth, the 311 men and women of Moonbase Alpha drift helplessly through the relentless expanse of nothing, chancing upon surreal cosmic phenomena and alien lifeforms far-stretched from their own understandings of life, culture and physics. Alienation is rampant for Commander John Koenig and all on Alpha for the simple reason that each and every day appears to bring a fresh horror for the base, one in which the Alphans are continually underprepared for, unable to call upon outside assistance. Quite often, individual members of Moonbase Alpha are struck by invasive cosmic forces, who accidentally or deliberately come into contact with the base, enforcing alienation upon these crew members. Often, the inability to communicate is a key source of separation from humans and aliens. And all too often, these Alphans cannot be saved from the strange forces that envelop them. Like *Doppelgänger* before it, death is the only release from the smothering confinement the Alphans must permanently tolerate.

'Ring Around the Moon' sees Helena Russell's mind captured by a cosmic entity, with Helena exploited to become some manner of biological super computer, oblivious to her fellow Alphans. 'Guardian of Piri' sees all of Alpha, bar Commander John Koenig, gradually become entranced by the siren call of Piri itself and slipping into an almost drunken state of euphoria. 'The Troubled Spirit' sees the time-displaced ghost of Alpha botanist Dan Mateo terrorise the base when his attempts to communicate with plants goes horridly wrong. Desperate for some form of communication with plant life and thus being freed from Alpha's remote state, death remains the harshest consequence of trying to break down those barriers. Curiously, *Space: 1999*'s most direct addressing of confinement comes not from the Alphans but from the aliens, specifically in 'The Infernal Machine', in which a sentient alien spaceship named Gwent imprisons Koenig, Russell and Professor Bergman just so that the machine may have some company when their original pilot, the aptly named Companion, dies. 'The Testament of Arkadia' sees Alpha members Luke Ferro and Anna Davis unplug themselves from Moonbase Alpha entirely and become convinced by spiritual forces to leave Alpha behind to start a new life on the planet Arkadia, whose ties into human history are so deep that they claim it to be destiny that the moon should drift into contact with the planet at all.

'The Testament of Arkadia' in particular is regarded as the final chapter in the series' loose story arc of the events throughout the entire series is a predetermined course of action for Moonbase Alpha, that some undefined cosmic force is quietly guiding them through the universe and that it was always their destiny to be wrenched away from the safety of Earth. Year 2 of *Space: 1999* mostly abandons this idea, unintentionally cementing the Alphans' isolated state within this grand cosmic plan. The mystery of their cosmic journey is hidden from them. What state Moonbase Alpha may be in by the time they reached their journey's end, if at all, is up for debate. Despite the aforementioned figure of Alpha being a home to 311 crew, that figure undoubtedly grows smaller almost with each episode, as various personnel are killed, whether through alien invasion or becoming ensnared by other cosmic powers they can't grasp. But these strange deaths offer more than cosmic dangers, validated by the disposable nature of the one-off characters these forces so often wrap themselves around. The constant invasion of death that grapples individual members of Moonbase Alpha, who are regularly seen only in their respective episodes, serves another and deeper function than giving Moonbase Alpha an enemy to tackle against every week. The strange deaths endured by so many on Alpha can be taken as a physical manifestation of the collective trauma that the Alphans experience on a regular basis, a side effect of this unexpected and never-ending isolation. The main characters are spared this fate, enabling their shared emotional state to continue producing inexplicable physical and cosmic forms.

Space: 1999 elevates the morose mentality of *UFO* to a truly cosmic scale. The philosophical diversions and unexplainable galactic experiences of the series weren't exactly rubbing shoulders with *UFO*'s comparatively down to earth explorations of the toll felt by those who defend the Earth from unpredictable aliens. And yet, just as *UFO* builds on *Doppelgänger*, *Space: 1999* stretches out *UFO*'s emphasis on the human, emotional consequences of space exploration and cosmic conflict. That sense of distress is however rendered to rather limp standards throughout *Space: 1999*'s second series in comparison to its first. Much of the urgency of Moonbase Alpha's situation simply isn't there during the notorious Year 2's jokey, light-hearted attitude to the seriousness of the Alphan's state, but Year 1 succeeds in standing on its own merits in depicting abandonment in its most enigmatic form.

Reflections in Isolation

This shared motif coils itself around these three productions on their own terms, but it becomes all the more apparent when the Supermarionation era pushes ideas that are the opposite in moods. As discussed at the beginning of this chapter, the rescue and security organisations in action when Gerry and Sylvia were producing entertainment for children are led by family units, both literal ones and symbolic ones. But you don't even strictly need to be a family in Supermarionation to have a shared sense of belonging, of being part of a team that has each other's backs. From the publically known World Aquanaut Security Patrol to the vigilante nature of International Rescue to the secretive Spectrum and World Intelligence Network, these organisations don't begin and end with their respective headquarters. They all have pockets of resources spread across the world, signalling to the worldwide influence of security they keep the world secure in, but also their direct and openness to the world itself. Even when Moonbase Alpha can be seen as continuing that sense of community, it has no such resources beyond Moonbase Alpha itself. Even when SHADO's combative outlets stretch to the moon, it's done under the strictest confidence, much like its Earth-based counterpart. Neighbouring space vehicles aren't permitted to know of SHADO's moonbase, cutting themselves off to the same extent as the film studio back on terra firma.

Now that Gerry and Sylvia had abandoned the marionettes they so often saw as tying them down creatively and found themselves producing the more adult-orientated dramas they were in a permanent state of reaching for throughout the 1960s, those family ties and worldwide familiarity for their security organisations were dispensed with. The comfortable attitudes aimed at younger audiences are there to give some sense of security and familiarity. But the Andersons were now living in the real and grown-up world, where life is not so straight-forward and safe. It's as if the Andersons are saying that in the real world, no amount of security or rescue outfits can save you from becoming lost in in a cosmic sea of displacement. The real world has its own duplicate that's forever out of reach. The real world is under threat from humanoid aliens who are after your hearts and lungs and kidneys. The real word doesn't even have a moon. All of these are utilised as metaphors for their human protagonists locked in a state of abandonment.

Glenn Ross and Jason Webb are unable to inform anyone of their parallel plights because no-one would believe them. SHADO is unable to reach out and tell any possible empathetic ear of their intergalactic Cold War because they're forbidden from doing so. The people on Moonbase Alpha cannot tell anyone of their trauma because there's no-one to tell. All three groups of characters, those who inhabit the Andersons' forays into adult-focused, live-action sci-fi adventure, are trapped in isolation.

Worn down by the bright, technologically-driven optimism of the far-future worlds crafted in Supermarionation, *Doppelgänger*, *UFO* and *Space: 1999* (its first series, at least) saw the Andersons step into more alienating territory. It's as if they drenched these productions in a downcast thrill of existentialist musings on the more negative consequences of space exploration and cosmic adventure. The dark emotions experienced by these characters acts like the great leap away from puppetry, as those marionettes couldn't possibly have communicated the themes ever-present in this trilogy as convincingly as genuine human actors. *Doppelgänger* may end on a conclusive note of false realisation found in one's own reflection, but *UFO* and *Space: 1999*'s lack of genuine conclusions comes with the implications that the members of SHADO and Alpha can never break free of their respective emotional imprisonment.

STRAKER'S OFFICE:
21ST CENTURY EPISODES

FIREBALL XL5: 'THE GRANATOID TANKS'

Before Technicolor production techniques gripped AP Films as it was then known, like the Hood's hypnotic glare, the company was doing its best to produce entertaining television using methods that were rapidly becoming antiquated. At the time of *Fireball XL5*'s production, Lew Grade hadn't yet bought the company. They hadn't yet set-up shop in Stirling Road. Dennis Spooner and Alan Fennell, who would become mainstays in the company's scriptwriting department during *Stingray* and *Thunderbirds*, were still finessing their narrative chops with *Fireball XL5*. And yet a separation is felt between the monochromatic and the Videocolor eras of Supermarionation. The black-and-white *Four Feather Falls*, *Supercar* and *Fireball XL5* are much more whimsical, carefree even, than the hard-nosed, straight-faced attitudes that would begin to creep in with *Stingray* and *Thunderbirds* before erupting into the much darker vibes of *Captain Scarlet*. These earlier worlds were ones where animal sidekicks were integral to the team's set-up and you could breathe in space without the need for oxygen helmets. As an overall package, *Fireball XL5* suffers in its aged form compared to the more robust offerings AP Films would produce afterwards, but gems are to be found within individual episodes, and 'The Granatoid Tanks' is a fine example of how *Fireball XL5* matched brawny hardware with characterful whimsy.

Fireball XL5's space-age ambitions often fails to match the general quality of the series. Villains are often exaggerated to the point of losing any menace that was surely intended. Alien worlds are often lacking in imagination or budget. The infinite misogyny directed towards Venus is undeniably there and makes character interactions hard to stomach at times. Much of *Fireball XL5*'s concepts would be strengthened as we dived from the stars to the seas with *Stingray* but this ends up making 'The Granatoid Tanks' all the more a unique offering, as it's one episode in which *Fireball XL5*'s balance of the quirky and the serious is relatively harmonious.

In this episode, quaint and homely character workings are bolted onto smouldering special effects sequences. It's preposterous that two seemingly jarring, conflicting elements should slot into each other so well, yet the self-aware bizarreness of *Fireball XL5*, somehow all too knowledgeable of the limits it was under, helps to make this work, the end result feeling like it's setting the stage for *Stingray*. It's a case of the archaic finding common ground with the advanced. The elderly, dotty-minded Ma Doughty single-handedly goes up against a small yet deadly army of destructive robotic warriors desperate to claim Planet 73 away from its human inhabitants, who are stationed there deducing whether or not the planet is fit for human life. Only in these early days of Supermarionation, as the AP Films crew were still untangling themselves from their newly moulded marionettes, can such a daft premise be pulled off with wit and enthusiasm. The whimsical attitude that surges through *Supercar* and *Fireball XL5*, and that would gradually fade away as *Stingray*, *Thunderbirds* and *Captain Scarlet* took hold (and still further with *UFO*) is on wonderfully upbeat display here in 'The Granatoid Tanks'.

Interestingly, the Granatoid robots themselves give the episode a tangible dollop of jeopardy, evidenced in the episode's early moments as the sight of the alien tanks themselves charging over rough terrain, like an army on the march, opens the episode, establishing a militant mood. The undetailed, chunky appearance of the Granatoids themselves haven't aged gracefully in the least, and their undefined motivations leaves you asking more questions than having those questions answered. However, the sheer number of their choice of vehicular transportation is what makes them so much fun to watch, like something out of a B-movie. *Fireball XL5*'s special effects department has rarely dabbled in land-based vehicles until now. The nature of the series obviously held a focus on space-based adventure, with satellites, rockets and alien craft being the order of the day. Seeing these tanks in action is a miniature masterclass of Derek Meddings and his crew, a rugged prototype of the large-scale disasters of *Thunderbirds*. It's terrific fun because it's not just a single tank rumbling into view (like so many other guest vehicle appearances in *Fireball XL5*); it's an armada of them, an unstoppable mass of vehicles scrambling for attention. With their protruding antennae and sharp, stylised lettering on the front of the vehicles made to look like open jaws, it's akin to seeing a swarm of deadly insects bearing down on you, relentlessly.

The overall blankness in the Granatoid robots themselves is really the episode's chief downfall. The only robot heard is the Granatoid robot commander, and he has the same voice as *Fireball* XL5's Robert the Robot with little change in tone or style. The marionettes of the robots themselves would become repurposed in the far more thematically engaging episode 'Trial by Robot'. Sophisticated backstories for villains weren't entirely within *Fireball XL5*'s vocabulary anyway, but to forgo any actual explanation for their presence entirely certainly asks just a bit much from the series' young target audience. Things get even stranger when the audience bears witness to Steve Zodiac's response on hearing the news that the Granatoid tanks are attempting an invasion of the human-manned research station on Planet 73 that they're out to destroy in the first place, exclaiming that he believed that they'd oppressed the Granatoids already in a past mission. Don't let Steve fool you. This episode is the first and only time we see the Granatoids in action, Steve referring therefore to an off-screen adventure that's surely defined subcanon, ie out of the regular continuity yet all but alluded to still occur, in this case a sly confirmation that these characters still enjoy some space-based adventures when the audience's backs are turned. It remains a curious bit of dialogue to let slip through the admittedly loose editorial standards held by *Fireball XL5* and really doesn't add a great deal of advancement to the plot in itself. If anything, it does the opposite and bogs the episode down, with the audience scrambling to recall if and when Zodiac and crew last fought the robots, given his very direct dialogue.

The Granatoids represent the advanced attitude of the episode. Even if we never learn of the genesis or motivations behind this race of stampeding robotic demolishers, it's still a fun divergence from camp, child-friendly alien lifeforms the *Fireball* crew were often pitted against. Magical gnomes, sentient plants or merely humanoid-esque characters that weren't otherworldly enough to be convincingly alien were commonplace in *Fireball XL5* at this point. The lesser explored angle of mechanical marauders, surface-level here in execution but advanced further in 'Trial by Robot', remains a welcome addition to the series' narrative platter.

At the other end of the spectrum, Ma Doughty provides the episode's thematic balance by representing the anarchic aspects of the episode. The aged owner of Space City's own music store dutifully attends to Steve and Matt's wishes to purchase a harmonium for Venus' birthday. Her store itself, stylised as a then-contemporary 1960s music arcade, highlights a retro futuristic angle of the Andersons' output, visible only with the benefit of hindsight as we view these shows from the far distance of over 50 years since the Supermarionation era in particular was produced. As villainous robotic tanks are bearing down on a man-made scientific research station, two pinnacles of techno-hardware of the future, the scenes back on Earth with Ma Doughty present a different story. It's as if we veer from the alien future to the homely past. It's in this episode that we see that Space City is equipped with shopping arcades for all its resident's needs. With its retro décor and in-person listening booths enabling customers to sample the music before purchasing, it's endearing how Supermarionation shows often pulled us away from presenting their far-flung futuristic worlds by reminding us with scenes like these that these worlds, however futuristic, were still rooted in the 1960s. The greatest charm of 'The Granatoid Tanks' is its back-and-forth between the past and the future perspectives, assembling together a retro futuristic swirl that becomes all the more apparent as time passes when we watch these productions.

Ma Doughty herself, ably performed by Sylvia Anderson dipping into one of her stock character accents, is a charmingly insistent one-off character for *Fireball XL5*. Her determination to join the *Fireball* crew to help rescue the scientists falls on deaf ears, despite her protestations that she, somehow, possesses the ability to ward off the otherwise indestructible tanks. Her domesticated appearance and thick Irish accent makes her appear eccentrically out of place in the advanced community of Space City, but as mentioned, that clash of cultures only adds to the warmth of the episode. Her eventual stowing away on board *Fireball XL5* comes across as endearing rather than annoying.

Ma Doughty herself gives 'The Granatoid Tanks' its comically offbeat and curious finale, which also succeeds in packing in that rarest of things into *Fireball XL5* – a sense of threat. *Fireball XL5*'s creative staff does its best at several stages throughout the show's run to insert a palpable feeling of true danger in the other-worldly exploits faced by Steve Zodiac and company, but the series' almost anti-sophisticated stance in its art direction and story-telling all too often render this venture redundant. This is made all the more apparent when viewing Gerry and Sylvia's output backwards, for those who may have blasted off into their worlds via their more well-known properties first and worked their way backwards to the earlier days of Supermarionation, when the shortcomings were evidently rescued in later entries. In this particular climax, the danger succeeds by being simple, uncluttered and genuine.

Stranded outside of the research laboratory with the two doctors they came to rescue, Steve, Venus and Matt find themselves unable to outmanoeuvre the Granatoid tanks, which have arrived to claim their victims. Their gradual encroaching of the trapped humans gives further weight to their animal-like designs, as if they're some wild animal preparing for the final, savage leap into their prey. Out of the blue (or rather, out of the *Fireball*), Ma Doughty emerges onto the scene, demanding that the tanks disperse. As the tanks unexpectedly comply, it's here that Matt discovers that the necklace that Ma Doughty is wearing is fashioned from Plyton, the only substance known to put fear into the artificial minds of the Granatoids. In keeping with the episode's whimsical half, it's never quite made clear if Ma Doughty is aware that her necklace is in fact a rare space mineral or whether she sincerely believes she possesses robot tank-repelling powers. One can't help but imagine that Venus would have a field day from a psychiatric perspective in having a one-to-one session with Ma Doughty, prizing her away from her precious music store, to enquire about just how deeply she believes in her mysteriously defined powers, particularly when Ma herself makes no reference to what her supposed abilities are. Instead, we conclude the episode on a musical number with the electronic harmonium Steve and Matt bought for Venus' birthday. Very twee. Very *Fireball XL5*. After all, it would be a fair few years until *Captain Scarlet* and *Joe 90* began implementing psychological undertones to Supermarionation. The light-heartedness so characteristic of these earlier, simpler times is firmly in place here.

'The Granatoid Tanks' isn't the greatest episode of the Supermarionation era by any means, but it is one of the most definitive adventures for the art form. 'The Granatoid Tanks' is a delightful joy rather than a frivolous outing because it carries its criss-crossing themes with a carefree confidence that would slip away as the stage, and pressures for commercial momentum, became grander for AP Films.

The nimble balance between Ma Doughty and the Granatoids themselves gives the episode a gently kinetic zig-zagging, just enough to cover the cracks over *Fireball XL5*'s admittedly surface-level qualities. There's a reason that *Stingray*, *Thunderbirds*, *Captain Scarlet* and *Joe 90*, all produced after *Fireball XL5*, are celebrated more and discussed in more extensive detail than this earlier entry in AP Films' canon and episodes that are as cohesive as 'The Granatoid Tanks' are few and far between. But with its winning mixture of engaging characters and robust special effects sequences, 'The Granatoid Tanks' is slight but splendid fun, free from the need to be as substantial as other later classic entries in the Supermarionation era, and a firm reminder that the earlier days of Supermarionation carried with them a certain innocence that would gradually get worn away as the years passed.

STINGRAY: 'SUBTERRANEAN SEA'

Stingray episodes can generally be categorised into two distinct genres that help to give the series such a characterful stamp: action or comedy, or sometimes both. *Stingray* is a series that keeps humour, adventure and characters in near-perfect balance throughout its 39 episode run. Much of *Stingray*'s spirited approach to characters, in personality and design, comes from the juxtaposition between the all-American, handsome, daredevil heroes of the World Aquanaut Security Patrol and the imaginative mixture of aquatic aliens – some genuinely evil, some driven by sheer survival, and some misinterpreting WASP as a destructive force and ultimately ending up as allies through the course of the episode. What makes 'Subterranean Sea' stand apart from much of its easily definable output then is how this episode dispenses with both of these established genres.

Stingray is a series littered with unique ideas, yet they're mostly spread across the series, rather than confined to individual episode. Admittedly, some episodes do blend together in their identity, failing to live up to repeated viewing and will devolve into atypical science-action tropes of Century 21 Productions. Whilst this didn't equate to some episodes being strictly bad, they simply become less unique and engaging. 'Subterranean Sea', for want of a better phrase, pushes the boat out on *Stingray*'s thematic dealings away from its favoured styles into something infinitely mysterious. It's plotless, but not listless. Atmospheric, but not ponderous. Glamourous, but not sickly. Alan Fennell's seventh outing as writer for the series, and the third episode directed by Desmond Saunders, sees the pair flexing their respective creative muscles, taking the *Stingray* crew to genuinely alien landscapes, without the need for an actual alien antagonist, when *Stingray* is tasked with exploring a newfound ocean beneath the Earth's crust. Indeed, this is the only episode of *Stingray* that doesn't feature a villain for *Stingray* to do battle against.

Writing on *Fireball XL5*, *Stingray*, *Thunderbirds* and editing *TV21* all showcased how Fennell was a writer who could easily prioritise rapid-paced adventures. 'The action stories were my bag because of my background in comic strips,' Fennell recalled in 1992. 'With comics, kids tend not to want to read too much, so you had to keep the story moving, unlike television where you have room to talk and room for the characters to develop dialogue.'[25] 'Subterranean Sea' is therefore one of *Stingray*'s greatest examples of allowing Fennell to stretch away from his action-driven comfort zone.

Fennell and Saunders work in tandem to create an exotically inviting yet tense, unknown landscape for *Stingray* to indulge in that widens the thematic vision of the series and presents viewers with a bespoke entry in the series' catalogue. The episode opens with a recognisable Anderson sight in the form of an undersea drilling camp that's pierced through the Earth's crust, discovers the new ocean and calls upon Marineville to assist with the discovery. The theme of humanity using advanced technology to discover more about the world around them and to better their understanding for the benefit of science is a tried and tested Anderson trope that serves to open the door for many a supersonic adventure. As 'Subterranean Sea' demonstrates, this takes the form of a civilian or private enterprise inadvertently chancing upon something that requires WASP, International Rescue or Spectrum to resolve the situation.

Prior to these events, the *Stingray* crew's attempts at going on a much-needed holiday allow a jovial atmosphere to compliment the earlier scene of scientific triumph, only to be recalled by Commander Shore just before their departure to travel to the drilling rig. In an intriguing exchange between Atlanta and Shore, Atlanta quizzes the commander as to why he wants to utilise *Stingray* on this mission when he has other vessels at his disposal. This could be interpreted to refer to the infamous number 3 marking on *Stingray*'s upper rear fin, with different sources explaining that this number refers to either: the most recent version of the *Stingray* craft, or the fact that this is the third of several submarine craft Marineville has elsewhere, otherwise unseen throughout the entire series. Whilst it can be seen as Atlanta referring to the other mythical numbered submarines used by the WASPs, it's more likely that this dialogue was written merely to create further tension between Atlanta and her father.

From here, the meat of the episode starts gain flavour. A pleasing aspect of 'Subterranean Sea' is how the episode makes well-paced room for emphasising the journey to and from the sea as much as the *Stingray* crew exploring the subterranean sea itself. As *Stingray* is lowered down the excavated tunnel down a manmade elevator, this man-made wonder gives way to a jagged complication of rock faces, like a low-hanging, misconfigured jaw, as *Stingray* gracefully slithers into the subterranean ocean, rising steam foreshadowing the colourful landscapes they'll soon encounter. It's a simple yet neatly effective bit of set design that quietly establishes the fact that we're now embarking into genuinely unknown

---

[25] Archer, S. Fennell, A. (1992) 'Alan Fennell Talks To C21'. *Century 21* (ed Reccia, M). No. 11, pp. 27-29.

territory.

A gradual build-up of aesthetic details culminates in a roaring mid-episode cliff-hanger that captures the freakishly otherworldly landscape *Stingray* journeys into. The nature of *Stingray*'s overall purpose as a security mech defending the peace of the world means that every dive into the depths of the ocean is unknown, but in 'Subterranean Sea', it's all kicked into a higher gear. Saunders' cohesive direction brings Fennell's numerous details to life – the sickly black-coloured oceans, *Stingray*'s jittering depth gauge proving eventually unable to record the depths they're diving into, and the magnificent fluorescent rock faces (the appeal of which must have been undoubtedly lost on first-time viewers in 1964, when black-and-white was still the norm) add an immensely colourful depth to the episode, *Stingray* gliding past the aquatic rock faces eventually giving way to more turbulent offerings as the crew become caught in an unstoppable downstream current. Again, Saunders steps up to the plate. Barry Gray's soundtrack blossoms from a fairyland-like tinkle that accompanies the multi-coloured rocks to a more dramatic pace as *Stingray* gathers speed and passes numerous seaweed all leaning in an oddly uniform forward direction.

A superbly edited scene comprising of long shots of one of *Stingray*'s smaller models, mid-range shots of a large model and interior shots of the *Stingray* crew being thrashed around as a new and terrifying form of mother nature grabs hold of *Stingray* and flings it down into the bowels of this horrific world. The cutting between small and larger *Stingray* models is seamless, a trick the Century 21 crew had become versatile with after *Supercar* and *Fireball XL5* and would continue to be so when crafting the action set pieces for *Thunderbirds*, *Captain Scarlet* and beyond. Stock footage of this spectacular crash scene would be reused in several other *Stingray* episodes, a testament of how well made it is.

The second half of the episode opens with an unnerving sense of calm as the *Stingray* crew awaken in the aftermath of the tidal wave, *Stingray* partially swallowed into the seabed, having crash-landed. Troy and Phones' attempts at launching *Stingray* back into action are met with failure, at first for unknown reasons, but clarified when Troy discovers that the ocean that was attacking them has completely vanished. In a sublime bit of forward thinking, this is shown by a visual clarity in the sight of the beached *Stingray* struggling to launch. The glass tank usually placed in-between the underwater model set and the cameras when filming aquatic scenes, not just in *Stingray*, but all of Century 21's output, has been removed to further impress upon the viewers that the ocean has been snatched away.

It's at this point that any form of plot is abandoned for the episode, as Troy, Phones and Marina opt to explore the petrified seabed on foot, all other means of transport rendered useless without water to operate in.

Unsure of the atmospheric quality of this newfound world, all three trek out into the open adoring breathing equipment, even Marina. So often, her underwater prowess was often use as a scapegoat to rescue Troy and Phones should their air supply run short or be compromised in some other form. Now with her own safety brought to the surface, she fails to contribute a great deal, acting only as a passive onlooker to Troy and Phones' exploration, but it also enhances the surreal situation the characters are in.

As Troy, Phones and Marina venture out into the unknown, we're treated to one of the most spectacular pieces of set design in all of Supermarionation. The trio's exploration of this waterless paradise has more in common with some far-flung, Videocolor style planet from *Space: 1999*. Unnatural plants and trees jerk upwards to the ... sky? Compact pools of mysterious liquid ooze with thick smoke. Tropical skylines seem to stretch forever behind the trio, like a permanent nuclear sunset. The length of time given to exploring this space crafts a mood that's both unsettling and inviting, and not something seen elsewhere in *Stingray*, with Troy, Phones and Marina utterly vulnerable to the mysteries around them.

Context is gained for this tropical wonderland when Troy suspects they must be close to the centre of the Earth, accounting for the heated atmosphere. Marina's previously scuppered role in this episode salvages itself somewhat when she's the first to hear the thunderous approach of the returning ocean. Another finely-tuned bit of editing comes into play when the ensuing tidal waves come crashing down on the trio, rapidly enveloping them, as we witness juxtaposing shots of the marionettes being soaked along with close-ups of real-life actors filmed from the waist down fiercely consumed by the ocean. With *Stingray* now able to traverse as normal, they depart this mysterious land, with some half-baked reasoning from Troy and Phones as to how this ocean functions. Simple explanations of the disappearing ocean simply functioning like a tide, but on a much larger scale, and the centre of the Earth drying out the ocean seabed in an instant, transforming it into a desert, when the water vanishes close the book on the subterranean sea. Now, the episode shifts in focus and details how the crew attempt to navigate their way out of the subterranean sea without the help of their sophisticated tracking equipment, now severely shattered, reinforcing the group's vulnerable state.

It's here that 'Subterranean Sea' is at its weakest, never quite recovering from abandoning the plot from earlier in favour of atmospheric exploration of the unknown. We're now left with a simple, not so thrilling case of the *Stingray* crew trying to break the surface before their oxygen levels run out (did they forget they had their breathing equipment with them?). What saves these scenes is another batch of dynamically captured sequences of *Stingray* itself dragging itself through more untraceable seas. Eventually, all is well for Troy Tempest and company, as *Stingray* surfaces into a Hawaiianesque lagoon, ensuring that the group, minus Atlanta, are able to have their holiday as planned. The episode concludes with Troy, Phones and Marina in blissful decadence, the mysteries of the subterranean sea left as just that.

'Subterranean Sea' is a thoroughly seductive entry in *Stingray*'s canon. It really only falls flat in its third act, after the well-crafted build-up to the subterranean sea itself and the gorgeous set pieces of the sea itself, the episode can't quite figure out how to end on an equally satisfactory note. No resolution is offered of *Stingray*'s earth-shattering findings – a tropical world beneath the Earth itself that tears between being a paradise and a nightmare. It's as if Fennell recognised that a moment of light-hearted characterisation was needed to steer the episode to a decent ending, but at the expense of the episode's lingering plot elements.

Fennell would revisit claustrophobic themes in the far more menacing 'Invisible Enemy', the foundations of which are laid here in 'Subterranean Sea'. The warm, exotic flavour that make 'Subterranean Sea' such an appealing watch continue to fizzle with eye-popping colour over 50 years after its initial broadcast, but it's also a glamourous embodiment of *Stingray*'s emphasis on exploration of unchartered, aquatic worlds and how there are some secrets that the world's oceans will never divulge. The sense of adventure remains tightly coiled throughout the episode, as if the promise and possibility of danger is more thrilling that the danger itself, illustrated through the spellbinding adventure that Supermarionation can bring. 'Subterranean Sea' ultimately stands as one of the most delightfully strange and engaging adventures *Stingray* would embark upon.

JOE 90:
'SEE YOU DOWN THERE'

From a perspective like mine, the marvellous thing about Gerry and Sylvia Anderson's filmography is that its cult status ensures that it hasn't been overexposed by an abundance of retrospective analysis. *Joe 90* is a prime example of this. Cratered in-between the dual peaks of *Thunderbirds* and *Captain Scarlet* on one side and *UFO* and *Space: 1999* on the other, *Joe 90*'s stature has grown overtime, unlike the diminutive boy hero himself, but it remains a cult entry within an already cult catalogue of work. We've previously explored how *Joe 90* is a thematically complex and violent affair, which other forms of discourse have taken up in pointing out too, such as video essays from Anderson Entertainment. When selecting the key episode from *Joe 90*'s 30 episode run, one that captures the series' darkly witty soul unlike any other episode, it makes perfect sense for us to explore the cheery sadism of 'See You Down There'.

'See You Down There' captures the kind of series *Joe 90* is trying to be, whilst at the same time, no other episode quite has the gumption to combine the witty with the surreal and the sadistic quite like this episode does. 'See You Down There' is the final episode of the series before the obligatory greatest hits clip show that closes out the series, making this episode the last true, full-length adventure that *Joe 90* offered. With that context in mind, the amusing nature of the episode becomes clearer. By this point in the series, it had neatly settled into its format of Joe being dispatched across the globe to utilise whatever brain pattern had been plastered onto him mentally that episode in order to stop various villains as violently as possible. Indeed, physical battery against Joe and enemies alike is commonplace, with the series never afraid to show blood and bodies on a scale close to, if not exceeding, *Captain Scarlet*.

In 'See You Down There', the physical violence takes a backseat in favour of something closer to attacking the very soul of WIN's latest antagonist. Having established how enemies are defined by their breakaway from the rules and morals of society, 'See You Down There' plumps for a villain who, in all technicality, doesn't do anything illegal, but sure does villainous things. The ruthless actions of financial vulture Ralph Clayton catches the attention of the World Intelligence Network. Clayton knows no low in consuming his business rivals, amassing a gargantuan empire (not unlike the Century 21 Organisation itself at the time of *Joe 90*'s broadcast), but remains wise enough to operate within the boundaries of the law. Unable therefore to outright arrest him, WIN opts to teach Clayton a lesson in morality. Falsely alerting Clayton to the fact that they have slipped some narcotic substance into his drink when visiting his workplace, Joe, Professor McClaine, Sam Loover and Shane Weston set to work bringing about these fake hallucinations that will haunt Clayton until he rights his wrongs. It's ingenious of scriptwriter Tony Barwick to unplug from the established formula like this and introduce a greyer area of what defines a villain to a young audience such as *Joe 90*'s and a handsome reminder that Anderson productions weren't in the habit of talking down to their viewers.

A distinct pattern emerges in AP Films/Century 21 Production's style of making episodes towards the end of each successive Supermarionation venture. Although clip shows didn't become apparent until *Stingray* with 'Aquanaut of the Year', episodes towards the end of each series took advantage of the winding down state of affairs by offering episodes stretching beyond the normal roll call. As we'll discover during Brains' Lab, 'The Cham-Cham' in particular is a wonderfully robust claim for giving Lady Penelope, Parker and Tin-Tin their own spin-off series. *Captain Scarlet*'s 'Attack on Cloudbase' undeniably frustrates viewers with its reliance on dream sequences to push the envelope of the series' format, but the bloodthirsty drama within the dream remains breath-taking. In that other context, an episode like 'See You Down There' makes a lot more sense. One can't help but imagine the reactions to those who may dive into 'See You Down There' as a much earlier introduction to *Joe 90* without the benefit of the otherwise regular narrative patterns established by previous episodes.

With that context in mind, you almost don't notice that *Joe 90* is that rare beast for an Anderson production – an adventure without explosions. Very little in 'See You Down There' gets blown up; a further sign that we're in fresh territory here, as Joe, Mac, Sam and Shane all participate in making Clayton's life utter hell by subjecting him to random hallucinations of them masquerading as curious individuals from countless professions intent on persuading him to abandon his nefarious business ways. If not, these attacks will continue, and thankfully, Clayton holds out long enough for these hugely entertaining 'attacks' to demonstrate what a witty, character-driven affair *Joe 90* could be. The constant bombardment of amusing invasions of Clayton's professional and personal life feels like a rapid attempt to make the episode more engrossing without the benefit of futuristic vehicles or explosions, but ultimately, it rarely feels as though 'See You Down There' is trying desperately to cover up for itself. It's having terrific fun stretching *Joe 90*'s thematic legs.

The vocal performances are an undeniable highlight of the episode, as series regulars Keith Alexander and David Healy lap up the opportunity for the absurd, so too do regular guest performers Jeremy Wilkin and Gary Files as Clayton and his put-upon assistant Molineaux, respectively. The episode's opening scenes displaying Clayton in bullish attitude and Molineaux being overly enthusiastic is superb in immediately setting the tone for these characters. When Joe performs his inspection of Clayton Enterprises, utilising his tactic of putting the enemy off-guard by his youthful age, eagle-eyed viewers may spot that the literature he's brought with him to appear inconspicuous is a marionette-scale edition of the magazine *TV21*. If you subscribe to the idea that most, if not all, of the Century 21 Supermarionation series existed in the same shared universe and that *TV21* itself was also a fictional newspaper within the world of *TV21* itself, but also that *Joe 90* exists in a much earlier period than *Fireball XL5*, *Stingray*, *Thunderbirds* and *Captain Scarlet*, then that ought to give you a brain scratcher to contemplate worthy of being subjected to the BIG RAT itself.

However, the comedy becomes stiffened in its delivery when transmitted through the hyper-proportioned marionettes that were the uniform style of Century 21 at this point. It's both enjoyably odd to see these super formalised puppets made to act out such bizarre comedy and also reminds you how much more effective this sort of humour-focused episode would be in the hands of the playfully brighter era of *Stingray* or *Thunderbirds*, depending on how creatively successful you think the transition between the two styles was. But again, it's sign of welcome awareness on director Leo Eaton's part that the darker attitudes of *Captain Scarlet* were just as applicable to these marionettes as the lighter aspects of *Joe 90*. It would seem that where the new puppets, introduced in *Captain Scarlet*, gave directors and puppeteers a more limiting task of manoeuvring them effectively, *Joe 90*'s more jokey nature in fact expanded the remit of these marionettes rather than tie them down even further.

The delightful arrogance of this episode is a thrill to watch unfold, as WIN's attempts at persuading Clayton grow in their intensity, from visiting him at Clayton Enterprises to actually trespassing on his property. Joe masquerading as a trumpeter playing an ear-piercing slab of rough jazz whilst Mac hovers their flying car outside of Clayton's open window in the dead of night isn't the most common usage for a brain pattern, but the inescapable oddness is terrific fun. Clayton does his best to convince himself that these strange invasions can be brushed aside, but it isn't until he witnesses Joe on his television screen and speaking in Clayton's voice (having procured the brain pattern of a mimic) that Clayton is convinced of the insanity that surrounds him. Succumbing to the lies that WIN have placed in his brain, his fear-mongering business days are over as he happily consumes the 'antidote' provided to him by Mac and Joe – nothing more than jelly babies. The episode ends on a note of charming pleasantness as Clayton, a reformed man, promises a pay rise to Molineaux (whilst also showing his change in worldview by referring to Molineaux by his first name, Jim) whilst setting about righting the wrongs that he's committed in the business world.

At a time when *Captain Scarlet* had gone to great lengths to erode the sense of humour and character established in previous Supermarionation efforts, *Joe 90* swung those elements back to the forefront, wrecking ball-like. The oddity of a boy hero trouncing international villains worked to the series' advantage time and time again in providing an offbeat manner for any given episode's action to conclude on satisfactorily, but 'See You Down There' is where *Joe 90*'s sense of humour is pushed to the very limits of what can be passed off as another win for WIN. As such, the comedy in 'See You Down There' is strikingly self-aware, to the extent that you can argue that the episode is trying too hard to be funny. It doesn't have the natural flow of *Stingray*'s 'Titan Goes Pop' or the gentleness of the Tracy brothers' constant ribbing of each other. However, like all good comedy, it's played entirely straight, highlighting the absolute bizarreness of the whole affair and ensuring that the episode doesn't collapse under the weight of itself. Having comedy in whatever form throughout *Joe 90* suggests there was a conscious effort to reverse engineer the psycho body horror vibes of *Captain Scarlet*.

With its focus on humorous character depictions and less reliance on supersonic vehicles, 'See You Down There' points the way to *The Secret Service* (which surely would have been in production at the time of the making of the episode), and with it the finish line of Supermarionation comes into sight. 'See You Down There' is by far the last stand of the art form, but there remains the nagging acknowledgement that the medium had delivered all it could offer at that time. Sandwiched between *Thunderbird 6* and *The Secret Service*, this penultimate outing for Joe and WIN came during an era for Century 21 that felt like it was growing tired of Supermarionation's tropes and so set about implementing quirky, spur of the moment angles to invigorate some fresh momentum. 'See You Down There' coming so late in *Joe 90*'s run suggests that this logic was an afterthought rather than planning well in advance. Standing on its own merits, 'See You Down There' is a wonderfully daft outing for *Joe 90* on the surface, yet boasts a moralistic stance against a capitalist empire through anti-violent means. A surprisingly topical route for an episode to venture into with little attempt to mask its overall themes of taking down big business, but therefore even further evidence that the Century 21 crew wanted to take advantage of *Joe 90*'s comedic spirit, coupled with its lessened reliance on overpowering mechs that partly encapsulate Supermarionation, and attempt an episode that's heavily laced in witty, expertly executed character dynamics.

Those coming into *Joe 90* expecting the usual explosive flair and mechanical muscle atypical of an Anderson production may come away disappointed with the series. However, for those who don't define

Supermarionation as explosions, who appreciate how the medium was capable of shepherding in comedy and characters just as successfully as science fiction or espionage action, then 'See You Down There' is a welcome and recommended breakage from the norm and an absolute highlight of the twilight years of Supermarionation. If 'See You Down There' is any indication of a future in which Supermarionation dispensed with having to detonate its narrative momentum using a barrage of supersonic vehicles, a surface level tactic devoid of the kind of interplay that comes naturally with characters like those in *Joe 90*, then that future is sorely missed.

UFO: 'A QUESTION OF PRIORITIES'

When debating which episodes from Gerry and Sylvia's filmography to write about for this book, I found myself faced with a similar dilemma that Ed Straker must face in one of *UFO*'s most astounding episodes, albeit on a much less traumatic level. The Anderson fandom, like all others, adheres to a select few pieces of work from Gerry and Sylvia that are unquestioned in being fan favourites, so much so that there's almost an unspoken acknowledgement that they're untouchable in debate. You don't need to analyse or critique them in any shape or form. They're just *that* good, as indestructible as Captain Scarlet. 'War Games' and 'Dragon's Domain' are regarded as undisputable highlights of *Space: 1999*. 'Terror in New York City', 'Trapped in the Sky' and 'Attack of the Alligators!' are the highlights from *Thunderbirds*. As such, 'Sub-Smash', 'Timelash' and 'A Question of Priorities' are considered to be the cream of the crop for *UFO*. But from another perspective, the fact that such episodes are held up in such sky-high regard makes them all the more complicated to discuss. It's not as if they're a tangled mess that's impossible to unravel, it's more akin to such episodes being so masterly crafted that to attempt to deconstruct them would be an act of heartless destruction.

When dealing with a television episode that's deemed to be so perfect in its ingredients, construction, delivery and impact, it becomes frustratingly difficult to write about from a critical perspective. By *critical*, this doesn't mean purposefully nit-picking at the episode in question, determined to find fault in it. In the context of this book, *critical* refers to something much more three-dimensional; the act of disassembling an episode to uncover its capabilities to function. The good, the bad, the ugly and the everything else about it. Episodes classified as *perfect* traditionally don't lend themselves well to this sort of analysis, because there would be no difference between me proceeding to write two to three thousand words saying 'A Question of Priorities' is brilliant and me writing that only once.

However, 'A Question of Priorities' is considered the apex of *UFO* and by extension Gerry and Sylvia's live-action output for considerably convincing reasons. 'A Question of Priorities' is the definitive episode of *UFO*, chiefly because it clutches the heart of the series and squeezes emotional devastation out of it unlike any other episode. It's an episode of two halves – one focusing on the accidental death of Ed Straker's son, John, and the other detailing the events of a calm, non-violent UFO invasion in Ireland, in which the UFO's alien pilot breaks into an elderly woman's home to presumably try and make contact with their own kind. Tony Barwick's great strengths as a story-teller are on full display here as he gently overlaps the events of both stories, neither overpowering the other, both halves in delicate tune with each other.

UFO does much to show of how the various members of SHADO are forced to conceal their life-saving work from their loved ones, hammered home by Straker in the closing moments of opening episode 'Identified'. But it's 'A Question of Priorities' that really shows us this distance maintained by SHADO, rather than tell us. Straker has already endured heartbreak and suffering all in the name of SHADO when his marriage to Mary is eroded away, resulting in the forced and secluded experiences he's permitted to enjoy with John. The episode's opening moments of Straker and John careering through Harlington-Straker studios, a valuable period of father-son bonding as John live with his mother, is a bittersweet insight into seeing Straker's determined demeanour slip away into something more carefree and loving. Ed Bishop and Suzanne Neve are convincing in their awkwardness as Straker returns John home to Mary following their time together, Straker's authoritarian mask falling off entirely when he overruns his allotted time with John and is forced to deal with Mary's frustration.

A freak roadside accident when John rushes to his father before he can leave shows how 'A Question of Priorities' was venturing into more drama-driven territory than *UFO* was experienced in doing so prior, showing its audience that this was an episode that's going to be markedly different from what they're used to. Following John's admittance to hospital, attempts to inject him with antibodies prove useless when he reacts negatively to them. It's here that the episode allows us another unique insight into the inner workings of SHADO and its impact on the outside world. Straker's answer is to abuse his position of authority to order a SHADO transporter to deliver an experimental antibody from overseas that could cure John's injuries, if there's enough time for the transporter to arrive. Straker maintains a curtain of secrecy around his orders, unable to even inform Mary of how he can resolve the danger.

The consequence of SHADO's enforced secrecy mixed together with Straker's abuse of power, like a volatile cocktail of authority gone wrong, comes when Colonel Freeman orders the transporter to investigate the UFO landing that's taking place in Ireland. These sections of the episode should function as the episode's subplot, the lower-scale story that compliments the main narrative, allowing an ease of flow into the proceedings. Instead, the two work in equal tandem, Straker and Mary's strained heartache as they attempt to save their son gives the episode the drama it's celebrated for, but it's the UFO invasion that gives the episode a muscular undercurrent of genuine terror. This is far from the first time we've seen an alien horrifically encounter an unsuspecting human victim, but it's rare for us as the audience to be permitted such intimacy with someone constantly on the verge of becoming a victim, but ultimately evades their organ harvesting ways.

Mary Merrall's portrayal of the vulnerable yet compassionate Mrs O'Connor, blind with only a pet parrot for company, is a highlight of an episode chock full of notable highs. When the UFO itself crash-lands off the Irish coast and its alien pilot, escaping their damaged craft, quietly and calmly enters her home in an effort to find a suitable position to set up his mobile communication equipment, it's a riveting moment. Her unease at this sinister intrusion gives way to empathy when her constant questioning of the intruder falls on deaf ears. Throughout these tense moments, the alien doesn't respond to her, barely even acknowledging her existence, only doing so when she attempts to make physical contact with the alien. The sense of physical threat against Mrs O'Connor is permanent in these scenes, enhanced by her defenceless state, yet it never comes. Throughout *UFO*, the aliens are shown to be driven to acts of their violent organ harvesting by sheer survival, yet the alien featured in 'A Question of Priorities' doesn't appear to be fixated on such ideas. They appear to be driven by a different form of survival, one of escape from their alien colleagues. Eventually leaving the safety of Mrs O'Connor's cottage, the alien attempts to dash deep into the neighbouring countryside, only to be assassinated by another passing UFO. Whatever reasoning's or motivations this alien had for sparing O'Connor's life are rendered mute as the creature is taken to their otherworldly grave.

SHADO themselves remain nonplussed, helpless even, in trying to make sense of the situation before them. Straker's demands as to why the transporter was called off course is met with timid bewilderment from his staff as he proves unable to contextualise his frustrations, opting to keep the state of his son a secret. The alien's transmissions from O'Connor's cottage had attracted their attentions, diverting the transporter craft that's carrying the vital medicine for John, but the situation is snatched away from them to resolve as the aliens manage to shroud their own circumstances in the same level of secrecy as SHADO does theirs. This strange set of events dealt with, the transporter is allowed to continue on its original journey to England from America, but it's all in vain. SHADO's regular mission of saving the world results in them not being able to save John.

In a superbly directed piece of human drama, not once are the words actually uttered that John has died. Instead, Straker arriving at the hospital with the experimental antibodies is met with exiting sobs from Mary and bitter disdain from Steven Rutland, Mary's subsequent partner, smoulderingly performed by Philip Madoc. The breakdown of former marriage is given a final stab through the heart when Mary declares that she never wants to see Ed again. The episode ends on the striking image of Ed Straker alone in the hospital reception, shot from above, gazing down on him from behind, Mary and Steve dragging themselves away from the hospital drowning in their own grief. Director David Lane crafts a simple yet iconic image for the episode to conclude on, one that's not reliant on pyrotechnics or perfectly formed models. It's a distant view of a broken man, but the act of capturing Straker from behind reads as if to say that Straker can never show the world that he's broken. That's the price paid for remaining in the shadows.

Gerry Anderson too had a price to pay for daring to venture out of the pyrotechnic route with this episode. One person who didn't regard 'A Question of Priorities' as a classic was Abe Mandell, the head of ITC's New York branch. Essentially Andersons' American equivalent of Lew Grade, Mandell's reaction to the episode was to accuse Anderson of wandering into derivative, soap opera territory and had no business breaking *UFO's* otherwise firm science fiction formula. From a purely marketing perspective, it's understandable to see how Mandell reacted this episode. *UFO* struggled to secure a satisfactory American deal for broadcast in the States, ultimately resulting in the cancellation of the proposed second series that would have shifted focus away from Earth-based settings, which itself resulted in this concept becoming reformatted into *Space: 1999*. From Mandell's point of view, trying to find a home for a costly and complicated science fiction television, imported from overseas, was a struggle enough, but having to contend with an episode that snapped the threads that *UFO* had otherwise weaved for itself probably didn't help. During a time when science fiction television was still in an infant stage compared to the abundance of productions offered by today's standards, hindsight gives us the benefit of being able to understand how not everyone could perceive what kind of series *UFO* was attempting to be.

Nevertheless, his insistence that further scripts of this nature being avoided unintentionally enables 'A Question of Priorities' to stand proud and brave away from other episodes. 'A Question of Priorities' wouldn't be the first or last episodes of *UFO* to dabble in adult themes. Death, marital affairs, drug taking and implications of sex surrounds the series from all sides. But there's precious little in *UFO* that delivers on these themes with such poignancy. Despite having no clear explanations for its perpetrator's movements, the UFO invasion in this episode is mysterious rather than muddled, all reinforcing the idea that 'A Question of Priorities' pulls all the stops in maintaining a tragic, uneasy atmosphere. It's another unplugging from the routine state of affairs as this particular UFO deliberately avoids destructive acts. The shock of John's death and the assassination of the unarmed alien crystallise *UFO's* duelling appealing premises of human drama intertwined with technological sci-fi action.

Unsettling, unexpected, precisely heart-breaking and incredibly well delivered, 'A Question of Priorities' is justified in its status as an absolute classic. As we'll explore later on in this book in the chapter **Ironmongery vs. Agony**, there can be continued debate as to whether or not UFO was stronger as a human drama against a sci-fi backdrop or a science fiction adventure series that gave emotional depth to its intrepid pilots, astronauts and rampaging aliens. With its human heartbreak light touch of mecha, 'A Question of Priorities' is the strongest case UFO ever made for being at its best in being the former identity.

SPACE: 1999: 'THE TROUBLED SPIRIT'

The more Lew Grade witnessed *Space: 1999*'s first series, the more he must have had his patience tested by Gerry and Sylvia Anderson. Having canned pre-production on *UFO*'s second and more moon-based series but invigorated by Century 21's workaround of fashioning something new from their efforts (by now the company itself had completed its contracted run with Grade and its core members of Gerry, Sylvia and Reg Hill had regrouped under the name Group Three), his heart must have sank once more when seeing the finished result. *Space: 1999* marries exaggerated science-fiction adventure with intense, philosophical conversations that put the series at odds with much of its contemporaries. Intergalactic battles are often metaphors for musings on meaning and identity in a relentless, unforgiving universe and humanity's relationship with it. From Grade's perspective, the deeper *Space: 1999* burrowed into its cerebral mindset, the less exportable it became as a commercial product, as evidence by how the second series wiped the slate clean of anything resembling an intelligent plot. But *Space: 1999* always made room to explore some fascinating ideas, and yet 'The Troubled Spirit' diverts from the series' regular path and in doing so arguably fails to answer the thematic questions it poses.

Despite *Space: 1999* frequently dabbling in painful horror inflicted upon its characters and a general fear of the unknown hanging over Moonbase Alpha, 'The Troubled Spirit' marks the first and only instance of *Space: 1999*'s so-called Year One attempting a full-on ghost story, a tale in which the alien is transplanted with the occult. The extravagant, melodramatic alien menaces are replaced by something calmer, but no less sinister and terrifying. With its restrained, unhurried direction, claustrophobic atmosphere and lack of genuine alien creatures or intelligences at work, 'The Troubled Spirit' sets itself up as a standalone entry in *Space: 1999*'s run but crumbles in its inability to grapple with its own themes as it reaches the finish line.

The troubling issue at play here is that 'The Troubled Spirit' struggles to make coherent sense of its own story – Alphan botanist Doctor Dan Mateo becomes haunted by the disfigured ghost of his own self, a string of murders following in his wake when experiments in communicating with plants go horridly wrong, before an attempted exorcism results in Mateo's death, accidentally foreshadowing his ghost's existence. Through this mind-bending experience, Commander John Koenig can only respond with confusion; 'What's that all about?' he ponders by the episode's end, as the death of Mateo doesn't just result in his ghost's existence, but ends up killing the ghost too. Koenig's reaction is the closest the episode comes to offering a substantial answer to the question of life after death posed by the episode's events. *Space: 1999* prides itself on being a series where much is questioned but a great deal is also answered, to the point where the series is interlinked by a suspected overall mission of destiny at work in how Moonbase Alpha's drifting through space is in fact not some freak accident but a deliberate chain of events set in motion by higher cosmic powers. 'The Troubled Spirit' gives us a rare instance of the Alphans unable to unravel the mystery of their latest adventure, unable to find a moral centre within the baffling events surrounding it. Without that centre, the episode appears hollow.

Perhaps that's the point. The ebb and flow of any *Space: 1999* episode (Year One, at least) comes from the action stopping and starting to allow scenes of scrambling reflection to take place, as the Alphans engage in a race against time to try and make sense of their latest dangers and formulate a plan against that danger. 'The Troubled Spirit' sticks to that format well, but in doing so gives credence to the idea that this is an episode that very purposefully isn't meant to have a moral centre. In the aftermath of Mateo's initial experiments overwhelming him and the emergence of his ghostly doppelgänger causing havoc on Alpha, the idea gradually dawns on Alpha's senior figures that they are dealing with something beyond the realms of science, that an occult presence has infected Moonbase Alpha. This is met with scornful derision from some corners, but when the Alphans conduct their own makeshift séance to entice the ghost Mateo into the open, they see the phantom for themselves. Throughout 'The Troubled Spirit', seeing is believing, and the episode's best moments come from when less is told and more is shown.

The gradual rise of an occult force tightening its grip on Moonbase Alpha swells to great effect. The opening long shots of drifting through an empty base as the majority of Alphans attend an evening of music is searchingly tense, as if we're looking for something frightening to happen. Likewise, the tracking shots in the botany crackle with further danger, enhanced by the electric sitar being played, somewhere between Santana and Tangerine Dream. Like all good horror stories, the perpetrating fear isn't shown immediately, but the mood is entirely set. The glimpses of Mateo's ghostly form lurking within shadows and obscured by varying camera angles are enticing to watch, implying the arrival of a threat that can't entirely be cemented, so close and yet so far. The sharp, intense zoom-in into the petrified face of Mateo's partner Laura Adams when she confronts Mateo's ghost, dying from sheer fear, is bare and uncluttered in communicating the horror of the moment. The speed of the zoom helps to obscure Mateo's face, yet we can just make out some form of distorted features, but only just, and that's where the fear lies.

This brief, partially invisible moment within the scene neatly manages to summarise the qualities of 'The Troubled Spirit'; viewed from an attempted linear breakdown, the episode's storyline doesn't make sense, because that's the point. 'The Troubled Spirit' produces its dramatic power by the immediacy of the moment, the shock, the horror, the fear. The fear of the moment overpowers any need for in-depth narrative analysis, which rather makes this chapter's job all the more difficult, but for a series that continues to be probed more so than many other of Gerry and Sylvia's creations, there's a commendable salute to bestow upon an episode of *Space: 1999* which appears to rally against that approach so many people come to the series with. 'The Troubled Spirit' ultimately feels as though it's affirming the series' setting of the cosmic compass to explore internal themes within a very external location, ie the enveloping bleakness of the universe.

Held up under the scrutiny of repeated viewing, 'The Troubled Spirit' can't help but corrode in other areas. It's disingenuous to give the episode brownie points when nobody appears to recognise that, during the séance scene in which contact is made with the doppelgänger Mateo, the death that this version of Mateo warns of is ... his own? Nobody appears to make that connection and, in doing so, attempt to prevent his death, not even the ghost rendition of Mateo himself. This incarnation is fully aware of the death being foreshadowed, but joins his human counterpart in succumbing to the final grave, the two forms of Mateo appearing to bond once both have been struck. Why the ghost version of Mateo doesn't warn his former self of his impending doom when he appears to be the only one fully clued into this predicament is another mystery the episode leaves unsolved.

'The Troubled Spirit' avoids being confused by its own concept. Instead, it feels muddled by its own execution, content to focus on the piercing moments of fear at the expense of quality control in its other elements. The episode's efforts to ensure that fear overpowers logic only becomes more apparent when repeated viewings highlight that exact lack of logic. An episode that takes great pleasure in being inscrutable, but in doing so takes too much pleasure to be thought of as cohesive. It's both refreshing for the series to shackle its chains like this and frustrating when attempting to make sense of it.

Then again, it wouldn't do to come away from any chapter of this book without some attempt at prizing open a final send-off. Towards the end of each *Space: 1999* episode, characters will converse and attempt to make a final summary of the events that have just preceded, a summary of the jigsaw that they've finally put into place. As mentioned, Koenig's 'what's that all about?' is this episode's equivalent of that statement. It's dismissive. It's throwaway. It's anticlimactic. It points to the Alphans' lack of understanding as to what's just occurred before their very eyes. If one interpretation can be applied to 'The Troubled Spirit', maybe it's just that – that the possibilities and the very definition of life after death cannot be understood by anyone who's actually alive. They have to be deceased to comprehend it. It puts a rather perverse spin on the idea of having a lived-in experience.

It's a rather all-encompassing interpretation that scrubs away the need for close analysis of the aforementioned problematic story elements, simply because one can wave them away as being not intended for living minds. But it helps to tie into the episode's wider atmosphere of the characters unable to make sense of being invaded not by an outside alien force, but by something far more internal, that this is a threat they cannot simply expunge into the derelict outcasts of space. As the exorcism and the séance scenes show, this is a threat they have to entrap if they've any hope of not merely understanding it, but fighting back against it. So often in *Space: 1999*, threats need to be removed, but in 'The Troubled Spirit', the threat is contained, embraced even. This is a danger that spends much of the episode obscured and out of reach, yet it's much closer to home for the Alphans than a black sun or a space dragon. The ghost Mateo speaks their language, but there remains a communication barrier in saving both the present and future Mateo. The danger in 'The Troubled Spirit' is attempted to be embraced as if the Alphans harbour a desire to make sense of something unexplainable – life after death, something that no living person can explain.

Through a variety of far-reaching elements from story-telling inconsistencies, muted direction and a lack of alien antagonists, 'The Troubled Spirit' stands apart from a lot of the competition, for better or worse. It's aversion to make sense of its own story in an effort to strike fear into our hearts is commendable but flawed. On further viewings, fear without logic doesn't embellish the fear, it only embellishes the lack of logic. But the idea of the Alphans unable to successfully communicate with some otherworldly force feels achingly in-tune with the series' cursed attitude of Moonbase Alpha never being able to succeed in finding a new home, permanently destined to wander through space. 'The Troubled Spirit' succeeds in being one of the most confounding episodes of *Space: 1999*. Regardless of how creatively decent the episode may be deemed to be (which can really only be defined by the individual viewer), this is an extraordinary accomplishment.

'The Troubled Spirit' doesn't have the staying power of 'Breakaway', the time-displaced engagement of 'Another Time, Another Place', or the sheer, exhilarating terror of 'Dragon's Domain', but it does have a quiet power that arises from the piercing moments of fear it conjures up. It may have a confused soul, but it's not rushed or misguided, and boasts a concept that's well worth exploring within *Space: 1999*, chiefly because other episodes don't concern themselves with this concept. Where much of *Space: 1999* focuses on its characters surviving from one danger lurching to the next, 'The Troubled Spirit' stretches away from this and ponders what may occur once Moonbase Alpha has drifted as far as it can go. What may happen to its valiant crew members, doctors, Eagle pilots, scientists and commanders once they've reached their final destination, when they are unable to explore anymore new worlds? 'The Troubled Spirit' doesn't have the answer to this, but deliberately so. It's an episode that asks its audience to accept that there are times when the question is more revealing than any answer that may be plucked from deep space. On first inspections, such a venture doesn't tie in with *Space: 1999*'s ethos at all. An episode that forbids its audience from interpreting a clear-cut moral centre? What's that all about?

TERRAHAWKS: 'THE ULTIMATE MENACE'

The opening episode to *Terrahawks'* third and final series acknowledges its static set-up of characters, admitting that for all of the personality these heroes and villains exuded, it had gone as far as it could with such a set-up. 'Two For The Price of One' introduces It-Star, the transgender Goy-Birl offspring of Cy-Star, born with the same exposed mechanics as their elders, yet blessed with a wit and intelligence only matched by Zelda herself. Their presence gives *Terrahawks* a welcome zest, but before It-Star's arrival, *Terrahawks* had attempted to stretch itself in another fashion with 'The Ultimate Menace', the last true episode of the second series, not counting the clip show 'Ma's Monsters'.

'The Ultimate Menace' was originally broadcast within the second series of *Terrahawks*, but has since be revised to function on home releases as the intended finale to the second series, evidenced further by its production numbering as a much later episode. The standalone nature of many of *Terrahawks'* episodes results in most episodes having no real distinction as to what's meant to function as properly sequenced episodes, the aforementioned 'Two For The Price of One' and the two-part 'Expect the Unexpected' being acceptations. 'The Ultimate Menace' is another excursion from the standalone approach to so much of *Terrahawks'* output. It's an episode that feels like it really could be a grand finale with its end-of-the-universe scenario, played entirely straight and yet its sheer ridiculousness a neat highlight of *Terrahawks'* tongue-in-cheek story-telling.

Once *Terrahawks* disregarded its serious tones from early on in the series and began embracing its slapstick surrealism, it did so with enthusiastic aplomb. But 'The Ultimate Menace' playing things straight makes the episode hark back to those earlier attitudes seen in 'Thunder-Roar' or 'Close Call'. But unlike those earlier episodes, 'The Ultimate Menace' doesn't feel awkwardly executed in its serious stories delivered with these bizarre characters. 'The Ultimate Menace' comes with the lived-in feel of *Terrahawks* having been a series everyone involved in was readily familiar with what made the series function so well, hence it takes the opportunity to stretch its legs like this.

The episode opens with a solid burst of communicating the dangers our heroes and villains alike find themselves in. Ninestein leads the Terrahawks in *Spacehawk* to meet with Zelda herself on her Mars complex, for reasons neither leader is willing to divulge to their respective parties at this juncture. It's soon revealed that Ninestein and Zelda have agreed to call a temporary truce in response to a threat that could easily destroy Mars and Earth alike – the Zyclon. A colossal spaceship controlled entirely by artificial intelligence, silently stalking the universe, ready to pierce its pronged forks into its existence. Its presence is such a danger that human and android must put aside their differences and work together to fight a common enemy. This premise elevates 'The Ultimate Menace' to distinguished levels within the *Terrahawks* canon. 'A Christmas Miracle' may have seen Ninestein dream of a temporary but peaceful union between his friends and enemies, right down to being seduced by an flamboyantly-dressed, smooth-talking Zelda, but this is no fantasy. Here, this is a very real and urgent danger and it's worth praising *Terrahawks* for knowing when to treat a serious situation with the seriousness that it deserves.

But of course, this being *Terrahawks*, it doesn't get away with this concept entirely scot-free. The details surrounding the Zyclon's actual presence are never explored, a symptom of how *Terrahawks* was prone to being superficial in its story-telling. The size of this concept feels like something from *Space: 1999*, in which those hour-long episodes would have spent some considerable time diving into the possible origins of such a creation as the Zyclon. In *Terrahawks*' context, not so much. The irreverence of *Terrahawks*' stories makes it both a joy and a hindrance, none more so than 'The Ultimate Menace', given that we learn next to nothing of what this ultimate menace actually is. We never learn of its origin or how Ninestein and Zelda alike knew of the threat so much that they agree to combine their forces against it. *Terrahawks* never quite made the time to explore such roots of its stories and 'The Ultimate Menace' is a prime example of how much that drags the series down, where other episodes would have cheerfully flirted their way out of any narrative complications.

Strangely enough, that sense of irreverence, so typical of *Terrahawks*, isn't hugely at work elsewhere here. The episode's opening cluster of scenes, prior to the revelation and main attack on the Zyclon itself, display how *Terrahawks* is capable of being more mature and serious than it often let on. The scenes of confusion amongst Ninestein and Zelda's respective crews and *Spacehawk* comes into range of Zelda's complex, only for neither side to open fire, feel natural and convincing. Once the episode has established the perimeters set by Zelda and Ninestein in tackling the Zyclon, we get out first glimpse of the creature itself. Well, perhaps not creature. Creation is a more apt term. Alien entities exist in *Terrahawks* with no genuine exploration. Zelda, Yung-Star and Cy-Star's presence as androids manufactured by humanoids yet overthrowing their creators goes undefined throughout the series and its specific details wouldn't flourish until the series' audio continuation some 30 years later. In this context, the Zyclon's lack of specifics isn't totally gregarious. And yet this feels all the stranger in this episode, oddly helping 'The Ultimate Menace' to stand as one of *Terrahawks'* most distinctive episodes.

This impossibly gargantuan mechanized lifeform drifts into view in near-total silence, the hum of its metallic soul the only audible giveaway, like a robotic ghost. Without doubt one of the most striking vehicle designs not just in *Terrahawks* but in a Gerry Anderson production as well, the Zyclon feels like something carved out of Unicron or the Death Star. The robotic beast is so colossal it struggles to have its entire form fill the screen. Whenever it does, it appears diminutive, as if the Zyclon has to be filmed from such a long distance away just to capture it all in one shot. It's pronged front, jaw-like entrance make for awesome viewing. Even *Terrahawks'* plentiful amount of naysayers rarely have a bad word for the series' special effects, and the Zyclon helps to deliver some mecha-heavy jeopardy. The cosmic dogfight experienced by Hawkeye, Space Sargent 101, Kate Kestral and Sergeant Major Zero as they attempt to travel to the Zyclon itself in a pair of ZEAFs is the only moment the episode allows for mech-heavy action.

The plan is to exploit the Zyclon's programmed prejudice against all life, biological or artificial, ie human or android, by sending Zero into its dark heart and attempt to stop it. 'Tiger' does let slip that the Zyclon is built and programmed by a massive computer system, resulting in the episode being hacked by questions of how does one define personality and identity within machines and the superiority of computerised lifeforms over organic life, an age-old question that many works of science fiction have dabbled in. Even if *Terrahawks* doesn't have the sophistication to put a fresh spin on the question, it does have the scope to ask the question itself, which other lesser children's sci-fi TV shows wouldn't have explored. *Terrahawks* could surprise you by taking an oddly moralistic stance in its episodes, such as freedom of animal life in 'The Sporilla' or whether to destroy a newborn life if it could grow up to become evil in 'Two For The Price Of One'.

'The Ultimate Menace' brings the comedic juxtaposing relationship between 'Tiger' and Zero to the surface, one a stern, militant authority figure, the other carefree and frivolous yet keen to gain approval from his superiors. The comedy is to be found in how the robot Zero has a more flexible range of emotions than the stoic human Ninestein, yet both were created by artificial means, which Zero reminds 'Tiger' of early on in the series. The plan to destroy the Zyclon is to send one of the Zeroids into the heart of the metallic beast, 'Tiger' hedging his bets on the uncertainty of whether or not the Zyclon will open fire on a fellow machine. In a superb bit of acting on Windsor Davies' part, Kate's deployment of Zero from the ZEAF before the Zyclon can obliterate them both is met by a monotone performance from Zero, who responds to Kate's well-wishes as if stripped of his robust personality. Prior to their combat scene, 'Tiger' attempts, for the umpteenth time in the series, to convince Zero that he is no more than metal and wire. It's likely that he was informing Zero of this to get him in the right frame of mind to confront the Zyclon, but Zero doesn't fully catch on with this. He successfully approaches the Zyclon, entering its form, almost fully convinced he is as without emotion as the Zyclon itself.

Venturing within the belly of the beast, the interior of the Zyclon is as eye-catching as its exterior, but significantly smaller and curiously built to allow non-computerised forms to have access around the insides. A further sign of its mysterious genesis? The Zyclon itself, presumably portrayed by Robbie Stevens, has a personality as cold as its physical form. Represented by some grotesque, artificial glowing eye, Stevens' low-key, oily performance adds a delicate touch of menace to the Zyclon. This becomes matched by Davies' own performance, who continues portraying Zero as if his personality has been cut clean away. For the purposes of infiltrating the Zyclon, doing so makes sense, but Zero still doesn't appear to have been clued into this.

With this muddled mission in mind, it's unclear if Zero is genuinely lured in by the Zyclon's promise of an infinite, perfect existence if he and the other Zeroids join the Zyclon, creating the ultimate computerised intelligence. Only with the confirmation that doing so would mean the annihilation of his human friends does Zero regain his sense of self. Remembering his personality and identity, Zero enjoys his finest hour by obliterating the hypnotic eye before him, setting off a chain reaction that destroys the Zyclon in a fireball of computerised rage, the Zyclon's last feelings being one of utter confusion at the idea of a fellow machine exhibiting a personality. The episode ends on a comical high as 'Tiger' bemoans his cursed existence at having to work alongside what he sees as an idiotic character when Zero declares that he saved the universe because the Zyclon deemed him to be illogical, but it's those exact characteristics that have saved the universe from total destruction. No amount of heroic endeavours is going to get in the way of 'Tiger' and Zero having their bickering relationship sustained.

'The Ultimate Menace' demonstrates many of *Terrahawks*' strengths and weaknesses in fairly equal balance, but it also captures the series at an oddly crucial moment. It's not the first time *Terrahawks* had a go at dispensing with the comedy and focused on being a more hardnosed affair, but unlike earlier episodes such as 'Close Call' and 'Thunder Roar', it doesn't feel awkward in doing so. The impact of the episode comes from the comfortable assumption that the further you get into *Terrahawks*, the further the humour asserts itself. Whilst that would be the case for episodes after this one, 'The Ultimate Menace' feels earnest and sincere in the serious moods it conveys, something *Terrahawks* wasn't always preoccupied with.

The episode's eventual focus on Zero grappling with the Zyclon results in the truce between human and android going underserved. The androids themselves aren't hugely involved in the battle against the Zyclon, but it's appreciated to know that *Terrahawks*, of all the Anderson series, made room to explore what kind of scenario would necessitate barriers being broken down like this. We never saw that between Tory Tempest and Titan or Jeff Tracy and the Hood. The key message that 'The Ultimate Menace' seems to say is that having an individual personality and identity is a positive thing, that to think differently and be an individual is better than to be a colossal creature devoid of a heart. If that's the case, then 'The Ultimate Menace' succeeds as a pretty definitive episode of *Terrahawks*, a series that often disregarded logic, continuity, and other perhaps sterile elements in order to allow its own vibrant, offbeat and hugely enjoyable personality to be its defining characteristic.

NEW CAPTAIN SCARLET: 'DOMINION'

'Dominion' had an unintended significance heaped upon it. Not only is it the last episode of *New Captain Scarlet*, it's also the final episode of television that Gerry Anderson would make in his lifetime. Other projects born after *New Captain Scarlet*'s run such as *Lightspeed*, *Eternity* and *Gemini Force One* would amount to fleeting lifespans in the form of concept art and trailers, but would venture no further before Gerry's passing in 2012. Numerous attempts to revitalise *Thunderbirds*, channelled through Gerry Anderson's own vision of what a twenty first century International Rescue would look like, would similarly come to nothing. 'Dominion' wasn't planned to be any of this, of course. It's even possible that it wasn't meant to be the definitive end for *New Captain Scarlet*, in the hopes that the series would continue after its two preliminary seasons. However, the abysmal manner in which it was broadcast, lost within the schedule of the children's Saturday morning variety show *Ministry of Mayhem*, ensured its demise before the series had even begun. The end of *New Captain Scarlet*'s story is less frustrating than the end of *New Captain Scarlet*'s production, but 'Dominion' is also an episode that carries many of the series' braver and timid elements to the end.

It's practically impossible to approach *New Captain Scarlet* without having previously experienced the original series, thus making comparisons between the two so inevitable that this book is doing so right now. Nowhere is that comparison more applicable than 'Dominion', because it gives us something the original series never had in order to compare to – a finale. *Captain Scarlet and the Mysterons* is a rare instance in the Andersons' back catalogue that firmly begins with an overarching story to tell, but it wouldn't be until some 40 years later that another Anderson production would end that story, albeit set in an entirely different world to the original. 'Dominion' delivers a final strike in the war of nerves against Spectrum and the Mysterons, doing so with some handsome symmetry in ending the series as it began with Captain Scarlet and Captain Black journeying to Mars. In 'Instruments of Destruction', they had both left Mars in the hands of the Mysterons but in 'Dominion', both men return to the planet as human and Mysteron hybrids, a quirk of the series meant to offer some more modernised explanation as to how Scarlet's indestructible prowess is meant to function as neither fully human nor fully Mysteron.

'Dominion' sets the scene not on Mars, but on another cold, barren landscape – the rugged, snow-laden mountains of Russia, where a rumbling rampage of Druzynik tanks do battle with the fate of the Tereshkovo Nuclear Power Planet hanging in the balance. With one tank piloted by Black and the other by Scarlet and Captain Blue, it's a statement of intent to open the episode with that two such brute tanks should begin the episode. This is the kind of action that would usually conclude an episode of *New Captain Scarlet*, not open it. That's how serious this episode is. The ensuing blitz ends in victory for Spectrum. Not only is the Nuclear Plant saved, but Captain Black, knocked unconscious from the blast against his own vehicle, is finally captured and brought back to Skybase. Eventually recovering, his unbelievable claims of being freed from the Mysterons' control is enforced by his further claim that he knows how to defeat the Mysterons.

New Captain Scarlet always paid closer attention to its characters than the original series did and it's in these moments that 'Dominion' truly shines in how *New Captain Scarlet* portrays the human consequences of the war of nerves. In past exploits, Black has attempted to trick Destiny Angel, his former lover, into believing he really is the real Conrad but here, Destiny's acceptance of Conrad's claims is met with rejection from Conrad himself. His pushing away of Destiny for their joint safety is a feverishly welcome piece of humanisation and empathy for a character whose whole purpose in *Captain Scarlet*, whatever the incarnation, is to be the exact opposite of human. The exact opposite of empathetic. Considering that *New Captain Scarlet* was an action-driven affair, albeit very slick and nimble action that rarely diverted sensible story-telling, these minute moments of character interactions are a welcome touch, the icing on the cake. Merging that emphasis on characterisation with drastic action is when Captain Scarlet himself, willing to accept the risk of Conrad's claim, breaks Black out of confinement and the pair making a dash for Mars, Scarlet adopting an anti-authority stance following Colonel White's flat refusal to believe Black's suggestion of knowing how to defeat the Mysterons. The colonel himself is granted some interplay in all of this, eventually relenting and allowing Scarlet and Black to proceed to Mars, the fate of the world now resting on both men's hands.

As 'Dominion' progresses, its heavy emphasis on striking character-focused action takes desperate turns. When Scarlet and Black return to Mars, they become confronted by the Mysterons just as they had done back in 'Instruments of Destruction'. Whilst the Mysterons are at first keen to murder their former operatives by sending their projected green rings in hot pursuit of their Bison mech, Black's begging for an audience seems to win the Mysterons over. It's only once Scarlet and Black are inside the Mysteron complex that Black succumbs to their power once more, with the horrific revelation that he wasn't acting as a double agent in order to lure Scarlet to Mars, but that he was tricked into believing he really was free of their control. This is the Mysterons at something of a peak in how sadistic they are in *New Captain Scarlet* and quite honestly, it feels like a regression.

The whole point of both incarnations of *Captain Scarlet* is that the war of nerves is an accidental one and how in the original series the Mysterons were portrayed as a welcoming group, only to be antagonised by Captain Black's trigger-happy attack. In *New Captain Scarlet*, that sense of communal friendliness on the part of the Mysterons' is utterly absent. The Mysterons are shown to be evil from beginning to end and this episode's act of tricking Black and Scarlet to return to Mars in a final, desperate attempt to eliminate them paints the Mysterons into a confining corner. The original series episode 'Dangerous Rendezvous' is so effective because the idea that the Mysterons can be negotiated with feels incredibly genuine due to their existence before Captain Black introduced himself and his firepower to them. We have none of that in *New Captain Scarlet*. 'The Achilles Messenger' comes close with the arrival of a Mysteron agent who proposes that there are some in the Mysteron world who wish the war would end, but that doesn't get explored in any great depth.

The Mysterons are unfortunately so two-dimensional in *New Captain Scarlet* that it merely becomes dull, saved only by their intimidating appearance. 'Dominion' builds on the Mysterons' visual aesthetic first seen in 'Instruments of Destruction' but more fully in 'Enigma', when they launched a colossal Mysteron obelisk to the Earth to confound Spectrum whilst another attack was launched elsewhere. We've never come this close to seeing the interior of the Mysterons themselves, especially since the craft seen in 'Enigma' was a false projection. When you don't have that much engaging character development, you've got to take your positives elsewhere. The design of the Mysterons in *New Captain Scarlet* matches their permanently antagonistic status, a sinister mass of electrified green energy, pulsating throughout the curious yet menacing physical layout, not designed to facilitate human beings.

It's within this untameable, undefinable alien swarm that Captain Black meets his ultimate fate – or does he? In an act with Mysteron-worthiness of bloodlust, Captain Scarlet retaliates against the re-Mysteronised Black by flinging him into the dark heart of the Mysteron complex, a swarming black sphere. This triggers a chain reaction that gradually engulfs the entire city, vanishing before Scarlet's eyes as rapidly and totally as it first emerged during the series' opening two-parter. The final words *New Captain Scarlet* delivers offers something akin to hope and relief, a rare thing in *Captain Scarlet*. Paul makes contact with Skybase, altering them that he's leaving Mars, seemingly for good, and coming home. What *New Captain Scarlet* shows us is something quite different.

The parting shot *New Captain Scarlet* gives us is one that demonstrates how the series wasn't as brave and bold an extension of its source material as you might believe. As Captain Scarlet blasts off from the planet, we see him being watched by Captain Black, alive and well, who allows Scarlet to leave before being swallowed into the planet's surface by a pair of glowing green rings. The implication the series leaves us pondering over is Captain Scarlet's failure to rid the universe of the Mysterons, that they remain alive and well and that the war of nerves can never have an end. It's no crime to leave your audience wanting more, but 'Dominion' leaves us with the sensation that *New Captain Scarlet* wasn't entirely brave enough to provide a conclusion to the war of nerves. For a series to heavily-rooted in an overarching plot where a grand, climactic finale is greatly hinted at, this can't help but leave a bitter aftertaste. For Black's appearance to come so swiftly and disappear in an instant after Scarlet is led to believe he's won, it's also prickly, uncomfortable, an annoying thing to be reminded of.

'Dominion' ultimately leaves you feeling cheated, but it chooses which moments to cheat you with quite deliberately. Leaving *New Captain Scarlet* on an open-ended note is no accident. Instead of actually aiming to conclude the war of nerves, the open-ended site of Captain Black swallowed up by the Mysterons is a target that the episode meets with nimble pacing and eloquent direction. After all, if any Anderson series can boast the virtues of a horrific intergalactic war that forbids either side from encountering success, but remain a thoroughly entertaining bit of science fiction, then it's *Captain Scarlet*, whichever incarnation is your preferred one. It may be dispiriting how 'Dominion', much like the Mysterons, leads you to believe that you're engaged in one scenario when in fact another one lurks beneath the surface, but it's also gratifying that *New Captain Scarlet* took the opportunity to at least shift beyond the story-telling boundaries the original series imposed on itself.

Despite the episode's defining moments come in the form of how the war of nerves is resolved (or rather, unresolved), it's full of well-played out character interactions that paint a bitter and paranoid image of Spectrum, one in which no-one can ever be sure how deep the Mysterons' roots run and how love, friendship and authority are tangled emotional upheavals within the fiercely regimented functionality of Spectrum as an organisation. Much like *UFO*, the dramatic abilities of *New Captain Scarlet* come less from the all-powerful threat the Mysterons present to the Earth and come more from the human lives caught in the Mysterons' web, unintended consequences of their attacks. These lives may be small in comparison to the genocidal possibilities that the Mysterons have the Earth on the edge of their seats for, but this is how *New Captain Scarlet* succeeds over the original series. It succeeds in getting you to care about these characters because it shows their heartbreaks they must endure. Before this episode's portrayal of Scarlet and Black's relationship, there was how 'Heist' shows Colonel White's position within Spectrum's hierarchy is an undesirable and vulnerable one due to the life he's forced to leave behind. Even before that, there's the depiction of Lieutenant Green navigating her grief when her father is overtaken by the Mysterons in 'The Homecoming'.

'Dominion' serves as another but firm reminder of how the Mysterons impact these lives without even Mysteronising them. The thrill of seeing Captain Black surrendered from Mysteron control, convincingly performed by actor Nigel Plaskitt shows that 'Dominion' never lost sight of how the action-orientated nature of *New Captain Scarlet* is firmly married to a focused approach to depictions of its characters. Even when 'Dominion' can't fully deliver on the finale it sets up, it remains a riveting, emotionally-charged final outing for *New Captain Scarlet* and for Gerry Anderson.

THUNDERBIRDS ARE GO: 'THE LONG REACH'

Thunderbirds Are Go's blast off in April of 2015 generated an atomic-powered level of media interest. The opening two-part story 'Ring of Fire' was given an hour's slot at primetime viewing on ITV. Internationally recognised publications such as the *Guardian* and the *Radio Times* spoke highly of the two-part adventure in their respective reviews. The series' arrival was treated as an event 50 years in the making, a precursor to *Thunderbirds*' actual 50th anniversary later that September and ultimately enabling *Thunderbirds* to become part of contemporary remake culture that populates modern popular media consumption.

And then something strange happened. *Thunderbirds Are Go* continued, but everyone else didn't. As the show moved from its primetime slot to a Saturday morning slot of 8:00 AM, the interest dragged to a slow, grinding momentum rather than being propelled along at supersonic speeds. National media coverage stopped. It was as if everyone had forgotten that *Thunderbirds Are Go* existed. Across three seasons and numerous mid-season breaks (some unexpected and some lasting up to a year), *Thunderbirds Are Go* drew to a weary conclusion with the two-part story 'The Long Reach' in February of 2020, enough time for the series' young target audience to have grown older since 'Ring of Fire' and to lose interest in the series. This two-part story sees the Tracy brothers locate and rescue Jeff Tracy, who had been missing since the series' beginning, his fate left a purposeful mystery. This was the payoff that fans had been waiting for little under five years to enjoy. But which fans were watching at this point?

In the space of five years, it's highly likely that *Thunderbirds Are Go*'s target audience had grown older, but more importantly, outgrown the series. By the time series 3 had aired, fans were forced to become accustomed to mid-season breaks that stretched to a year. During series 3 itself, two mid-season breaks stretched the series to span three years. Adding to this interminable wait for resolution, teaser material scattered throughout series 3 made it abundantly clear that the mystery of Jeff's disappearance would be fully resolved. Despite series 3 beginning in March of 2018, it wouldn't be until June 2019 with the broadcast of 'SOS Part One' that the pieces of Jeff's puzzle grew more substantial. A hell of a long time to wait for a fandom that was growing tired of the drawn-out nature of *Thunderbirds Are Go*'s last hurrah. All that remains of the storm kicked up by the years' worth of following the clues to Jeff's vanishing is to determine whether or not 'The Long Reach' was worth the wait.

It's a thoroughly aptly named way to send off *Thunderbirds Are Go*. The titular reach itself refers to the distance the Tracy brothers must journey in the experimental, makeshift *Zero-XL* across the stars to retrieve their father, but it can also refer to the pains endured by the Tracy family in adjusting to life without International Rescue's founder and leader. It can also refer the length of time *Thunderbirds Are Go* has taken to reach this stage. The one overarching story the series has prioritised has been the disappearance and fate of Jeff Tracy and the impact his apparent loss has on International Rescue. What strikes you most about 'The Long Reach' is just how modest such a finale is for something that had so much riding on it. Written by series head writer Rob Hoegee, these two episodes resolve something that has been a core part of *Thunderbirds Are Go*'s DNA for the 76 episodes that had preceded the finale.

First and foremost, it delivers on what's been teased since 'Ring of Fire' – the rescue of Jeff. In that regard, 'The Long Reach' is the least surprising adventure of the series. It's the one rescue everyone has been expecting to occur since the series began, helping to quietly emphasis its modest nature. In ambitious fashion, a mixture of other multi-part episodes and standalone episodes have built up towards this mission, sometimes at the forefront and sometimes lingering subplots sketched into the background of otherwise episodic adventures. The loose four-part story within 'SOS' and 'Signals' confirm that Jeff is not only alive, but has sent out a distress call to be rescued by his family. A further and even looser four-part tale occurs within the events of the otherwise standalone sequence of episodes from 'Break Out', 'Buried Treasure', 'Venom' and 'Firebreak', which focus on the awkward realisation that the only one who can secure International Rescue's chances in finding Jeff is the Mechanic, the main villain from series 2. These four episodes sees the construction of the *Zero-XL*, but also sees the emergence of the Mechanic's uneasy alliance with International Rescue, agreeing to help Brains construct the necessary T-Drive engine to power the *Zero-XL* in exchange for the organisations help in attempting to free the Mechanic from the Hood's cybernetic psycho-control.

Eight episodes' worth of material and we haven't even reached 'The Long Reach'. Clearly, *Thunderbirds Are Go* was in no mood to mess around. This is the rescue to end all rescues. Inevitably, the background plots overshadow three of the individual episodes' comparatively light-hearted plots ('Break Out' being the exception), with stories of cheery treasure hunters and idolising firefighters clashing with Brains' probing the Mechanic's mind to free him of the Hood. *Thunderbirds Are Go* had never quite gone so physical with the cerebral. A sense of impatience clouds much of the series during which these episodes occur. When some of the best stories *Thunderbirds Are Go* had ever told occurred throughout series 1 and 2 as standalone adventures ('Extraction', 'Chain of Command', 'Earthbreaker', 'Deep Search', 'Home on the Range'), the standalone episodes throughout series 3 are somehow lesser. There's no discernible dip in style or quality (*Thunderbirds Are Go*'s story-telling qualities themselves are rather all over the place, really), but there's the inescapable feeling that all involved are far more invested in Jeff's arc and that individual episodes were now surplus to requirements. Some gems are to be found, including 'Deep Water' and 'Icarus', but they didn't focus on Jeff's arc and they weren't all that interesting compared to the longer, more complicated story that was brewing beneath the surface. The story arc of Jeff's rescue becomes stronger simply because that's what dominates and leaves little breathing space for anything else.

With these matters suitably attended to then, 'The Long Reach' opens with the fully assembled *Zero-XL* blasting off to Jeff's location within the Oort Cloud, piloted by all five Tracy brothers along with Brains, a further sign that this is a momentous occasion. Their launch is partially scuppered by an attack from the Chaos Crew, the Hood's main henchmen of series 3, whose actions ultimately deflate the true source of drama and danger this two-part episode hints at. In the run-up to series 3's release, an official statement from ITV teased the opening scenes of 'The Long Reach' by describing how the combined effort of all Thunderbird craft will leave Tracy Island vulnerable to a devastating attack. Cinematic-style posters for series 3 shows Thunderbirds 1, 2 and 3 soaring above Tracy Island, as if returning from rescuing Jeff, accompanied by a shower of flaming debris colliding all over Tracy Island. A hint at what was to come? Alas, no.

The much-hyped 'devastating attack' isn't devastating in the least, only occurs in a secluded area within Tracy Island and is quickly resolved. The attack boils down to the Chaos Crew targeting Brains' lab, activating a computer virus to target its electronic systems. Some robotic technology goes a little haywire, only for the combined forces of Lady Penelope, Parker, Brains, Kayo, Grandma Tracy and the Mechanic himself to quickly dispel the threat, capturing the pair for the final time. If the attack hadn't been emphasised in publicity material in such an important way, it would be possible to look upon these scenes in a different light, but it's an undeniable anti-climax. International Rescue saving Jeff and returning to Tracy Island, only for there not to be a Tracy Island to return to, could have been an event that placed both sequences on the same level, but such a move never comes to pass. It's an utterly missed opportunity for there not to be a greater threat going on here, because this is the side of the episode where unpredictability is allowed to be rife. The rescue of Jeff, whilst arguably more perilous, as mentioned, isn't surprising. He is going to be rescued, because this is what's been hinted at since the beginning. This is the payoff we've been expecting and thus the danger is grounded in safety, caressed even. The attack in Tracy Island is the dangerous flipside, but it's content to be unthreatening.

The mission to rescue Jeff is where the episode is truly focused and invested. The journey from Tracy Island to the Oort Cloud, where Jeff's distress call is transmitting from, is quick-fire and without peril, but once the *Zero-XL* arrives within its destination, the visual menace takes hold. The animation that brings the treacherous Oort Cloud terrain to life is breathtaking in its appearance and direction, as are most space-based scenarios in *Thunderbirds Are Go*. Combined with the Foster brothers' soaring orchestral soundtrack, the sight of Thunderbirds 1, 2 and 3 charging through uncertain cosmic danger is a thrill everyone involved has clearly been desperate to bring to life with as much enthusiasm and craft as possible. Nagging questions of how exactly the non-space Thunderbird craft are capable of travelling through such foreign territory struggle to assert themselves here when the visual thrills are this splendid. However, something else that raises suspicions of credibility is just how exactly Jeff manages to survive in deep space for so long. By the series' own maths, it's revealed that Jeff had been missing for 8 years, following the original *Zero-X*'s experimental engines propelling him to unknown danger when attempting to stop the Hood from sabotaging it. As if in response, several references are peppered throughout the series briefly explaining how Jeff was one of the world's foremost lunar explorers and that he wrote the book on space survival. Clearly, this rescue has been in the making since the series began.

The rescue of Jeff itself hits all of the right notes. It's entirely suitable that Scott, the oldest Tracy brother and the one who has spent much of the series forced to adjust to being the new, unofficial leader of International Rescue in Jeff's absence, should be the one to rescue him from the crashed *Zero-X*, now lodged within one of the many planetoids within the Oort Cloud and has been Jeff's makeshift home all this time. One of the episode's greatest moments comes not in the reunion between Jeff and his five sons aboard Thunderbird 2, but what happens after this reunion. Once recovered, Jeff's gratitude to Scott as he's hauled away by Virgil for medical examination is met by a simple, silent nod of acceptance from Scott himself. The young man who's been forced to bark out orders to his younger brothers can now return to being one of those brothers as his dad, the leader of International Rescue, returns. He no longer has to carry that unnecessarily heavy responsibility that he's never quite been ready for, evidenced by how International Rescue distinguish themselves in *Thunderbirds Are Go* from the original series by showing how they work most effectively as a team on an equal level, steering the ship in one cohesive direction, rather than one person in control of the helm.

Not even the Hood's attempted sabotage of this emotional rescue can scupper its impact. Having somehow stowed himself away on-board the

Zero-XL prior to take off, his final, desperate effort to outwit International Rescue is only moderate and lacks the punches he's managed to pull over the course of the series. It's really fun for it to be Jeff who sniffs out the Hood's disguise, attempting to pass himself off as Brains. In true *Thunderbirds Are Go* fashion, the Tracy family's last capture of the Hood lets slip some intriguing if lightweight backstory surrounding the Hood's reasoning for targeting International Rescue. The Hood reveals that he and Jeff were once colleagues, but the Hood's desire to use his abilities for evil didn't sit well with Jeff. The exact details of their relationship are sketchy and ill-defined, but that's in-keeping with how *Thunderbirds Are Go* has built its world from day one. Unlike the original series, *Thunderbirds Are Go* has never made it explicitly clear why or how International Rescue exists, how it maintains its security (if at all), why it operates from a secret island, and more. It leaves these details up to the minds of its audience to colour in the blanks and to be informed by having watched the original series, and this scene is no different.

Speaking of missed opportunities and vague backstories, this brings us to the Mechanic, one character whose development 'The Long Reach' was surely due to deliver but comes up short. The Mechanic has hung over *Thunderbirds Are Go* like an atomic cloud, somehow both the character least connected to Jeff's own story and yet the most intriguing and arguably interesting watch develop over the course of the series. If there's one other character 'The Long Reach' was duty-bound to resolve besides Jeff, then it was surely the Mechanic. Introduced at the beginning of series 2 as an antagonistic, anti-Brains with a mysterious past linked to the International Rescue inventor, his story underwent a seemingly haphazard reshuffle as his cryptic identity angle was dropped as soon as series 3 came along. His voice and facial features partially disguised as if to hide his identity, his teaming up with International Rescue results in no grand secret being revealed. It's as if his story was abandoned or forgotten. The series' attitude towards the Mechanic is revealed by his conspicuous absence from Alan's graduation. With his fate unresolved, he departs the series as he entered it – a complete mystery.

Despite these shortcomings proving how the foundations that hold the core story of rescuing Jeff are not being as tight as they should be, 'The Long Reach' succeeds in doing what it needed to accomplish – give *Thunderbirds Are Go* the closure it's been chasing since 'Ring of Fire'. It's not the most thrilling adventure *Thunderbirds Are Go* has ever produced, which on paper appears to be a step back for such an action-ready series. But this story wasn't about the adventure, it's about the emotion. Where 'The Long Reach' supposedly is meant to pack a more dizzying punch, it fails to do so, the end result being the entire episode is a pretty low-key affair compared to past frantic disasters that demand International Rescue's invaluable help. Fans across social media clamoured for this to not be the end and that a fourth series be made, with a changed dynamic of Jeff Tracy regaining his position of command would be something many would enjoy seeing. 'The Long Reach' all but confirms that *Thunderbirds Are Go* has landed safely at its destination, not in what it says, but how it says it. The leisurely attitude in how 'The Long Reach' transmits its end-of-the-road energy comes from the confidence that *Thunderbirds Are Go* has amassed over its five-year run. It's not been the smoothest of take-offs, but its journey has been fraught with adventuresome highs and dangerous lows, just like your typical International Rescue mission, and just like a typical mission, ends with lives being saved. In the case of 'The Long Reach', what a life it is. Driven purely an emotional momentum, 'The Long Reach' is the conclusion *Thunderbirds Are Go* has been journeying towards, finally caught.

BRAINS' LAB:
THUNDERBIRDS' DEFINITIVE EPISODES

5: 'SUN PROBE'

Throughout its original 32 episode run, *Thunderbirds* gripped its winning formula so tightly that repeated viewings can suffer from a feeling of having the life squeezed out of them. 25 of *Thunderbirds'* television stories are geared around Earth-based scenarios that primarily call upon Thunderbirds 1 and 2 to action. These are the two craft that inevitably have come to be most closely associated with the series, in much the same way that the Angel Interceptors and Spectrum Pursuit Vehicle are the most commonly used vehicles identified in *Captain Scarlet*, leaving the remaining three Thunderbird craft out in the cold. Some episodes bypass the need for Thunderbird 5 entirely when requests for International Rescue's help are made via public broadcast. Whether it's through production demands, audience expectations or the Century 21 crew simply getting comfortable within the series' formula, episodes that break the tradition are rare and thus noteworthy events, making 'Sun Probe' all the more worthy of unboxing here.

'Sun Probe' is an episode of many firsts and one-offs. The episode marks the true debut of Thunderbird 3 in *Thunderbirds*, only appearing in the series' opening and closing credits until now. Going by the original broadcast order of the series, 'Sun Probe' is in fact the second instance of audiences witnessing the space rocket, as 'The Uninvited' preceded the showing of 'Sun Probe'. ITC's recommended broadcast order shrewdly pushes 'Sun Probe' up to being the fourth episode, ensuring that the space craft's debut would be its own episode and that the episode appears as early as possible. 'Sun Probe' remains that rare beast in *Thunderbirds'* canon of being a space-based rescue, the first of only two episodes of the first series to be such a thing. 'Sun Probe' distinguishes itself further from much of *Thunderbirds* by having a rescue disaster attempted to be solved by International Rescue launching a dual mission, with Thunderbird 2 joining Thunderbird 3 in attempting to stop the Sun Probe rocket from crashing into the sun.

The greatest compliment one can pay 'Sun Probe' is how effective it shows *Thunderbirds* can be when it disengages from its established format. The quirky mixture of Thunderbird craft not usually seen together, character pairings likewise rarely seen elsewhere in the series and a tonal shift in story as the episode evolves from International Rescue saving the titular Sun Probe rocket to International Rescue having to save International Rescue, the first instance of this trope becoming semi-regular, all make for hooky viewing. However, even these creative leaps were a matter of circumstances

5: 'SUN PROBE'

rather than any sincere attempt to break *Thunderbirds*' quickly-setting mould. 'Sun Probe' was one of the earlier episodes of *Thunderbirds* to be produced, and thus falls into the era when the show was being created under its eventually scrapped half-hour format. An otherwise straightforward adventure that would have seen Thunderbird 3 pop off into deep space to salvage the Sun Probe before it can collide with the sun and dash back to Earth again in time for another of Brains' and Braman's chess matches is made all the more riveting via the inclusion of Thunderbird 2 and Virgil and Brains' subplot. What began as an inspired afterthought to stretch the episode to meet the newly found demands of the series now stands as one of the most far-reaching episodes of *Thunderbirds* ever produced, from frozen wastelands to darkest space.

Despite the initial broadcast of 'Sun Probe' meaning that audiences were already familiar with the craft, the shifting of 'Sun Probe' to earlier on in the series, cemented by official series guidebooks (despite DVD listings adhering to the original broadcast order), confirms its importance as the episode that introduces International Rescue's space craft. The first truly space-based episode that sees International Rescue engage in a cosmic disaster clearly had to hit the asteroid running and premise of the episode is reflective of its colossal ambitions. 'Sun Probe' is the third of 10 episodes written by Alan Fennell, one of Gerry and Sylvia's greatest and prolific screenwriters, and it's readily apparent that he had been paying attention to the disaster-ready world of *Thunderbirds*. Having successfully replicated the formula established by Gerry and Sylvia via International Rescue saving a malfunctioning atomic vehicle with 'Trapped in the Sky' and 'Pit of Peril' and proceeding to stretch *Thunderbirds*' thematic reach via an entire metropolis descending into terror with 'City of Fire', 'Sun Probe' sees Fennell taking the vehicle disasters of *Thunderbirds*' first two episodes and placing them on a hellishly cosmic scale.

Strapping a bomb to the undercarriage or collapsing into a hollow pit are some of the more modest ways International Rescue have been called out to action. By comparison, Sun Probe's fraught mission to collect a portion of the sun itself spiralling into chaos as the craft accidentally has its controls set for the heart of the sun itself was confirmation that *Thunderbirds* meant business. Where 'Trapped in the Sky', 'Pit of Peril' and 'City of Fire' occur in something close to real time, the events of 'Sun Probe' span over a week. Fireflash and the Sidewinder are undeniably big mechs and International Rescue is an undeniably big organisation, but with the galactic scale of 'Sun Probe', *Thunderbirds* was now showing how big a series it could be. The added bonus of its subplot also shows what a creative series it could be.

'Sun Probe' doesn't hint at its disparate origins. The duelling landscapes of the unknown depths of deep space and the barren, snow-drenched landscapes of Mount Arkan, the two locations where much of the episode takes place, swell together to create an atmosphere that's rich in oppressiveness, providing a grimly exquisite backdrop for this drawn-out duo of rescues. It's these juxtaposing operations of the crews of Thunderbird 3 and Thunderbird 2 that give 'Sun Probe' its buoyant narrative thrust, even if it occasionally succumbs to its own trappings. 'Sun Probe' tests your patience with its rather hefty handful of scenes where characters spend time projecting retro beams from their rescue craft in an effort to reach the Sun Probe, only to see them fail. It's in these moments that 'Sun Probe' risks collapsing into becoming droning and tedious, as characters watch and do little. But 'Sun Probe' often remembers to pull itself up by its bootstraps before these moments drag the episode down to the point of no return.

Ironically, despite 'Sun Probe' being an episode designed to showcase Thunderbird 3, it's most pedestrian elements become Thunderbird 3's successful rescue of the Sun Probe itself. Thunderbird 3 doesn't have the novel gadgetry that Thunderbirds 1, 2 and 4 have (perhaps explaining why the craft was seen so little) and so the episode rummages around for other means of making the rescue engaging. Alan, Scott and Tin-Tin's daring venture to capture the Sun Probe before the sun can do the same forms the initial meat of the episode, with the episode's remaining events scattered around it, added later on. Captivating performances from Shane Rimmer, Christine Finn and Matt Zimmerman and the Sun Probe crew and the ever-meticulous special effects that show the slow crippling of the Sun Probe as it starts to break up from the Sun's relentless attack make for compelling viewing that shows how effective *Thunderbirds* is in building up a terrible sense of threat thanks to its extended format. What also makes this sense of danger feel very real is Alan's steadfast command of Thunderbird 3's attempts to rescue the space craft. So often, Alan is painted into a corner as the family brat. Immature and sometimes the butt of his brother's sense of humour, all for committing the crime of being the youngest of the family. Here however, given command of the rescue operation, the bratty nature is nowhere to be seen, as Alan remains mature and composed throughout the mission, a welcome injection of understated character growth amidst the tech-heavy adventure.

Humanising the mecha-driven drama of Thunderbird 3's initial rescue further is the presence of Tin-Tin joining in with Scott and Alan. The sole rescue mission in which she's an active member in, Jeff's concern for Tin-Tin after the trio have blasted off in pursuit of the Sun Probe foreshadows the disaster later experienced by Thunderbird 3, but is also an unexpected and welcome bout of concern on Jeff's part. His questioning of whether it's morally right of him to ask Tin-Tin to risk her life by being part of a rescue operation touches upon the everyday risk of sacrifice the Tracy family put themselves through on a daily basis, yet Jeff is never outspoken about this matter over his own children. It's an all-too real admission on Jeff's part that these are the dangers he regularly places his loved ones in and although it's never quite spoken about again in such direct terms, it's refreshing to see that human element made room for into the techno-disaster world of *Thunderbirds* every so often. The integration of Tin-Tin and Jeff's note of the risks involved conflict with Sylvia Anderson's perspective on the episode, declaring it to be a 'boys' own adventure minus Lady P, but this time with a more space-age theme. Too much space and too many machines for my personal taste, but again cracking special effects.'[26] Creators aren't always the best judge of their own works.

Inevitably, the Sun Probe is rescued by Thunderbird 3's own retro beam, proving to be more effective than Virgil and Brains' attempts to propel their own beam back on Earth. However, it's here that the episode shifts into a different gear as Thunderbird 3 succumbs to the same fate as the Sun Probe. This fresh nightmare enables Brains and Virgil to become heroes as much as Alan, Scott and Tin-Tin, with this bolted on sub-plot providing further character-heavy touches via Brains stepping up to the spotlight, his first time doing so, and the earlier comedic interactions between himself and his robot understudy Braman becoming contextualised. In classic *Thunderbirds* style, it would have been all too easy for Brains to have calculated the formula necessary to neutralise Thunderbird 3's transmitter on the super computer he and Virgil had thought their had brought with them. Instead, bringing Braman along by mistake adds a quirky punch of black comedy, jeopardy upon further jeopardy, as the fate of Thunderbird 3 and its crew are placed in the hands of this experimental, temperamental robot.

Dragging the tension out to one last thrill comes as the unconfirmed formula, calculated by Braman, is fed into the Transmitter Truck's own circuitry and Brains and Virgil proceed to probe a newly launched beam towards Thunderbird 3 in the hopes of pulling it off course. On Tracy Island, Jeff, Kyrano and Gordon (whose role in the episode is minimal, but remains useful as being the one to suggest that Thunderbirds 2 and 3 attempt the same rescue in a gamble to see who's more successful) remain frozen, awaiting the call from the Thunderbird 2 crew, whether it's in the positive or the negative. This final and greatest stretching of the drama to hit home with maximum impact makes the successful payoff all the more satisfying. Braman's calculations succeed, the beam makes contact and Thunderbird 3 swings away from its solar coffin, mission successfully completed for both Thunderbird 2 and Thunderbird 3. A final droll send-off comes in the aftermath of both craft's homecoming back on Tracy Island when Braman succeeds in beating his master against a game of chess, a final validation of

---

[26] Anderson, S. (2008) '*Thunderbirds* Episode Guide' *Sylvia Anderson*. Available from – https://web.archive.org/web/20080503080402/http://www.sylviaanderson.org.uk/html/episode_guide.html.

Brains and Braman's positive contribution to the episode's events (Brains invented Braman, after all), whilst Scott, Alan and Tin-Tin's declaration of thanks for Brains' efforts cements his own efforts to the episode.

'Sun Probe' marks the first bold yet rare steps of *Thunderbirds* going beyond its comfort zone, and does so with some narrative sagging yet ultimately great aplomb as the finale drives the events with a focused blitz of energy. Other episodes made during the extensive reshooting of the first eleven episodes of the series and the remainder of the series would dip their toes into these bracing waters to novel effect. '30 Minutes After Noon' weaves together two separate rescues themed around a single spy-fi caper, whilst 'Vault of Death' would go to great lengths to paint an intricate backstory for Parker. 'Sun Probe''s settled status as the fourth episode after the comparatively regular structures of 'Trapped in the Sky', 'Pit of Peril' and 'City of Fire' make its demolition hit with all the more atomic impact.

Curiously, the impact of 'Sun Probe' is specifically felt across one other particular episode of the series. By some accounts, 'Sun Probe' forms part of an oddly loose two-part story with 'The Perils of Penelope', via the launch sequence footage early on of 'Sun Probe' blasting off from Cape Kennedy Space Centre being recycled into the early moments of 'The Perils of Penelope'. The explanation is that 'Sun Probe' is powered by rocket fuel converted from sea water, a creation that sees its inventor captured and Lady Penelope hot on the kidnapper's trail. The reasoning for the episode's connection is explained in various series guides that the events of 'The Perils of Penelope' occur within the week of Sun Probe's flight to the sun, definitely a wide enough gap to allow a convenient slotting in of an entirely separate series of events that don't conflict with the events of 'Sun Probe' itself.

The fact that neither story impacts on each other questions the diagnosis that the pair are connected together via continuity at all. Any eagle-eyed Anderson viewer would understandably pass this off as a simple case of footage recycling, a common feature in Supermarionation series. In the *Thunderbirds* 50th anniversary bookazine, Alan Barnes describes how episode writer Alan Pattillo, who was also the script editor for the series, eased the process of the episode's expansion by falling back to weaving in previously shot footage.[27] It's likely that this cost-saving measure was meant as just that, rather than any grand attempt at elaborate story-telling. It's an admitted stretch to ask that the events of 'The Perils of Penelope' sit within the events of 'Sun Probe', and it's worth noting that only *The Complete Book of Thunderbirds* makes this allusion. Neither the *Thunderbirds* bookazine, the 1990s *Thunderbirds* series biography nor *Thunderbirds: The Vault* confirm this

---

[27] Barnes, A. (2015) 'Sun Probe' *Thunderbirds: A Complete Guide to the Classic Series* (ed Hearn, M). p 19. Panini Magazine.

theory. It's therefore more likely that 'Sun Probe' and 'The Perils of Penelope' function without each other.

It's ironic that for a Thunderbird craft that doesn't quite *do* a great deal, its debut adventure has a lot of originality and novelty going for it. From dynamic rescue scenarios to character synergy that swing from being welcome to being unexpected, 'Sun Probe' asks you to expect the unexpected as what begins as the triumphant debut rescue for Thunderbird 3 evolves into something enjoyably different. Two episodes later, *Thunderbirds* thematic reach would be finalised with the debut of Thunderbird 4 in 'The Mighty Atom', but the stars were now firmly in the series' eyes.

4: 'TERROR IN NEW YORK CITY'

The episode that many consider to be the greatest television-based story *Thunderbirds* ever told has been held in high regard over the decades. The cinematic special effects and disaster-riddled story of 'Terror in New York City' has been celebrated by fans and critics alike. Writers from national broadsheet the *Guardian* to the more niche-marketed publication *TV Zone* single out the episode as a high point for the series. *Thunderbirds* co-creator Sylvia Anderson (2008) described the plot as 'ingenious' and captures screenwriter 'Alan Fennell at his best.'[28] Of *Thunderbirds*' 32-episode run (35 if counting the trio of specially produced anniversary episodes), 'Terror in New York City' is one of the ten episodes to have its own entire page on Wikipedia, at the time of this book's writing, further evidence of its importance. The devastating collapse of the Empire State Building, the event that triggers the episode's central rescue, is an endearing image that crystallises *Thunderbirds*' obsession with wrangling life-threatening human drama from techno-disaster, whilst the accidental sabotage made against International Rescue early on in the episode marks a mature move to show that the Tracy family are not infallible.

At odds with the overall perceived quality of the episode is its haphazard genesis. Like 'Sun Probe' before it, 'Terror in New York City' captures *Thunderbirds* at a transitional point as production on the series was shifting from its original 25 minute-per-episode format to its 50-minute incarnation. Curiously, whilst 'Terror in New York City' was original written under the initial 25-minute rule, the episode wasn't ultimately produced as such, and managed to scrape through as being filmed under the newly revised 50-minute guideline. Only the first eleven episodes of *Thunderbirds* to be produced were fully filmed as 25-minute episodes, and thus had to be revisited and expanded upon. Evidence suggests that 'Terror in New York City' however only appears to have been written as a 25-minute adventure, rather than filmed as a 25-minute episode. This then brings to mind just how much of the episode was newly written material and what exactly formed the original, earlier edition of the story. Gerry Anderson's biography *What Made Thunderbirds Go!*[29] and *Filmed in Supermarionation*[30] suggest that only

---

[28] Anderson, S. (2008) '*Thunderbirds* Episode Guide' *Sylvia Anderson*. Available from – https://web.archive.org/web/20080503080402/http://www.sylviaanderson.org.uk/html/episode_guide.html.
[29] Archer, S. Marcus, H. (2002) 'Calling International Rescue' *What Made Thunderbirds*

the opening rescue and Thunderbird 1 pursuing Ned Cook comprised of the freshly produced material needed to pad out the episode. However, it's possible that things stretch further.

Much of the drama that arises from the episode (and which helps to fill the episode out, time-wise) is the partial destruction of Thunderbird 2. This catastrophe forces International Rescue to work at a much slower pace than usual, which neatly stretches the episode out more than the opening rescue would have achieved alone. A more digestible rendition of 'Terror in New York City' then might have opened with the collapse of the Empire State Building, trapping Ned and Joe, and Thunderbirds 1, 2 and 4 arriving at the danger zone to perform the rescue, allowing the episode to carry on much as normal from there. The entire subplot involving Thunderbird 2 being put out of commission ties in with what Gerry Anderson tasked his scriptwriters to do from December of 1964, ie to expand upon existing material, which in turn created a rather controlled chaos for A P Films as 1965 dawned, with multiple puppet stages essentially finding themselves making two versions of *Thunderbirds*.

It's incredible, almost preposterous to think then, that the iconic image of Thunderbird 2 being almost totally destroyed was little more than an afterthought. The complicated, layered narrative of 'Terror in New York City' that evolves from its additional material is also evidence that *Thunderbirds*' writers were willing to experiment with different methods of script expansion compared to how 'Trapped in the Sky' and 'Pit of Peril' widened their running time simply by adding in an attempted civilian rescue that would inevitably fail before International Rescue would arrive. If we presume that the original version of 'Terror in New York City', then called 'Terror of New York', was a straight forward rescue mission for International Rescue, then the finished episode is a testament to how gripping *Thunderbirds* could be in its 50 minute format.

Thunderbirds' greatest and most common story tactic is to create an impossible situation so gargantuan in its unsolvable nature, so uncontrollable in its capacity for carnage, that it can only be resolved by a single, specialist organisation: International Rescue. 'Terror in New York City' gives us this recognisable dilemma in an evolved manner compared to *Thunderbirds*' usual formula, chiefly through the Empire State Building and Thunderbird 2. Metropolitan landmarks being destroyed is a regular sight in *Thunderbirds*, but the disintegration of the Empire State Building, the event that propels the core rescue into motion, is something markedly different. Audiences in 1965 would bear witness to the destruction of such properties

---

Go! The Authorised Biography of Gerry Anderson. p. 123. BBC Books. 2nd edition.
[30] La Riviere, S. (2009). 'Calling International Rescue' *Filmed in Supermarionation: A History of the Future.* p. 122. Hermes Press. 1st edition.

as the Thompson Tower, the Allington Suspension Bridge and the Hudson Building. But unlike those fictional hot spots, the Empire State Building disaster is a very real termination of a very real building, lending the episode a stranglehold on reality, rather than the detached approach that the rest of the series takes in portraying a futuristic reality that's close to our own, but with its own unique, fictional landmarks.

'Terror in New York City' makes the characteristic danger of *Thunderbirds* all the more palpable with the destruction of the Empire State Building, giving the episode an eerie foreshadowing of the events of 9/11 when the series was rerun in its digitally remastered form on BBC Two between 2000/2001. However, what enables 'Terror in New York City' to stand out even more is the attack Thunderbird 2 suffers from an accidental strike by the US Navy. This attack has a substantial effect on International Rescue, as the outcome of Thunderbird 2 being put out of action spirals into weary dread for the Tracy family when the disaster in New York strikes. 'Terror in New York City' is the closest *Thunderbirds* ever came to presenting International Rescue with a scenario even their herculean might cannot resolve.

The episode embraces the newly grounded 50-minute rule of *Thunderbirds* via its series of seemingly unconnected events that prolong the arrival of the story's main drama. Several scenes pile on top of each other, like the debris of the Empire State Building itself, seemingly without consequence, yet they ultimately find themselves slotting together to contextualise the heart of the episode. The arrogant news reporter Ned Cook and his long-suffering cameraman Joe find themselves in a battle of perseverance as they attempt to film Thunderbird 1 during the episode's opening rescue, the only time *Thunderbirds* begins in the heat of the action, mid-rescue. This opening rush has an amusing edge that's wildly juxtaposed with the nerve-attacking sight of Thunderbird 2 sustaining damage from the US Navy. The sight of Ned being covered in spools of electromagnetically wiped film footage when Scott resolves his media intrusion of International Rescue's activities amusingly clashes with the sight of Virgil Tracy being smothered in smoke and flame as his Thunderbird craft explodes all around him. This clash of images allows the opening comedy to ease the viewer into the drama that occupies much of the episode.

Thunderbird 2's attack sees the AP Films' special effects department in fine form. A visibly-stricken Thunderbird 2 plummets downward from the skies towards the oceans of nearby Tracy Island, only for it to pull out and crawl mere inches above its watery grave. The interplay between Shane Rimmer, Peter Dyneley and David Holliday as Scott and Jeff guiding Virgil to land back on Tracy Island is full of tension, culminating in the craft's dramatic crash-land on Thunderbird 2's runway, now prepared in emergency mode. In true *Thunderbirds* fashion, the danger isn't over yet. The image of Thunderbird 2 instantly leaping back into the air as it crashes to the ground is downright eerie, as the craft's undercarriage's destruction makes a safe landing impossible. The final image of Thunderbird 2 being drenched in firefighting foam as the flames continue to belch out of the craft, to the point where the very sky above becomes polluted by foam, smoke and flame, is strikingly otherworldly, and a testament to Derek Meddings' attention to detail, along with directors David Elliott and David Lane. It's a tightly compacted shot that makes Thunderbird 2 appear as if it's crash-landed on an alien planet.

'Terror in New York City' methodically and slowly has now set the stage for the episode's titular event to unfold, but before we dive deeper, let's examine another factor that these two scenes demonstrate about *Thunderbirds*. Both of these attacks made against Thunderbirds 1 and 2 respectively, one slightly intrusive and easily resolved and the other downright devastating, highlight the vulnerable, exposed nature of International Rescue's vigilante stance, an aspect not hugely discussed at any great length elsewhere. International Rescue's humanitarian nature, in the minds of many, place them above the traditional image of a lawless Robin Hood or Batman figure. The organisation's actions are excused by any governing power due to the heroic work they do, yet the two events in 'Terror in New York City' that catapult the episode towards its main focus go one further by pitting International Rescue against civilian and military personalities taking exception with the group's outsider status. It's highlighted still further by Joe and Ned interfering with International Rescue because they know exactly who they are and the US military interfering because they, at first, don't know who it is. International Rescue's accepted status as do-gooders who operate outside of law and order without disrupting it comes to the forefront when the US Navy call off their attack once they discover who it is they're attacking.

However, 'Terror in New York City' ceases providing any comment on International Rescue's vigilantism at this point, as Ned and Joe succumbing to their intrusive journalistic desires still further by capturing the attempted moving of the Empire State Building results in them needing International Rescue's help and the US Navy providing transport assistance to Gordon in Thunderbird 4 as an apology for their unconsidered missile attack. The status quo of International Rescue not having their security set-up tampered is quietly resumed. Other episodes of *Thunderbirds* would toy with International Rescue's secret work ethic, most notably 'The Imposters', but a that episode's story of stern militant eyes cast over International Rescue's activities when rogue impersonators tarnish their name doesn't quite have the moral complexity of what 'Terror in New York City' offers. This episode may be best known for the thunderous sfx-driven drama its name carries, but closer inspection also shows that it offers a curiously two-sided perspective on how the world perceives International Rescue and allows them to operate. And we haven't even got to the Empire State Building collapsing yet. We can take that as a reflection of how effective and inspired *Thunderbirds* as a story-telling machine can be now that the fifty-minute runtime has been hardwired into the series' DNA.

With these subplots neatly tied up with and their effects spilled out for us to great effect, a lull in the episode takes over, the calm before the other and much larger storm rears its head. It's safe to assume then that the scene of the Empire State Building being moved to a new location and the event televised around the world, including being watched by the Tracy family, was where the original, earlier incarnation of the episode began. It's strange to think that all of the drama that's occurred over the last 15-20 minutes were just the prelude to the main adventure that gives the episode its title. This scene gives us 'Terror in New York City's other most striking image, that of the Empire State Building's collapse. As the building begins to move along its colossal mechanical tracks towards its new intended home, nature strikes back against the might of technological decadence that so often dominates the world in *Thunderbirds*. The ground begins to crumble, as if a concrete jaw opening beneath the Empire State Building. The building itself violently lurches into the transportation section that's pulling it along. Ned and Joe appear once again, contextualising their earlier appearance by not only filming the building's moving but are caught in the ground's collapse, the episode's ultimate victims. The implied destruction of the Empire State Building is tremendous. We never actually see the building be destroyed. The screen fades to black in-between its collapse and reappears to a scene of concrete waste, indicating where an advert break would have occurred during the episode's debut broadcast. Ned and Joe gazing up helplessly through the hole they fell in from at the building itself gains an odd grandeur as the building is filmed in slow motion, descending upon them, but also the small hole can only pack in so much visibility of the building, the intention being that the building's collapse is so huge it can't be fully captured on screen.

It's one of *Thunderbirds*' most unnerving moments, the drawn-out nature of the Empire State Building's devastation somehow atypical of how *Thunderbirds* would establish its disasters, and yet treated as a distinct event; a genuine, real-world landmark now eyed up by *Thunderbirds*' vision. After this, real-world monuments would go untouched. No disasters involving the Eifel Tower or Big Ben, but more fictional properties, making this an event as feel like a genuine tragedy.

It's arguably from this point on that 'Terror in New York City' becomes less interesting. With the disparately intriguing subplots dealt with and interconnected, the episode now settles into a routine affair for *Thunderbirds* – rescue Ned and Joe before the rise of the underground rivers that caused the Empire State Building to collapse in the first place consumes them, a case of nature intending to claim back what humanity took from it. What sets this rescue apart from others is how fatigued it feels. With Thunderbird 2 damaged beyond being helpful to the rescue, Scott and Gordon are dispatched in Thunderbirds 1 and 4 to New York, with the Sentinel making a further appearance in transporting the minute sub to the danger zone. Such is the drawn-out nature of International Rescue desperate to reach the danger zone in time that there isn't a huge deal of actually plot occurring here. The dizzying energy of the episode's opening blitzkrieg of seemingly unconnected scenes and the unstoppable, Godzilla-sized threat of the Empire State Building's accidental annihilation gives way to smooth yet tense waiting on Ned and Joe's part as the river water slithers upwards around them, the knotted tangle of events earlier now neatly ordered with this almost languid series of events.

As the episode creeps towards the inevitable rescuing of Ned and Joe, because even with Thunderbird 2 out of action (it's still impossible for International Rescue to fail), the dread takes a much firmer hold. Because despite no episode of *Thunderbirds* being able to function without a life being saved, just as no episode of Captain Scarlet can function without a life being killed, 'Terror in New York City' uses this otherwise traditional series of events for International Rescue to do its hardest to make you believe that International Rescue could lose. Thunderbird 4 traversing a totally alien underwater terrain whilst the land subsidence spreads to further buildings, risking Ned and Joe's life even more, is slick in how electrifying it is. 'Terror in New York City' expertly piles on the pressure for the rescue to be a success, but like the episode overall, it's not in any rush to deliver on its many elements. Whilst other *Thunderbirds* episodes unintentionally show up the shortcomings of the fifty-minute format, 'Terror in New York City' remains an intense, inventive and captivating sprawl of tense and dangerous situations, swelling together into a satisfying package.

Just as the Fulmer Finance Building tumbles to its death as the land subsidence spreads, Gordon salvages the swiftly declining Ned and Joe, rapidly losing consciousness as the underground rivers have risen to the point where they need their limited oxygen masks and tanks. In a telling sign of just how unhurried 'Terror in New York City' is to slow the events down, the rescue's final moments on screen is the shot of Thunderbird 4 being thrown back into the aquatic rocky undergrowths as the Fulmer Finance Building collapses near Ned and Joe's pilot hole, sending cascades of debris and surges of water into the submarine like a missile. We then cut jarringly as the commotion of Thunderbird 4's impact bleeds into the fanfare of The Ned Cook Show, as Ned himself appears on stage in a wheelchair, battered and bruised, but alive, fast-forwarding the events onward. Possibly unbeknown to him, much of International Rescue is in the audience as he tells of his and Joe's dramatic escape and thanks International Rescue for their efforts. Humbled by the actions International Rescue performed for he and Joe, Ned's fanfare resumes as he ends his opening speech, but the fanfare shifts in meaning. It's as much for welcoming Ned back to the stage, but it's also a triumphant cheer for International Rescue, their most complicated and nerve-wracking mission yet a success.

'Terror in New York City' isn't a *Thunderbirds* episode that tackles any drastically new subject matter – man-made machinery malfunctions, disaster strikes, Thunderbirds are go. The closest the episode gets to adding to the *Thunderbirds* mythos is how the attack on Thunderbird 2 calls into question how effective the secretive nature of International Rescue is, but the episode doesn't dwell too much here. If the US Navy's reaction in discovering just who it is they tried to bring down out of the sky is a universal one, then the world appears to give International Rescue the privilege of unquestionably accepting its vigilante status as an outfit. What makes the episode such a thrilling watch is how its elements are executed, and what makes it such an interesting watch is seeing how the pieces of this narrative puzzle slot into place. Through the strenuous circumstances that made the early days of production on *Thunderbirds* all the more complicated, 'Terror in New York City' demonstrates the well-tooled propulsive thrust that *Thunderbirds* is capable of delivering.

3: '30 MINUTES AFTER NOON'

Thunderbirds grappled with such a bountiful array of concepts throughout its original run of 32 episodes and two movies that its non-techno-adventure aspects become not just overshadowed but drowned out by the roar of rocket engines igniting into life. The secondary roles of Lady Penelope and Parker for instance, always on standby and ready for action and often brought to the foreground whenever the duo are onscreen, gives *Thunderbirds* a lingering spy-fi presence that rubs shoulders with the series' chiefly sci-fi modes. Whenever Penelope and Parker are on screen, they bring with them charm, elegance and deadly danger of prime, post-Bond spy-fi entertainment, always ready to deliver a cool, sexy, stylish defeat to the baddies of the day. What this tells us then is that where *Thunderbirds'* sci-fi explorations come from multiple avenues and aren't restricted to International Rescue's actions, Lady Penelope and Parker act like a lightning rod, bringing with them *Thunderbirds'* spy-fi mentality. This makes '30 Minutes After Noon', an episode known for its stylistic diversions, an even more unusual affair, stripping away much of the glamour of Lady Penelope's perspective of the spy-fi world. It's such an unusually thrilling outing for *Thunderbirds* then, because it presents us with the darker, seedier, sadistic world of covert villains and the harm they incur upon civilians and heroes alike.

With their extroverted espionage action, 'The Perils of Penelope' and 'The Man From MI.5' are the strongest indications that *Thunderbirds* gives as to how a Lady Penelope spin-off may have proceeded, but '30 Minutes After Noon' is the episode that dives deeper into the world of murderous criminals and super spies. '30 Minutes After Noon' shouldn't just be remembered for its unusual visual direction. It should be remembered as an espionage themed duo of missions for International Rescue where Lady Penelope and Parker, who so often are relied upon to bring the non-rocket energy of Thunderbirds with them, are barely brought out of their background presence. This is confirmation of the fact that the kind of espionage Penelope and Parker dabble in is glamorous, exciting and fun, because the espionage at play here is dirty, deceitful, hurtful, with murder in its eyes. The disjointed feel of '30 Minutes After Noon' actually enables a well-paced rise and fall to occur, which feels quite natural once you accept that this isn't an episode about rescues – it's about spies.

But let's attend to the reasons why this episode is already memorable to begin with. '30 Minutes After Noon' pulls apart at *Thunderbirds'* 50-minute structure by featuring two rescues performed by International Rescue, rather than the usual single operation that's built up towards throughout the episode, or the lesser-seen rescue attempt tactic, whereby a civilian rescue fails, validating the need to send out a distress call. 'Atlantic Inferno' would re-approach this tactic in the second series. There's been some debate as to whether or not '30 Minutes After Noon' began life as one of the original half-hour episodes during the early days of *Thunderbirds'* production before its upgrade by Lew Grade. As previously explored, 'Sun Probe' and 'Terror in New York City' were born from those early days, but where 'Sun Probe' was fully filmed initially as a half-hour production, 'Terror in New York City' was only written as a half-hour venture, and had its story creatively extended to the required 50 minutes in time for it to go into production.

ITC's recommended broadcast order places '30 Minutes After Noon' quite late in the series as the 18th episode out of the first series' overall 26 episode run. However, the original broadcast run of *Thunderbirds* tells a more interesting story. '30 Minutes After Noon' was broadcast originally as the eighth episode, alongside other freshly minted, hour-long adventures as 'End of the Road', 'Desperate Intruder', 'Day of Disaster', 'Edge of Impact', 'Terror in New York City' and 'The Perils of Penelope'. 'The Uninvited', 'Sun Probe', 'City of Fire', 'Operation Crash-Dive', 'The Mighty Atom' and 'Vault of Death' were all broadcast in succession, and were all episodes subjected to frantic extensions, suggesting that the earlier batch of episodes were transmitted earlier on in an effort to afford breathing space for episodes that were being hastily re-produced, thus likely confirming that '30 Minutes After Noon' was fully made as an hour-long production, and all the more intriguing. *Thunderbirds* having to break out subplots involving multiple rescues is the core giveaway to that episode being one that was extended, but '30 Minutes After Noon' isn't. It was a creative choice of script writer Alan Fennell to push International Rescue into a background role and drag the seedy underworld of crime and spies to the forefront. Sylvia Anderson (2008) wasn't exaggerating when she described the episode as 'a vehicle for live action than the limited emotions of our puppet cast.'[31] After diving into a pair of episodes where much of the core line-up of *Thunderbirds'* craft get seen and their intrepid pilots with them, it's a case of thematic whiplash to have an episode where much of the *Thunderbirds* are rarely seen.

The first half of '30 Minutes After Noon' rolls like a slick slice of standard but effective spy-fi fare, the kind that ITC were exporting around the globe. The ensnaring and blackmailing of Hudson Building employee Thomas Prescott by the nameless Erdman Gang member to destroy the Hudson

---

[31] Anderson, S. (2008) '*Thunderbirds* Episode Guide' *Sylvia Anderson*. Available from – https://web.archive.org/web/20080503080402/http://www.sylviaanderson.org.uk/html/episode_guide.html

Building in exchange for Prescott's own life reads like scriptwriter Alan Fennell having glanced at a synopsis for an episode for *The Saint* in ITC's office, rather than a straight-forward *Thunderbirds* techno-disaster. There's something deliciously atmospheric about night-time settings in Supermarionation productions, and '30 Minutes After Noon' is no exception. It adds a suitable layer of tense atmosphere to what's going on, and a nice backdrop for Prescott's humanisation throughout the episode's first half. One key benefit of *Thunderbirds* being 50 minutes in length is the dedication some episodes would go to in developing their guest characters. Ironically, where Prescott's characterisation seems like a good example of this, the fact that this chunk of the episode could take up a regular half-hour slot seems to undercut this point.

Whilst the rescue of Prescott itself hardly ranks alongside the most creative and nerve-wracking heights *Thunderbirds* would soar to, it's well executed and its build-up is arguably superior than the event itself, but also reinforces the fact that this episode is one where the rescuing takes a back seat in favour of humanised espionage danger. An amusing link between the two rescues can also be found in their respective Pod vehicles utilised. The compact, slug-like Laser Beam tractor is one of several tractor-like International Rescue vehicles that can serve multiple uses, but the Dicetylene Cage is an unintentional source of humour from Thunderbirds whereby their rescue equipment proved painfully plot-convenient to the demands of the danger zone. The real reason the Mole and the Firefly are the best remembered Pod vehicles is the simple reason that just about every other Pod vehicle around them is too niche, only used once. Such is the fate of both Pod vehicles here, but the Dicetylene Cage is one of the more obvious examples of this.

One of the episode's most effective and rewarding scenes comes in-between the two rescue situations when the Spoke City police department uncover the bracelet that Prescott was forced to wear from the wreckage of the Hudson Building. Police Commissioner Garfield is one of the lesser seen guest characters of the episode, but with Prescott relinquished to prison for his supposed terrorist attack on the building, Garfield is given a chance to shine. This inconspicuous scene provides links the two rescue scenarios together by Garfield choosing to believe Prescott's tale of being hijacked and blackmailed into obliterating the Hudson Building, his feelings validated by the recovery of the bracelet. Set within the cramped, untidy police office, the clatter of typewriters heard continually in the background, this welcome lull in the proceedings does much to shift the story deeper into its criminal tendencies.

Playing to the episode's strengths, there's a striking aesthetic clash between the two disaster scenarios that helps to make each other stand apart. Where the destruction of the Hudson Building occurs at night time and within a densely populated area, the Erdman Gang's attack on the plutonium store in Scotland takes place in broad daylight in a barren, mountainous location, not a soul for miles. The scenes during the plutonium store are where '30 Minutes After Noon' loses momentum and are more tedious to sit through when compared to the rapid race-against-time danger of the Hudson Building scenes. We're essentially made to sit through three instances where a series of metal doors are opened, one imagined by undercover British Secret Service agent Southern and the other two members of the Erdman gang that he's infiltrated, one played out in reality and one where Scott and Virgil must blast the doors back open when Southern's plans to apprehend villainous gang members Dempsey and Kenyon go awry.

A further handsome thematic balance is to be found in the distinction between the destruction of classified documents about enemy organisations including the Erdman Gang, a rather spy-fi method of taking out the enemy, to a much more physical threat of nuclear annihilation. But the episode's second half plods along, struggling to make effective use of the seriousness of the situation. It just doesn't have the spark that the first half does. Still, the trio of Southern, Dempsey and Kenyon gives series regulars Ray Barrett, Peter Dyneley and David Graham a fine chance to show off their verbal prowess, effortlessly slipping into their respectively heroic and villainous spy roles with great fun. Their performances are a lasting example of how the vocal qualities of Supermarionation's voice actors were such a necessary component on making effective characterisation.

From stellar vocal performances to humanised victims, '30 Minutes After Noon' likes to think that it's trying to work with human beings, not lifeless marionettes. From Prescott's empathetic framing as a victim caught up in a world of villainy he can't begin to grasp to Southern's attempts at selflessly demanding that the British Secret Service evacuate the area around the nuclear hub rather than attempt to rescue him, there's a very human heart beating at the centre of this episode's spy-fi exuberance. By that logic, despite my earlier definition of this episode shying away from International Rescue's influence, '30 Minutes After Noon' remains a prime offering of *Thunderbirds* for its emphasis on rescuing human life and the clashes of morals this may bring. Jeff Tracy isn't swayed by the news telecaster's concerns that Prescott's actions have caused the inferno that engulfs the Hudson Building, he's only concerned for the man himself. Likewise, the chief of police wastes no time in believing Prescott's outlandish story, an outstretched arm of authority shown to be empathetic that matches Jeff's own reach of vigilante humanism. The nuclear store scenario of '30 Minutes After Noon' has less material to work with in complimenting as effective a picture, yet Southern's willingness to die for the sake of others comes close.

This is all wrapped up in an effective spy-fi layer which, when unpackaged, shows how *Thunderbirds* could be subtle in its characterisations but rarely missing a beat in recognising the series' heartfelt humanism. The two halves approach '30 Minutes After Noon' has either disturbs the regular flow *Thunderbirds* builds for itself or is a welcome diversion into mild experimentation, depending on your view. But anything that toys with the established format should be worth investigating, however creatively successful it ends up being. '30 Minutes After Noon' balances its surface elements and deeper characterisations with plenty of success, its rescues recognisable enough to be something close to traditional *Thunderbirds* but distinct enough to make the episode stand out. It doesn't fully have the gumption to throw the rulebook totally out of the window in its structure, but it does have plenty of heart towards its characters by placing the focus on them instead of on techno-rescue extravaganzas.

2: 'THE CHAM-CHAM'

The fact that *Thunderbirds* opens and closes with the triumphant surges of 'The Thunderbirds March' illustrates the level of confidence it exudes. Throughout the series, it quickly and comfortably carved out its identity and maintained itself from beginning to end. Only when *Thunderbirds*' first series reaches its end that it decides to pull at various disparate strands that its displayed over the course of the series and weave together an episode that has no right to be as charming as it is. Offbeat and often downright ridiculous, 'The Cham-Cham' is rich in strong characterisations and enjoyably absurd story-telling. The last true full-length episode of the first series before the obligatory clip show 'Security Hazard', 'The Cham-Cham' is a delightfully colourful and curious espionage-flavoured outing for International Rescue.

The episode's opening moments set the scene beautifully. A calm, establishing shot of the super computer itself which bears the episode's name, housed within some concealed, undisclosed chalet, gives way to the launching of a UASF transporter craft taking off from Matthews Field Air Base. No soaring Barry Gray soundtrack accompanies the craft's launch as it taxies out onto the runway and takes to the skies. In its place is a delicious bit of swinging 1960s pop, 'The Dangerous Game', played not only over the launch but from the aircraft's navigator's radio itself. This slick little number continues to play out as a series of unidentified fighter jets burst onto the scene out of nowhere, attacking the transporter craft, sending the plane and its crew into a fiery descent. So begins the mystery surrounding the events that propel International Rescue into action, with this seductive pop number central to the episode's heart.

The episode's premise of coordinates hidden within the musical notes of a pop song that's being broadcast live in order for terrorists to track down secret American rocket transporters is downright ludicrous, but the greatest strengths of 'The Cham-Cham' is how enjoyable and convincing it makes this premise. The episode embraces it, as if Century 21 really wanted to try something abundant in a sense of fun, now that the first series was coming to an end. That sense of embraced fun ripples into the episode's flavoursome character moments. This is something Sylvia Anderson herself noted, saying that 'even though the plot is far fetched, it has charm and because of the lovely Swiss mountain setting, has credibility.'[32] The first of these arises from

---

[32] Anderson, S. (2008) '*Thunderbirds* Episode Guide' *Sylvia Anderson*. Available from –

2: 'THE CHAM-CHAM'

Alan Tracy, who is the member of the Tracy family to initially suggest that 'The Dangerous Game' could be the reason why this transporter craft, and several others before it, are being targeted. For reasons the episode doesn't divulge, Alan is somehow aware that 'The Dangerous Game' was being performed live on the radio on the other past missions in which the previous transporter craft had attempted their own dangerous game and that the song therefore could be less of an innocent tune and more of a weapon of war.

It feels like a conscious choice to have Alan be the one wisest to this move, even if Virgil is usually the more musically inclined of the Tracy brothers. But where Virgil's piano skills always did hint at a classical, sophisticated taste for music, Alan was the hippest of the bunch and it feels somewhat natural that he'd put two and two together via this pop song of death. Even Jeff is taken aback by Alan's knowledge that the song wasn't just played on the radio, but performed live by the Cass Carnaby Five. With this suspect knowledge, Lady Penelope is dispatched to the pop group's location, playing a season at the Paradise Peaks hotel. Accompanying her however is Tin-Tin, whilst Penelope slips into a disguise, not as her guise from 'The Perils of Penelope', but as Wanda Lamore. It's here that 'The Cham-Cham' establishes its winning formula, bringing together an unusual pairing of characters not often seen throughout *Thunderbirds*, but who make for a delightful combo. With another female presence to bounce off, Lady Penelope and Tin-Tin are blessed with solid character interaction throughout the episode as a pair of robust, capable female spies, with Parker eventually joining them as the brawny comic relief; the icing on this unusual cake.

'The Cham-Cham' quickly establishes itself from here as a Lady Penelope centric episode, automatically placing it into a distinct sub-category within *Thunderbirds* itself as spy-fi within sci-fi, as Penelope-focused episodes were want to do. But with its quirky premise and strong characters, 'The Cham-Cham' marks the point where espionage-themed episodes of *Thunderbirds* stopped trying to emulate *James Bond*, as 'The Perils of Penelope' and 'The Man From MI.5' had been so intent on being before. Instead, by embracing *Thunderbirds*' understated yet often odd and unexpected sense of humour, 'The Cham-Cham' steps out of the Bond shadow and confirms *Thunderbirds*' own unique spin on the spy-fi genre. In doing so, 'The Cham-Cham' as a whole feels like a prototype of *Thunderbird 6* – unusual character groupings with Penelope at the centre, exotic locations and foreign enemies using coded messages to get their way.

Predating *Thunderbird 6*'s emphasis on character-focused adventure, 'The

---

https://web.archive.org/web/20080503080402/http://www.sylviaanderson.org.uk/html/episode_guide.html.

Cham-Cham' is an episode that's held up by the charm of its performances. Lady Penelope is in regularly fine form, her feminine spy façade rolls like a well-oiled machine by this point in the series. Parker's role as Penelope's right-hand man is somewhat superseded by the presence of Tin-Tin, but he has little difficulty in making his own presence felt. A witty scene involving him making use of his underworld connections in show business to secure Penelope's spot under the guise of Wanda Lamore at Paradise Peaks is an absolute hoot as he blackmails a former impresario colleague of his to gain the gig for his employer. From there, he eventually joins in with Penelope and Tin-Tin's investigations, providing much physical humour, ranging from human snowball to Mary Poppins impersonator.

Tin-Tin provides the most to unbox in the episode. It's a sly but genius move to give Penelope a secondary female to engage with, but also to act as more than a sidekick but a fellow spy. Arguably, it comes at the expense of established character development. Throughout *Thunderbirds*, Tin-Tin has been sown to be a character of many traits – technical assistant to Brains, caretaker of her father and Tracy Island's resident tearjerker whenever one of the Tracy brothers fails to make radio contact with International Rescue, for whatever reason. What she hasn't displayed before now is the capacity to be as good an undercover agent as Lady Penelope. She performs much of the same skills as Penelope does in gathering her intelligence, ie wooing the key male suspects so that they divulge necessary details relating to the Cass Carnaby Five's connection to the transporter attacks. There's nothing to suggest that Tin-Tin can't be a spy, but the series hasn't built up towards this additional strand of her character in any shape or form, and wouldn't do so again. A great pity, given how well this gamble pays off here. The unexpected contributions she makes to the episode result in her character feeling changed rather than expanded, which feels like we're meant to accept without question. Where Jeff had held great concern for Tin-Tin joining in with the rescue of Sun Probe much earlier on in the series, his concern certainly appears to have subsided entirely.

Where 'The Cham-Cham' wins with its characters, it's arguably less successful in its story-telling. The sheer ridiculousness of the premise isn't the problem, though. The episode's bonkers plot wonderfully taps into vivid, retro spy-fi whose sense of camp enjoyment is enhanced by contemporary viewing habits. This was an era when spies were dynamic and fun and there's actually precious few of the spy-fi flavoured episodes of *Thunderbirds* that are this much fun. What fails to give 'The Cham-Cham' much support, whilst it's preoccupied in being a lively spy-fi caper, is how the various specifics of the story aren't explored or explained. Zero context is given to that opening sequence of enemy fighter jets shooting down the rocket transporter. We come away from the episode not being informed as to why a foreign government is targeting the United States' military vehicles, what exactly its contents is or what it's to be used for, or why the Cass Carnaby Five's thuggish manager Olsen is working in cahoots with the enemy government. David Graham puts on a splendidly snaky performance as the subdued villain, but the episode doesn't make adequate room to explore Olsen or its other components.

Where 'The Cham-Cham' may be light on its storytelling mechanics, its conclusive act brings some full-throttle storytelling back into the mixture that thrills in giving the episode a final jolt of excitement without shedding its comical oddness. Once Lady Penelope and Tin-Tin have uncovered the secrets of the Cham-Cham supercomputer itself as the true enemy of the episode, their game is up. Brains is able to feed in an entirely new code just in time to prevent another newly launched transporter craft from being attacked, but Olsen uncovers his own discovery of Wanda Lamore's true identity. A traditional way of securing the success of a rescue operation in *Thunderbirds* is to have Thunderbirds 1 and 2 dispatched, but 'The Cham-Cham' goes about this in its own creative way, emphasising its unique place in *Thunderbirds'* canon. Thunderbird 2 blasts off to Paradise Peaks on the assumption that Olsen will be less than kind to Penelope, Tin-Tin and Parker's efforts in outing his alliance with the enemy government that's been targeting the transporters, but Thunderbird 1 instead journeys to Matthews Field Air Base in a final, desperate bid to convince the authorities to prevent their latest transporter jet from taking off.

The rescue might be where the drama is, but Scott Tracy's brief visiting of the military base is an intriguing insight into how International Rescue is perceived by the world they protect. Thunderbird 1's desperate dash to the military base is only necessitated after Jeff's earlier radio call with the base goes awry. Having cracked the Cham-Cham's code, Jeff attempts to warn Matthews Field Air Base not to launch their latest transporter rocket, now that International Rescue have confirmation that the live performances of The Dangerous Game are being used to transmit coded coordinates that allow the enemy to locate and destroy the transporter jets. The military base scoffs at Jeff's claims. It's a world away from the military's grovelling desire to do right by International Rescue way back in 'Terror in New York City' and goes to great lengths to suggest that not everyone is grateful for International Rescue's services. Now that the code has been cracked, Brains' alters the code so that the message received by the enemy government will send their fighter jets directly past the military base, which Scott promptly alerts the general to when he arrives. Not even this welcome act is received with gratitude, as the general sarcastically comments how International Rescue have saved the day once again as the base's own strike forces are launched to take down the enemy fighters.

Away from these gritty, downbeat, militant vibes, Thunderbird 2's rescue of the cable car that's been sabotaged by Olsen is a further focus on 'The

Cham-Cham"'s character-driven enjoyment. It's not a rescue about the hardware, it's a rescue about the characters. In a superbly filmed sequence, Parker is the one who elevates his physical comedy relief to physical live-saving manoeuvres as he clambers onto the top of the cable car to secure Thunderbird 2's harnesses that's been deployed above them. The awkwardness in Parker's various positions along the surging car, which must have been a nightmare to film, do a great deal in showing the intensity of the situation, complete with the rattling and swaying of the cable car itself. From a production standpoint alone, but with the context of the quirky character pleasantries of 'The Cham-Cham' itself, it stands as one of *Thunderbirds* most underrated rescues. The parting shot of Parker, having been flung off the cable car as it draws to a halt, floating down to safety with the help of an umbrella, Mary Poppins-esque, is the high point of charm in a spirited oddball of an episode. And once again, logic remains defied – given that the cable car was at the very bottom of its tracks and the mountains when it stopped, just how far was Parker propelled in order to be able to give himself enough time to float down gracefully?

'The Cham-Cham' is that deceptive sort of episode that's funny without trying too hard. Parker may bring in the physical comedy, but the witty premise and scenes of these marionettes superspies ducking and diving out of each other's grasp highlights something rarely discussed in *Thunderbirds* – its sense of humour. *Thunderbirds* may have been the series where technological marvels often fell victim to disaster that could end life, but it was also the series that featured exploding dog food, accidental consumption of edible transmitters and glamourous secret agents sometimes needed assistance from superspy hillbillies. 'The Cham-Cham' rides on a wave of buoyant character action above almost all other elements, but its energy is infectious, along with a sharp eye for visual glamour. The sheer style of the episode can't be dismissed, as Gerry himself noted; '"The Cham-Cham" gave our art and design departments a chance to show what they could really do and they didn't disappoint … Bob Bell (art director) created some spectacular settings …'[33] 'The Cham-Cham' isn't an episode you see appear in many accounts of *Thunderbirds*' greatest episodes, and its status as such a thing is less solid than 'Terror in New York City' or 'Attack of the Alligators!' And yet the episode succeeds where other episodes were too tentative to execute their sense of humour or too serious in their spy-fi elements.

---

[33] Archer, S. Marcus, H. (2002) 'Calling International Rescue' *What Made Thunderbirds Go! The Authorised Biography of Gerry Anderson*. p. 128. BBC Books. p. 128. 2nd edition.

1: 'ATLANTIC INFERNO'

Such is the insistence that *Thunderbirds* places on its stories being driven by atomic vehicles and machinery that it's easy to overlook the rare instances where stories are driven by their characters and even rarer to show those characters perceived as getting things wrong. Such a scenario is just what 'Atlantic Inferno' delivers, the opening episode of *Thunderbirds*' brief second series and one of the greatest of the series overall. It's a commendable complication of colossal disaster and tricky father-son dynamics that presents the very real idea that, one day, Jeff Tracy will no longer be able to be the leader of International Rescue. For a series whose protagonists are the ultimate in unshakeable action men heroes, it's a mark of maturity in the series' writing department that 'Atlantic Inferno' positions the Tracy family as being susceptible to emotionally charged schisms like the ones seen in this episode and capable of making mistakes.

Too often, *Thunderbirds* unintentionally showed up how its ensemble cast could be its downfall in the story-telling department, as the series would succumb to having too many characters doing too little in the space of each episode. But 'Atlantic Inferno' succeeds in making clever, economical use of the majority of the Tracy family as everyone rallies around Lady Penelope's suggestion that it's time Jeff took a much needed vacation away from dictating rescue operations. Ironically, it's when these characters don't do anything that speaks volumes. Aghast at the idea, Jeff attempts to diplomatically throw Penelope's kind request back in everyone's faces, but Scott, Virgil, Alan, Tin-Tin, Gordon and Brains' collective cold shoulder, staying silent at Jeff's scrambling efforts to justify not leaving his family alone, is enough to melt him.

Once Jeff departs from Tracy Island to spend some enforced relaxation with Penelope and Parker on their Australian sheep farm, 'Atlantic Inferno' eases into giving us some of the loveliest character moments in all of *Thunderbirds*. Scott Tracy, Jeff's eldest son, is placed in temporary charge of International Rescue in Jeff's absence, and Scott and his voice actor Shane Rimmer lap up the scenario tremendously. Compared to the likes of the joker Gordon and the temperamental Alan, Scott remains the smooth talker of the Tracy boys. He has the calmest demeanour, giving him a stronger link to the equally stoic Jeff than the others. But once he's given the atomic reigns of Tracy Island, his visible elasticity is enchanting to see. The other Tracy boys crowding round Scott as he takes command of Jeff's desk has a boyish enthusiasm that's quite sweet to witness, matched by Scott's first task of contacting John in Thunderbird 5. Only once he's engaged in radio communication with John that Scott realises he has nothing to say, he's just so enthused by the idea of performing an act relegated to his father – until now. There's a delicate infliction in Rimmer's performance as he gives Scott a suitable excitement to match the episode's premise, and it's just great fun to see the actors relish the opportunity before them.

It's only at this point do we come to the traditional meat within any episode of *Thunderbirds* – the accidental disaster. Seasoned viewers of *Thunderbirds* ought to know by now that if the World Army, World Air Force or World Navy are featured in any Anderson production, there's going to be some explosive consequences to their presence, and 'Atlantic Inferno' doesn't disappoint. It's odd to think that some of *Thunderbirds'* grandest set pieces are obscured by lively character dramas, but that's what makes 'Atlantic Inferno' such an enjoyable outing for the series and demonstrates why it's such a fearless opening to the second series. The emphasis on the fallout between Scott and Jeff as his handling of International Rescue is poorly received by his father ensures that the episode slips into different gears when it comes to the delivery of the rescue operations. Like '30 Minutes After Noon' before it, 'Atlantic Inferno' features not one but two rescues, but engrained within the same scenario, one evolving out of the other. Rescue operations are often portrayed in black-and-white resolves in *Thunderbirds*. Once a rescue is performed, that's it. Disaster averted. Roll credits. 'Atlantic Inferno' proposes the notion that solving one disaster can easily slip into another, something not that commonly seen in *Thunderbirds*.

The second disaster is portrayed with much greater severity than the first. The situation involving World Navy's war games going askew when their testing of nuclear missiles go off course and detonating near the drilling rig Seascape is welcomed with open arms from Scott and recoiled disdain by Jeff. The explosion from the wayward missile causes an eruption of flame, igniting a gas field beneath the sea bed, spewing up a piercing jet of flame through the sea. The ensuing rescue performed by Thunderbirds 1, 2 and 4 provides another finely-tuned moment of anxiety for our characters. International Rescue aren't accustomed to having their efforts ungratefully received, let alone by their own commander. Jeff's retaliation against Scott following International Rescue's successful quelling of the fire breakout is so well executed, because neither character is in the wrong. Jeff's reaction feels very genuine, the thought of his precious organisation performing such a low-risk operation speaks volumes about how emotionally and mentally tangled Jeff is to his own outfit, whilst Scott's decision to launch the operation at all shows his desire to prove he can operate International Rescue just as well as Jeff can, but also try to impress his father. It's all superbly played out to full dramatic effect.

1: 'ATLANTIC INFERNO'

However, further expulsions of bulging gas later on encircle Seascape like a ring of fire, placing the platform in much greater danger than before. Seascape workers O'Shea and Hooper attempts to secure one of the platform's support columns after it's damaged from the onslaught of the unstoppable underwater onslaught sees the World Navy unable to assist them, their diving bell encroached in damaged metallic debris. A further signature of how closely *Thunderbirds* would pay attention to its characterisation comes in the clash between the upper class British commander of the World Navy sub, resplendent in his military uniform, compared to the working class vibes given by O'Shea and Hooper in their grimier working overalls.

The pair had previously called again on International Rescue for help prior to venturing down in their diving bell, but not wanting to provoke his father's wrath any further, Scott refuses, necessitating O'Shea and Hooper to take drastic measures into their own hands once Seascape itself becomes damaged. Only when the alert is given that O'Shea and Hooper are trapped at the bottom of the ocean, close to being crushed by the collapsing Seascape, surrounded by a torrent of belching flame chaos does Scott's sense of duty overpower his fear of his father. In classic *Thunderbirds* style, we finally have a situation where only International Rescue can save the day. Jeff's journeying back to Tracy Island having cut his holiday short in reaction to his perceived mistake of leaving the island in someone else's hands is rendered mute as the call is given for the Thunderbirds to launch.

This much greater danger now in full swing, 'Atlantic Inferno' succeeds in delivering one of *Thunderbirds*' most spectacular danger zones. The Seascape gradually collapsing into the ocean, soaring flames prowling around it and shooting out of the ocean is such an unnerving, unnatural sight to behold. Military evacuation efforts for those stranded on the Seascape whilst Thunderbirds 1 and 2 are positioned directing the rescue of O'Shea and Hooper gives a nice sense of visual depth to the proceedings. It's worth noting that this was all just another day at the office for Derek Meddings and his team, but there's no sense of things being lazy, rushed or forced. It's the sense of a team of film-makers in their moment, doing what they do best, doing what few others were doing at that time when producing children's entertainment. *Watch With Mother* this was not.

The rescue's eventual victory and the saving of O'Shea and Hooper remains conclusive proof that International Rescue is in safe hands without Jeff. As the Seascape succumbs to its watery grave, this image is countered by the triumphant emergence of Thunderbird 4 from the ocean depths with the Seascape diving sphere in tow. The mission a success, 'Atlantic Inferno' can't let you go without one last chef's kiss of character treatment. Jeff cuts his holiday short when hearing of Seascape's further danger, firm in his belief that this is a genuine emergency and that his guidance is demanded of him. Jeff's return to Tracy Island is refused by Scott to make way for the imminent return of the Thunderbird craft, a verbal reflection that International Rescue can run just as efficiently without its founder and with it the realisation that Scott isn't just going to make as an effective leader as Jeff – he already is one. This idea is cemented further by the fact that Jeff is unable to return in time to actually take over from Scott anyway. In this regard, Sylvia Anderson's thoughts on 'Atlantic Inferno' read rather hollow: 'Breaking the format is not a bad thing in a television series, but the team are not allowed to manage too well without him.'[34] 'Atlantic Inferno' succeeds *because* it breaks the format and quite deliberately shows that Scott and the others can manage without Jeff.

Aside from Scott and Jeff's own joint development, other characters also receive boosts of development. Penelope's framing as the voice of reason to calm Jeff's anger and frustrations is a handsome touch, with Parker adding in some deft touches of physical comedy to impede on Jeff's attempts at relaxation. Gordon and John receive some welcome but restricted presences, making 'Atlantic Inferno' a rare instance where all five Tracy brothers have substantial screen time. Alan's command of Thunderbird 1, therefore making him the new director of the danger zone, feels less focused than Scott and Jeff's own development, given Alan's previously established position as being able to take command of space-based missions, such as Operation Sun Probe. It's as if he's trying to receive character growth that he already has. Then again, any excuse to not bear witness to Alan's childlike temperament is a decent one, a tacky trope that ultimately reminds us how annoying Alan could be as a character and therefore how *Thunderbirds'* writers were culpable of resorting to tired ideas in an attempt to squeeze out some personality for their characters.

'Atlantic Inferno' stands as a defiant, proud statement for the series that's full of its own successful personality without sacrificing the central heart of what makes a solid episode of *Thunderbirds*. It's an effortless juggle of all the elements that *Thunderbirds* brings to the table and more often than not, when looking at episode preceding this one, struggled to keep those elements in balance. 'Atlantic Inferno' does more than balance its elements, however. It weaves its pyrotechnic thrills and its family upheavals carefully yet confidently in and out of each other, doing so with the characteristic cinematic atmosphere that gives *Thunderbirds* so much of its identity. From here, *Thunderbirds'* second series wouldn't be given many more opportunities to be as well-produced as 'Atlantic Inferno'.

'Path of Destruction' would continue the momentum of large-scale

---

[34] Anderson, S. (2008) '*Thunderbirds* Episode Guide' *Sylvia Anderson*. Available from – https://web.archive.org/web/20080503080402/http://www.sylviaanderson.org.uk/html/episode_guide.html.

disaster of 'Atlantic Inferno' but without the foundation of emotional character moments. 'Alias Mr Hackenbacker' would reduce that sense of threat entirely with a much quirkier rescue balanced by a focus on characterisation outside of the core Tracy family. 'Lord Parker's 'Oliday' pushes the idea that Century 21's minds were starting to drift away from *Thunderbirds* and more towards a spin-off series focusing on the exploits of Lady Penelope and Parker. 'Ricochet' would give us an unusual mixture of Thunderbirds 2 and 3 called upon as the main stars of the day within an otherwise mundane space-based rescue, albeit with a fun, retro-futuristic spin on pirate radio stations of the 1960s. The absence in 'Give Or Take a Million' of traditional *Thunderbirds*-style threat entirely would prove to be a divisive way to end the series. Nothing throughout the remainder of *Thunderbirds'* second series amounts to being as focused or muscular as this episode. The most robust quality of 'Atlantic Inferno' is how it toys with the status quo of the series without shifting the goalposts. The end result is one of the most determined efforts delivered by *Thunderbirds*.

THE AMBER ROOM: CAPTAIN SCARLET'S CHARACTERS

'FATE WILL MAKE HIM INDESTRUCTIBLE': CAPTAIN SCARLET

Paul Metcalfe is the ultimate heroic action man of the Supermarionation universe. His biography in the 1967 *Captain Scarlet* annual reveals that he was born into a family of military achievers. His father and grandfather before him excelled in the World Army, cementing Paul's own career path. His adventuresome military life earned him the nickname of Supreme Solider by his colleagues, whilst his joint time in the World Army and World Army Air Force caught the attention of Spectrum in their recruitment process. In both spin-off media and television series, Captain Scarlet is passionate, desperate even, to show you that the titular hero is the man born to be the hero of the series. Arguably, that action mentality embedded within Captain Scarlet's DNA comes at the expense of rewarding character growth and any sense of three-dimensional personality. Probing still further, Captain Scarlet's indestructible capabilities ultimately serves to ensure that the series can reach astronomical heights in delivering dynamic, blitzkrieg adventure.

On a strikingly basic level, *Captain Scarlet* is an action/adventure series first and foremost, meaning that having the protagonist be indestructible is the perfect way to compliment a series of *Captain Scarlet*'s genre. However, on an individual level for Paul, the aforementioned backstory is hardly a complex or engrossing one to untangle. It's not even a backstory mentioned within the context of the series itself, but delegated to supplementary material meant to accompany the series. *Captain Scarlet and the Mysterons* wasn't a show preoccupied with character growth, as Stephen La Riviere notes how the show's episodes 'were back to the 25-minute format and so, with 14 regular performers, any serious development of character was unlikely to happen for more than a handful of them.'[35] However, whilst *Captain Scarlet*'s characters are cold, robotic and static in personality and development when compared to Supermarionation's past character peaks, this hasn't been too much of a hindrance for the series. Genre fiction continues to show us how despite character arcs within stories of various mediums makes them more compelling to watch, media that's devoid of those characteristics isn't instantly

---

[35] La Riviere, S. (2009) 'This Is the Voice of the Mysterons' *Filmed in Supermarionation: A History of the Future.* p. 153. Hermes Press. 1st edition.

condemned to an early grave. Over 50 years since the classic era of Supermarionation drew to a conclusion, we're still here, watching, discussing and celebrating these works. Clearly, they boast an everlasting appeal, which arguably stretches beyond the eye-popping pyrotechnics. There's something much more internal at play in what makes Gerry and Sylvia's works last, and the mostly impersonal heroes of *Captain Scarlet*, a series seemingly stripped of the charming character mechanics of past glories, still offers plenty to discuss within its heroes and villains alike.

'His body may burn...'

The initial trouble that we're faced with when trying to assimilate Paul Metcalfe as a character then is the apparent lack of individuality within his own story. His militant upbringing places him firmly alongside the other men and women of Spectrum in terms of personality. At times, their colour-coded outfits are the only elements to these characters that sets them apart. The fact that he's the third of his generation to embark upon a military career is reflective of how he initially appears lacking in any form of uniqueness in his personality. This immediate lack of individuality is reinforced by the accidental nature of Paul acquiring his alien powers of reconstruction. As Captain Blue routinely points out to us with the opening of every episode, it's fate that's made him indestructible.

Captain Scarlet retains his cool, calm, collected action man persona throughout the course of the series; never breaking a sweat, never bursting into fits of laughter or tears of sadness. As if mirroring his physical construction as a mechanically advanced marionette, Captain Scarlet is secured in a state of permanent standby on Cloudbase, ready to spring into instant action whenever the Mysterons show their invisible hand. His function is to serve Spectrum by protecting mankind from annihilation – that's it. Within the television series alone, we know nothing of Paul's past or future. He remains trapped in a static present of war-ready adventure. This attitude didn't go unnoticed amongst the series' own production staff, with writer and director Leo Eaton recalling how 'I think it (*Captain Scarlet*) was humourless, I think that was the big problem, and I think that may also have been one of the reasons why it wasn't as successful. It was all action. Scarlet himself was a pretty humourless individual, as were all of them.'[36] Leo paints a rather damning picture of Captain Scarlet as a character, but it's a picture that was deliberate in intent. The strict military set-up of Spectrum and by extension the world of *Captain Scarlet* as a whole was no accident, as Sylvia Anderson recalls: 'Spectrum was a military organisation with no room for emotions and all of the things we'd seen in Thunderbirds... the show lacked heart and

---

[36] Interview with author.

humour.'[37] The absence of individualism within Spectrum's ranks at least makes sense.

Neither Leo or Sylvia are entirely wrong, but such summaries become all the more striking whenever humour and emotion do manage to slip through into the series as it progresses and a more eye-catching persona emerges for Captain Scarlet, which in turn helps to serve the series' more audacious qualities when delivering high-flying adventure. Once the series settles into its format of Captain Scarlet being Spectrum's living deterrent against the Mysterons, we see time and time again how he's fuelled by his desire to protect the world from villainous threats. That firm commitment goes a step further with Scarlet occasionally but happily adopting an anti-authoritarian stance against his superiors if there's a chance to stop the Mysterons, an intriguing attitude to take within the regimented world of Spectrum. Captain Scarlet is perfectly willing to disregard the rules to save the Earth. Quite a suitable attitude to take when Scarlet's indestructibility already makes him a stand-out recruit within Spectrum.

Scarlet and Blue's refusal to evacuate Base Concorde before the rocket can detonate with the base is a fine example of this, the pair throwing aside their Spectrum caps so as not to endure Colonel White's aggressive demands that they leave a visual reminder of the pair egging each other on into ignoring their superior. More intimately is Scarlet's actions in 'White as Snow' to sneak aboard a World Navy submarine to disguise himself as Colonel White to trick the Mysterons into attacking him instead of his commanding officer. It's in moments like these that Sylvia's comments in particular, thankfully, don't entirely hold up and that there is a complex human being within the marionette.

Alternatively, a convincing argument can be made for the complete opposite. Spectrum's vast influence across the Earth has undeniable Orwellian undertones. They are the ultimate gatekeepers of the status quo, maintaining social order for humanity. The Mysterons, otherworldly beings with violent powers that cannot be easily defined, are the ultimate disrupters of that status quo, possessing the ability to distort the social order so preciously held up by Spectrum. Captain Scarlet's actions of exaggerated heroics capture him as a visual symbol of being the ultimate defender of the status quo by being the only human being who can withstand the Mysterons' incredible, unforeseeable capabilities.

This thirst for heroics builds on the foundation of Captain Scarlet being a straight-forward, two-dimensional action hero, first and foremost. The very colour that Captain Scarlet is designated is another visual aid to this. Simon Archer theorises that the colour-coded agents of Spectrum were named to

---

[37] Anderson, S. Lewis, J. (2001) 'Lady Penelope Speaks: Interview With Sylvia Anderson' *Action TV* (ed Richardson, M). No. 4, p. 12.

encapsulate their personalities and their contributions to the structure of Captain Scarlet. He suggests that '… Captain Black was the villainous traitor, Colonel White the upright commander, Scarlet the dynamic man of action …'[38] It's an idea that holds merit. After all, scarlet is a close neighbour of the colour red, which itself is a colour that throughout popular fiction has been utilised as representing danger, excitement, passion and adventure. All of Spectrum's men are meant to be dynamic, but it's Scarlet who cannot be killed and therefore capable of being that more of a daredevil than his colleagues. Gerry Anderson however had a different explanation for Paul's colour designation and one that was far simpler than Archer's more in-depth interpretation – 'I wanted it to sound different,' Gerry explained.[39]

'But they know he'll return, to live again'

As mentioned, Captain Scarlet's insatiable need for heroic adventure may enable him to stand apart from his Spectrum colleagues, but it also serves a higher purpose for the series overall. Armed with his post-human capabilities, Scarlet is able to throw himself into a vast array of catastrophic situations against the Mysterons in which mere mortal men would surely perish. The transition Paul Metcalfe makes between 'The Mysterons' and 'Winged Assassin' may be strewn with head-scratching oddities surrounding how exactly the Mysteron doppelgänger of Captain Scarlet now reverts to being the original Captain Scarlet, particularly from Doctor Fawn and Colonel White. And yet Paul is just about the only person who doesn't question this strange state of affairs. He immediately accepts his newfound powers of indestructibility and is ready to face the Mysterons singlehandedly if needed. He does so without any bemoaning of living some kind of cursed existence now that he's virtually immortal. His reaction to Colonel White considering Doctor Fawn's medical report of Scarlet in 'Winged Assassin' is a simple 'I'm ready, Colonel'. No ifs, no buts, a determined acceptance of knowing he can put his powers to good use, evidence later on in the episode when he saves Captain Blue's life by ejecting him from their rampaging SPV so that Scarlet alone may face the terror of the Mysteronised DT19 from attacking the Director-General of the United Asian Republic. The Director-General's death, the first of several Mysteron victories over the course of the series, makes Paul's enthusiasm hit on a sombre note.

Interestingly, it's this action man mentality that put some of Century 21's production crew's noses out of joint. Scriptwriter Alan Fennell

---

[38] Archer, S. Nicholas, S. (1996) 'Chapter 16' *Gerry Anderson: The Authorised Biography*. p. 122. Legend Books. 1st edition.
[39] Anderson, G. (2001) *Captain Scarlet S.I.G.* Carlton International Media.

remained disparaging of the concept of having a hero who can't be killed; 'What works in film doesn't always work in comics. An indestructible hero presents problems because there is nothing that can threaten him and therefore there is no drama.'[40] It's immensely curious that Fennell should single out writing *Captain Scarlet* from a comics standpoint rather than a television standpoint, because he remains indestructible in both incarnations and therefore surely the same problems arise, if indeed they can be interpreted as problems. A looming irony here is that Fennell didn't write for either the *Captain Scarlet* TV series or its *TV21* spin-off.

Leo Eaton holds a different opinion as to how Scarlet's indestructible readiness enhances the drama of the series; 'The tension was how they were going to stop the disaster, whatever it might be, in time. I don't think the fact that Captain Scarlet was indestructible or not was particularly relevant. It was like James Bond – you know he was never going to get killed because he's got to come back.'[41] Indeed, how Captain Scarlet and Spectrum stop the Mysterons gives way to some thrillingly reckless actions on Scarlet's part. Alongside 'White as Snow' and 'Renegade Rocket', 'Winged Assassin', 'Flight 104', 'Crater 101' and 'Attack on Cloudbase' all feature Scarlet exploiting Colonel White's remark from 'The Mysterons' of being Spectrum's greatest asset in the fight against the Mysterons by performing acts of dangerous heroism that no other Spectrum man or woman could endure. From a character perspective, there's just something effortlessly endearing about Scarlet being able to take command of a situation that no-one else could and in such action-propelled style.

This then highlights Captain Scarlet's key contribution to the series. His fearless actions propel the series to engage with some of the most jaw-dropping special effect sequences that Century 21 Productions conjured up. When your protagonist is virtually indestructible, it reads like permission given to the writers, director and special effects crew to negate any concern for how Scarlet may evade death at the last possible moment and embrace pyrotechnic destruction on a spectacular scale, an unpredictable playground of vibrant death. 'It was a bit of a shock when I realised the implications of Scarlet being indestructible would affect the opposing fates of Spectrum and the Mysterons,' recalls scriptwriter Shane Rimmer. 'More imaginative methods of thwarting the Mysterons certainly had to be found and executed.'[42] This idea of kicking imaginations into overdrive is shared by Leo; 'I do remember there was a certain gruesome,

---

[40] Drake, C. Bassett, G. (1992) 'The United Colours of Anderson' *Captain Scarlet and the Mysterons*. p. 13. Boxtree. 1st edition.
[41] Interview with author.
[42] Interview with author.

dark humour about "well, let's see which way poor old Captain Scarlet's going to get squished or stomped on or blown up this time."'[43]

This Indestructible Man

Captain Scarlet's heroic persona may be in service to the series' pyrotechnic aspects and to make the series visually stimulating as an overall package of action/adventure entertainment, but Scarlet's character remains consistent throughout as an unflinching saviour of humanity. It's basic, it's two dimensional, but it also works and signals to one of several reasons why Captain Scarlet has stayed in the hearts and minds of viewers for over half a century. Captain Scarlet's posthuman heart is the beating nerve centre of the series, his fixed precision in stopping the Mysterons both captivating and oddly perverse. An early concept for him as a character was for Captain Scarlet to be a robot, presumably meaning that the Mysterons would have specialised in biological copies of their victims rather than the more biological ones that populate the series.

Gerry Anderson's reasoning for abandoning this idea was the apprehension of audiences not being able to empathise with a robotic character. Ironically, the Captain Scarlet we root for still remains a synthetic duplicate of the original, but it's a further sign away from Sylvia and Leo's earlier perspectives that those involved in creating Captain Scarlet still wanted to place believable, watchable characters to carry the adventures along. Placed in the context of previous Century 21's heroes, this approach to character construction resonated with Shane Rimmer in particular, even in the face of Fennell's earlier comments: 'The change to a darker feel came as a natural progression – we were now in a new territory. The crew jumped at it and delivered the goods – but as always Alan Fennell had a point and we had to tread carefully with the dangers that Captain Scarlet had to deal with.'[44]

The most recognisably human aspect in animated Captain Scarlet's personality is in Francis Matthew's performance of the character, who remained another naysayer of the series; 'the only things people ever want to talk about are Captain Scarlet and Paul Temple, which are not exactly high quality drama.'[45] He's wrong about that last remark. A fiercely handsome reminder of Captain Scarlet's positivity as a character can be found in that despite Captain Scarlet being the one Mysteron creation who displays any sense of agency and individuality is also the sole Mysteron creation that's entirely focused on saving life rather than destroying it.

---

[43] Interview with author.
[44] Interview with author.
[45] Matthews, F. Porter, J. (March 1994) 'This Is The Voice of … Francis Matthews' *TV Zone: Secret Agent Special* (ed Vincent-Rudzki, J). No. 12, p. 52.

'INITIATIVE SHOULD NEVER CLASH WITH DISCIPLINE': THE SPECTRUM MEN

There is a convincing case to be made that *Captain Scarlet and the Mysterons* is the most inhuman of the Supermarionation era of Gerry and Sylvia Anderson. This isn't strictly a reference to the act of Captain Black destroying the Mysterons' Mars complex in a fit of panic, and by extension the bleak, war-mongering attitudes of the series as a whole. It's more of a case that *Captain Scarlet* undeniably lacks the warmth in its characters when compared to the cast of *Stingray* or *Thunderbirds*. As we explored previously, it was a deliberate choice to fashion the men and women of Spectrum in this way, but further inspection points to a deeper and more personal cause. Speaking in 1992, Sylvia Anderson revealed the frustrations she was experiencing in working within this deadly militant landscape; 'Gerry and I did not agree on a lot of characterisation. He always wanted to make the characters a lot more rigid than I did. I wanted to start to give them human flaws, start to make them more important ... If you don't care about the characters, it doesn't work.'[46]

There is some harsh truth in the idea that *Captain Scarlet* 'doesn't work' in the character department. Biographical material is mostly left to spin-off material. Characters spend much of the series following Colonel White's orders without question or hesitation. When Paul Maxwell left his role of Captain Grey midway through the series, did anyone notice?

Sylvia's role within Century 21 Productions grew from production assistant to being more assertive in her contributions to the creative departments of their various productions. From overseeing production designs to writing story book and annual material, her role is most characterised by, well, her characterisations of the daredevil agents and astronauts within Gerry's concepts. Where Gerry was very much a hardware man, Sylvia embedded that hardware with the characters needed to engage the viewers with. With characterisation so firmly within Sylvia's territory by the time *Captain Scarlet* came along, it's little wonder that she felt frustratingly closed off from these characters when *Captain Scarlet* seemingly

---

[46] Anderson, S. Turner, S. (1992) 'Living in the Future: An Interview With Sylvia Anderson' *Time Screen* (ed McKay, A). No. 18, pp. 16-17.

places such little emphasis on the humanisation of the newly developed ultra-realistic marionettes.

However, much like Captain Scarlet himself, close probing of the series finds that there's a much less black-and-white scenario at play than Sylvia otherwise states. The men of Spectrum exhibit the characteristics that Sylvia speaks of (or rather, lack of those characteristics), whilst also not entirely freeing themselves from each other in terms of interchangeable personalities, something Sylvia also spoke of; 'there was a samyness with everyone in the same uniform.'[47] As a collective, the men and women of Spectrum elicit empathetic reactions from the audience due to the dangerous situation they're in. With the Angels confined mostly to their interceptor craft, the men in particular are the ones who deal the most with the unpredictable, Devil-like terror of the Mysterons. Alongside Captain Scarlet, Colonel White, Lieutenant Green, Captain Blue, Captain Ochre, Captain Magenta and Captain Grey are constantly thrust into the terror of the Mysterons with little to no expertise to combat them, a perverse thrill kicks into gear as we witness these men attempt to treat with something utterly untreatable.

Spectrum is shown to be a gargantuan outfit with numerous other agents, sub-headquarters and other resources scattered around the globe, but it's this core group of men who we focus on throughout the course of the series. As the series develops, strands of relationships are sewn together, hinting at the human heart beating beneath the surface of the war of nerves which Sylvia might claim was never there at all. Sub-groups of characters can be found within the relationships between Captain Scarlet and Captain Blue, Colonel White and Lieutenant Green and the remaining trio of background Captains. Through these instances of synergy, personality, drama and humour cautiously float to the series' surface.

'You'd better not let the Colonel hear you call me that'

Despite Captain Scarlet being the protagonist of the series, he's very rarely seen without Captain Blue, just as Captain Blue is rarely seen without Captain Scarlet. This character-driven concept of pairing the protagonist with a secondary character highlights something of a masterstroke the series pulls in executing its characters. By pairing Scarlet and Blue together almost constantly, the duo are able to bounce each other's characterisations off of each other, allowing a richer sense of personality to emerge for the pair than what might emerge by comparison if the two were left alone. The series establishes the friendship between Paul Metcalfe and Adam Svenson early on in the series' run, just as it establishes the professional relationship

---

[47] Anderson, S. Russell, G. (1991) 'The Power Behind the Rolls' *TV Zone* (ed Vincent-Rudzki, J). No. 20, p. 12.

between Captain Scarlet and Captain Blue.

Scarlet and Blue share the masculine, action man persona that defines the stereotypical Anderson hero. Their shared determination to defend the Earth for the Mysterons helps to make them an engaging pair to watch on screen in action. However, it's only when the pair are pulled apart from each other that they arguably become more interesting as characters. Captain Blue is prone to being easily distracted by his emotions, his on-off romance with Symphony Angel an effective example of this. 'Manhunt' sees him show an uncontainable agitation at the thought of Symphony held captive by Captain Black, a display of affection reiterated in 'Attack on Cloudbase', although that was more of a projection on Symphony's part, given the dream nature of the episode. Evidence of Adam's passionate feelings being returned, perhaps? Interestingly, this strand of Adam's personality would be extended in his incarnation in *New Captain Scarlet*, in which he's portrayed as entirely hot-headed and even more susceptible to aggressive outburst. He succumbs to his emotions still further in 'White as Snow', but in this episode it's done to delightfully comic effect, as he eagerness to lead Spectrum in the absence of Colonel White makes him hugely unpopular with Spectrum's staff. It's also a characteristic that goes against Sylvia's earlier comments.

In comparison to Captain Blue, Captain Scarlet is comparatively lax without being lazy. As explored previously, Scarlet is decidedly unperturbed by his newfound indestructible status in 'Winged Assassin', suggesting that he's more in-tune with himself than Adam. Given the indifference his colleagues have to him being a failed Mysteron clone, Paul remains the same man as he was before, not defined by his incredible powers and not tempted to abuse them either. It makes for an effective duo of characters to watch in action.

The relationship between Paul and Adam gains an emotional galvanising in 'Special Assignment', in which the Mysterons and most of Spectrum are tricked into thinking that Captain Scarlet's gambling additions have seen him fired from Spectrum and so he is instantly snapped up by the Mysterons. With Scarlet dismissed from Cloudbase, he retreats into the seedy underworld of alcohol abuse. It's all for show, of course, Captain Blue's concern for Scarlet sees him attempting to track him down and salvage his friend, suspecting that all is not as it appears. Adam's concern for Paul is a touching element of humanisation throughout the episode, emphasised further by the audience not being entirely clued in early on to the deception at work. We share in Adam's desire to ensure that his friend remains safe now that he's untethered from the safe harbour of Cloudbase.

It's episodes like these that demonstrate how Paul and Adam's relationship was more than mere superhero and sidekick and instead suggests a more equal footing for the pair, akin to Napoleon Solo and Illya Kuryakin's bond in *The Man From U.N.C.L.E.* Neither character allows Scarlet's indestructible powers to interfere with their friendship. Their aforementioned joint action man persona lends weight to the idea that they're equals, further by their aesthetic details – same uniform, same armoury, same abilities to pilot various Spectrum craft. Sylvia's comments about 'samyness' comes in pretty useful here in highlighting their friendship. A hierarchy in their relationship is enforced by Scarlet's powers, often resulting in him having to make the final assault against the Mysterons whilst Blue is left to witness the proceedings from the sidelines. It's an unspoken thing between the pair that Scarlet is ultimately the more qualified individual to engage whatever the Mysterons may throw at Spectrum, but Scarlet's actions in this regard are purely a matter of circumstance rather than being a case of one believing that they are in anyway better than the other. Blue still regularly joins in with Scarlet's actions until the last possible moment. A twist in the friendship is seen in the final act of 'The Mysterons' in that it's Blue who delivers the fatal shot to the Mysteronised Scarlet atop the London Car-Vu, sending him spiralling to the ground below and enabling him to become Spectrum's number one agent.

The lack of any clash between the pair in this regard does point towards Sylvia's perspectives, as *Captain Scarlet* rarely made exceptions for internal struggles between its heroes. This is particularly underwhelming when *Captain Scarlet*'s themes of paranoia seems ripe for exploring this angle. The series' distant live-action counterpart *UFO* would go to greater lengths to display the fraught relationships between its characters, worn down by constant alien battles. Perhaps this signals to the overriding influence Gerry had over the directions Captain Scarlet's character should take and further evidence that Sylvia's creative contributions were going ignored.

However, in this world where any one walking past you could be a Mysteron replica and in which the Mysterons could strike any time, any place and in any fashion, the unshakeable friendship between Captain Scarlet and Captain Blue is a pocket of optimism in a world that feeds off of destruction. Paul and Adam exhibit the healthiest and warmest relationship between characters throughout all of *Captain Scarlet*, aided by their protagonist roles. As if to demonstrate how intertwined these characters are, consider that despite the series being titled *Captain Scarlet and the Mysterons*, the first voice we hear in every episode is that of Captain Blue as he narrates over the opening titles, setting the tense, noir-tinged scenery. We see one but hear another as the scene swerves violently to Captain Scarlet himself before the titles bleed into the episode itself. One is inseparable from the other, a duo of characters whose cordial relationship gently pokes at overly rigid masculine stereotypes in companionship in sci-fi media.

'One more question like that, lieutenant…'

Compared to Captain Scarlet and Captain Blue, a more traditional commander/subordinate dynamic is found between Colonel White and Lieutenant Green. Charles Gray and Seymour Griffiths fulfil a standard Supermarionation trope of the militant commander and the dutiful yet occasionally sly lower ranking officer. Their relationship bears parallels then to Commander Zero and Lieutenant 90 of *Fireball XL5* as well as Commander Shore and his lieutenant daughter, Atlanta, from *Stingray*. Fiery dynamics are always struck up between these sorts of characters, and *Captain Scarlet*'s spin on this trope is no different.

There's plenty of handsome, indirect instances of White and Green having something of a mentor and apprentice attitude, as Lieutenant Green can often be counted upon to question various Mysteron methods of attack, only to be resolved by the colonel's aged wisdom colouring in the areas the Mysterons otherwise leave blank. Alongside this, actor Donald Gray hardwires a riveting sense of authority into his portrayal of Colonel White, enhancing the character's role as the fearsome yet fair commander-in-chief of Spectrum. Cy Grant counters this cold, ruling presence by integrating a natural, Guyanese drawl into his own performance as Lieutenant Green. It's through these distinct vocal performances that further subtle touches of the characters' relationship emerges. Lieutenant Green's affable nature gives the impression that he's one of the few on Cloudbase, if not the only one, who's not entirely intimated by the Colonel and can bypass or rebuke his stringent leadership. Complimenting this, Colonel White's almost fatherly treatment of the lieutenant indicates a more agreeable side to the Colonel than the series often allowed.

Within the action-driven demands of Captain Scarlet, where Scarlet and Blue can usually be counted upon to stop the Mysterons, White and Green spend much of their time over the course of the series stationed, or even entombed, within Cloudbase. They are the chief enablers of Spectrum's technological iron fist to slam down upon the Earth with brute force, as White orders Green to launch all Angels, Spectrum Passenger Jets and other supersonic creations to blast off into adventure. Their roles within the series aren't entirely captivating, but they are necessary in maintaining Captain Scarlet's para-military attitude.

Akin to Adam and Paul exhibiting more discernible traits of characters when separated from each other, so too do Charles and Seymour. Seymour undergoes more development than Charles, earlier episodes seeing him bemoaning of his ensnared status within Cloudbase and wishing that he could join in the fight with his Captain colleagues. This evolves into Green having a much more involved role alongside Captain Scarlet and Captain Blue, initially just with Scarlet during 'Avalanche' and proceeding to take a tremendous leap to the moon with Scarlet and Captain Blue for 'Lunarville 7' and 'Crater 101'. Whilst Green doesn't entirely shift the status quo established by Scarlet and Blue, he brings a welcome presence to the few adventures in which he's permitted to leave Colonel White's side.

The Colonel maintains his persona in typically upright fashion of that of a commanding officer and so doesn't undergo the same growth that Green experiences, but he succeeds in displaying some semblances of character. His fatherly attitude extends towards much of Cloudbase, a hangover of Commander Shore's patronage of Marineville in *Stingray* and Jeff Tracy's handling of Tracy Island in *Thunderbirds*, whilst most episodes sees the Colonel conclude the latest mission, whether it's ended in victory or defeat for Spectrum, with a note of reflective optimism, as if he's maintaining moral amongst his surrogate family.

Charles and Seymour work in tandem akin to Paul and Adam, albeit in not as adventuresome manners. They're the oil that keeps Spectrum manoeuvring in a slick fashion, and even if the pair aren't the most dynamic in personality or complexly written in arcs, there remains a fun combination of youth and experience between the pair and discipline mixed with playfulness.

Shades of Grey, Ochre & Magenta

When describing the house rules laid down by Tony Barwick in the writing department for *Captain Scarlet*, Shane Rimmer recalls that one of the rare guidelines set by Barwick was to 'make it interesting and your characters believable.'[48] Whilst the personas of our four central protagonists mostly ensures that Rimmer's words ring true, they can't be said for the forgotten trio of Spectrum's finest – Captains Ochre, Grey and Magenta. They make plenty of appearances throughout the series, but by the time 'The Inquisition' plays out, we know so little of them. Richard Fraser, Bradley Holden and Patrick Donaghue are the Spectrum agents we bond with the least over the course of the series. Often restricted to menial patrol work or other background duties when compared to the efforts of Adam and Paul, there's no possible doubt that the three characters present a missed opportunity to add some depth to the human side of the Spectrum organisation and that they ultimately often appear as little more than ghosts behind the main characters.

Curiously, it's not a question of these three lacking any personality or

---

[48] Interview with author.

history, it's that they're restrained from showing them. Of all of the men in the Spectrum ranks, Ochre, Magenta and Grey are the blankest of slates in the entire series. No episodes are devoted to their characters, the spotlight well and truly avoids them from beginning to end. They're little beyond human cannon fodder, props brought in to serve as back up whenever the story demands it. Within *Captain Scarlet*'s world, they do add some additional dimension to Spectrum as an outfit, but are far more diminutive in their roles than Seymour and Charles.

It's curious to know then that Ochre and Magenta boast the most compelling backstories of the Spectrum men. Like all of the characters in *Captain Scarlet*, such backstories aren't revealed within the series itself and we're forced to stretch beyond into the spin-off media, but it's a journey well worth undertaking for those who are curious. According to the 1967 *Captain Scarlet* annual, prior to joining Spectrum, Patrick (Magenta) was a criminal overlord in New York's crime landscape who joins Spectrum on the promise that he'll be pardoned for his offences and because Spectrum require a man with inside knowledge of the criminal underworld. In Richard's case (Ochre), he failed to be an academic high flyer like most of his Spectrum colleagues managed to achieve and instead worked his way upwards to become something of an underdog within the World Government Police Corps. Even though Shane Rimmer didn't contribute to Century 21 Publishing's output of comics, novels, annuals and storybooks, the advice given to him by Tony clearly transferred over from one department to the other.

Despite their detached role within the series, this threesome offer conclusive proof that *Captain Scarlet and the Mysterons* was a victim of its own ambitions, ie that it buckled under the weight of the sheer number of its own characters. This is another justifiable reason why it's a tricky thing to wrangle substantial investigations out of these characters. A common point of debate for *Captain Scarlet* is how its 25-minute run time per episode holds up compared to *Thunderbirds'* more extensive 50-minutes. The lack of characterisations in certain corners answers just how well *Captain Scarlet* stands up. Having that larger running time would surely have granted a more expansive canvas for the men of Spectrum to express themselves in more engaging ways.

Another indicator of *Captain Scarlet*'s slipping standards in the character department arises from Gerry and Sylvia's distanced role from the series at the time of its making. '…We weren't what I call 'hands-on' producers on that (*Captain Scarlet*). We were off doing a show called *Doppelgänger* at the same time, and although the team that did were excellent, we rather let it get away from us and the results was that the puppets were too perfect and the cast too big,' Sylvia Anderson admitted in 1991[49]. The lack of a 50-minute run time was another source of frustration for Sylvia; 'I'd always be saying to Lew Grade "Could we do an hour show?" Because as I was in control of the characters, I wanted time so that we could see more of them, you could talk about their past lives, and so on.'[50]

In Captain Grey's case, such logic would have changed the tone of the show considerably. Stephen La Riviere makes the claim that 'Captain Grey was originally intended to be as prominent, if not more so, than Captain Blue.'[51] Paul Maxwell's exit from the series dictated that Grey should be reclined to become a non-speaking role, appearing in only a fragment of episodes once Maxwell left, but this quote is curious. If Bradley was indeed meant to have a more visible role, why wasn't he featured more heavily in the batch of episodes spanning from 'The Mysterons' to 'Shadow of Fear'? Adding to the curiosity, Captain Blue's role as secondary hero is cemented via his role as the narrator for the opening credits.

The emphasis *Captain Scarlet*'s crew members placed on the visual flavour of the series, whilst undoubtedly stimulating, is the biggest price paid for an equal balance in engaging character dynamics. This is something that scriptwriter Alan Fennell took note of when explaining how he and the rest of the *TV21* staff took hold of the more character-focused aspects that had gone relatively untouched; 'The film people were more concerned with the visual side, so they didn't have time to produce character profiles. Instead, we'd get together round a table and decide where each character came from.'[52] Fennell's comments add further fuel to the fact that Sylvia was smothered in her role as character developer for the series. *Thunderbirds* had shown how to achieve a relatively harmonious mixture of such a large group of characters, but with the episode runtime chopped by half, *Captain Scarlet* had much shorter legs to stand on than its predecessor. Whether it was solely down to Gerry's insistence on preventing the characters from being more human, his and Sylvia's attentions focused elsewhere, or a mixture of both, the unfocused execution of the men of Spectrum point to one of *Captain Scarlet*'s less successful aspects. The questions that now remains is do the Angels soar any higher than their male counterparts?

---

[49] Anderson, S. Turner, S. (1992) 'Living in the Future: An Interview With Sylvia Anderson' *Time Screen* (ed McKay, A). No. 18, pp. 16-17.
[50] Anderson, S. Farrell, R. (2014) 'Sylvia Anderson Interview' *Andersonic* (ed. Farrell, R). No. 17, p. 7.
[51] La Riviere, S. (2009) 'This is the Voice of the Mysterons' *Filmed in Supermarionation*. p. 165. Hermes Press. 1st edition.
[52] Drake, C. Bassett, G. (1992) 'The United Colours of Anderson' *Captain Scarlet and the Mysterons*. p. 40. Boxtree. 1st edition.

'LAUNCH ALL ANGELS': THE ANGELS

The expunging of individual personalities within *Captain Scarlet*'s characters is not entirely confined to the men. The five-piece, all-female fighter squadron who function as Spectrum's first line of defence serve as yet another reminder of how a longer running time per episode would have better served the Angels. For the most part, they're as devoid of personality as Captain Ochre, Captain Magenta and Captain Grey, but the Angels manage to maintain a more palpable identity within *Captain Scarlet* through other means. When asked about creation behind Destiny, Symphony, Rhapsody, Melody and Harmony, Sylvia Anderson (1991) retained fond memories of her creations: 'I'm proud of the fact that I created the Angels … The Angels were a good mixture, we had a coloured girl mixing with an American Southern girl, a Chinese girl, all working together – strong characterisation.'[53] Counteracting this, David O'Brien defines the group as 'little more than a sexist fantasy.'[54] Can both of these perspectives have merit?

For starters, where it's possible that Sylvia's influence in *Captain Scarlet*'s characters was being prevented, she was very much responsible for the Angels. A potted biography on Glotime.TV speaks of how '… Women were rarely recognised as heroes, and so once again (Sylvia was) was ahead of her time.'[55] Whilst there's little individuality amongst the Angels, their collective presence adds welcome diversity to Spectrum's operations. Their very inclusion can't help but feel like a retaliation on Sylvia's part against the all-male hierarchy of Spectrum, aided by their racial diversity, which in turn becomes just about the only aspect that highlights their individuality. Their lack of uniqueness is furthered by the inconsistencies in their voice actors.

The Angels serve as the battle-ready heroines for Captain Scarlet, rarely seen anywhere else beyond the Amber Room or within the cockpits of their

---

[53] Anderson, S. Russell, G. (1991) 'The Power Behind the Rolls' *TV Zone* (ed Vincent-Rudzki, J). No. 20, p. 11.
[54] O'Brien, D (2000). 'Supermarionation, Superspies and Car Sickness' *SF:UK: How British Science Fiction Changed the World*. p. 84. Reynolds & Hearn Ltd. 1st edition.
[55] Anderson, D. (2021) 'Celebrating Sylvia Anderson On International Woman's Day – A Pioneer For Women In Television' *GloTIMEtv*. Available from – https://www.glotime.tv/celebrating-sylvia-anderson-on-international-womens-day-a-pioneer-for-women-in-television/.

Angel Interceptor craft. From that perspective, they add a stimulating dollop of aerial adventure to a series where its various Captains mostly engaged with the Mysterons in battle down on solid ground. However, is this really the highest compliment we can pay the Angels? That they flew around in the sky? The lack of focus the series places on the Angels as characters didn't go unnoticed by other corners of Century 21. *Captain Scarlet* script editor Tony Barwick spoke of how the Angels benefitted the series by giving it an international appeal for overseas television markets; 'To that extent, there's no deep characterisation.'[56] Barwick's comments point to a large role the Angels served within *Captain Scarlet,* one driven by commerciality than artistic desires.

Throughout their tenure under Lew Grade's thumb, Gerry and Sylvia Anderson were in the business of making business, rather than art. Grade's output of television productions championed commercial viability, thus necessitated commercial aspects to make them more appealing. The novelty of a group of female action heroes within a predominantly male setting such as *Captain Scarlet*'s undoubtedly enabled the series to meet Grade's standards. The Angels therefore traded in personality and character development for the commercial success of *Captain Scarlet,* an odd way of tapping into how heroes and heroines in Anderson productions often fought against their enemies for the freedom of the world, ie sacrificing themselves for the greater good. 'After the success of the *Thunderbirds* merchandise, the most successful of all, we had a whole merchandise operation to feed,'[57] Sylvia recalled in 1991, a logic that's entirely justified. If the singular character of Lady Penelope had spawned an unprecedented level of demand for merchandise, then surely five characters would produce even greater demand. Sure enough, just as Lady Penelope had been treated, The Angels were handled as a franchise within the *Captain Scarlet* franchise itself, right down to having their own distinct logo. This logo adorned comics, novels, activity books and more.

Once again, the lack of emphasis on the characters as humans rears its head. The slew of product based on the Angels comes with a materialistic mind-set; that these heroines are surface level characters without any tangible complexities within themselves, even if such a merchandise operation helped to establish further audience thirsts for future and better female heroes in science fiction media. The Angels are often treated with the disposability of the action figures they marketed.

The Angels are segregated from their male counterparts via them being

---

[56] Barwick, T. Drake, C. Howard, A. (1986) 'Tony Barwick: The S.I.G. Interview' *Supermarionation Is Go* (ed Nightingale, D). No. 16, p. 25.

[57] Anderson, S. Russell, G. (1991) 'The Power Behind the Rolls' *TV Zone* (ed Vincent-Rudzki, J). No. 20, p. 11.

on standby in the Amber Room ready for blast off, but evolving past Lady Penelope's ability to drive FAB 1, there's absolutely no questioning throughout the series of their combat abilities. The Angels are the strike force that the men know not to ever doubt in any Mysteron-induced scenario. Then again, as 'Manhunt' demonstrates, the Angels aren't apt at piloting every kind of vehicle in Spectrum's arsenal. Symphony Angel's inability to drive a Spectrum Pursuit Vehicle in her attempts to escape Captain Black's clutches whilst Black himself evades Spectrum's capture induces flashbacks to Penelope's own abilities to command FAB 1 in *Thunderbirds*' 'Vault of Death'.

Other episodes provide similarly drip-fed instances of character focus to varying degrees of insight. A minor scene from 'The Launching' sees Melody engage in a brief yet weirdly violent encounter with the Mysteronised news reporter Mervin Brand. Ordering the reporter to land after tracking him, the Mysteronised Brand behaves disarmingly towards the Angel before revealing a thuggish machoism towards her when he raises his hand as if to strike her. Melody succeeds in repelling him by informing Brand of her martial art skills. 'Model Spy' is the most substantial episode in offering a perspective of the Angels away from Cloudbase when Destiny and Symphony Angel accompany Captain Scarlet and Captain Blue to go undercover as models in a fashion show, the mastermind of which is a secret agent who's been targeted by the Mysterons. Prizing the two most regularly seen Angels away into a context of glamour and spies harks back to the espionage of Lady Penelope. 'Attack on Cloudbase' allows us the most striking insight into the psyche of one of the Angels. Symphony Angel's crash-landing in the desert and prolonged exposure to the harsh heat as she awaits rescue causes her to hallucinate the Mysterons' greatest assault yet – the complete and utter destruction of Cloudbase. Her nightmares come across as a projection of the paranoia the Mysterons force upon the world. Having spent much of the series relegated to background characters who implement a sense of visual femininity into the masculine roots of Spectrum, Symphony's experiences in 'Attack on Cloudbase' is a sudden and horrific rush of character development that's too late in the series to see more of.

The Angels' contribution to *Captain Scarlet* does manage to stretch further than O'Brien's dismissive comments would otherwise suggest, but arguably not by a great deal. There is a sense of progressiveness in how Spectrum recruits a multi-racial group of females to act as its strongest aerial defence, but it's only a slight sense, one that would be more fully rounded by stronger focus on the Angels as individual human beings. As a collective, the Angels would prove to be the last great leap Century 21 would make in giving its Supermarionation output a muscular female presence as *Joe 90* and *The Secret Service* are almost shorn entirely of regular female characters. Whilst the Angels' portrayal in *Captain Scarlet* remains problematic in its overall blankness, this is more rooted to the series' automated approach to characterisation, rather than a direct target on the women themselves. The sparing usage of the Angels in *Captain Scarlet* ensures that they're never overexposed, meaning that their appearances are always welcome as they dive, wing to wing, onto the scene.

'YOU KNOW WHAT YOU MUST DO': CAPTAIN BLACK

Captain Black commands a presence that few other characters in *Captain Scarlet* achieve. Nowhere else in the series does a character fill such a vital role whilst lacking any sense of their own agency. The indestructible Captain Scarlet, who's forced to routinely sacrifice himself for Spectrum's efforts in saving the world, and the omnipotent Mysterons being antagonised into a war that neither side wants may be justified in having a sense of tragedy wrung from them, but Captain Black trumps all. He's the one who initiates the war, transforming Spectrum and the Mysterons from relatively passive states of existence into active warmongers. The propulsion of *Captain Scarlet*'s story is the result of his man's cracked nerves when witnessing the Mysterons for the very first time, the end result of his actions being his own destruction and rebirth into the hands of the Mysterons. His reestablishment as the alien's main operative based on Earth is a stroke of underscored smarts in giving the series two levels of lingering threats – one based on Mars and the other based on Earth.

Relaying Instructions from the Mysterons

The Mysteronised Captain Black bears little familiarity to his past-self compared to every other Mysteron agent scattered throughout the series. Rather than simply being a replica of the human Conrad Turner, this new Captain Black is given a fresh identity and appearance altogether. Perhaps *fresh* is a poor choice of wording, given his actual appearance. The formerly clean-shaving, handsome features of Conrad become decomposed into something that looks like a corpse that doesn't realise that it's dead. The petrified face, permanent five-o-clock-shadow, and the exact same voice as the Mysterons itself enable Captain Black to be one of the most visually striking characters in all of Gerry and Sylvia's work, but with one notable absence. Throughout the series, the Mysterons' voice ripples like an atomic explosion across the airwaves of Earth, an unstoppable wave echoing across the world as they deliver their threats. Captain Black on the other hand has no echo whatsoever. Whilst his voice remains the same as his masters, it's coldly intimate, lacking the imposing boom of the Mysterons. This lends credence to the idea that Captain Black could very well be the closest we ever come to seeing a biological embodiment of the computer-defined Mysterons themselves.

It's through this physical identity that Captain Black distinguishes himself from other Mysteron agents. Whilst the series establishes that victims must first be destroyed and their bodies replicated in order to become Mysteron agents, the process in transforming Captain Black is markedly different. Once the Mysterons have reconstructed their own city which Captain Black orders the destruction of, and which prompts the war of nerves, the Mysterons seemingly ensnare Conrad from the comfort of his command within *Zero-X*, not replicating Conrad's body, but hijacking it entirely, as if forcibly plugging his physical being into some vast Mysteron hive mind.

Whatever alien mechanics go into Captain Black's resurrection into the Mysteron cause, he goes on to provide a multi-layered purpose for the series. Where the Mysterons are the series' chief antagonists, Captain Black provides an additional sensation of horrific jeopardy, a lingering Mysteron presence secured on Earth. As the Mysterons' chief operative on Earth, he intermittently orchestrates attacks devised by the Mysterons whilst delivering orders to newly formed Mysteron agents. Given that the Mysterons are clearly shown to be able to deliver their threats directly from Mars, the presence of Captain Black at all arguably comes off as unnecessary. However, it can also be said that Captain Black's inclusion is a sign of weakness on the Mystersons; part, that for all of their omnipotence, a human hand is still needed to pull the trigger on occasion. Black's usage in the series gains a further undercurrent of tension thanks to his sparing appearances. Like *Thunderbirds*' Hood or *Stingray*'s Titan, Captain Black doesn't appear in every episode. It's as if the Mysterons restrict using him unless all other options are exhausted.

Whilst deceptively human in appearance and able to blend in with crowds without raising suspicions, Captain Black possesses similar otherworldly qualities to his masters. His recruitment of people into the Mysteron cause is as deadly as anything his masters can deliver. His hypnotic capabilities regularly place human beings under his command. Before Major Reeves' watery demise in 'Renegade Rocket', Captain Black observes the Major from a nearby costal vantage point, fixing him with a deathly glare before Reeves succumbs to his queasiness and falls into the sea. Similarly in 'Big Ben Strikes Again', as Macey's truck slithers past Black, he gives the truck a solitary stare before the truck convulses into a life of its own. Whilst much is hinted at and rarely explained when it comes to the Mysterons, the underlying tactic of Captain Black's ability to control machinery and human beings from afar is another side of the Mysterons' horror that's thrilling to watch unfold.

Additionally, Captain Black's actions result in him having a far more successful hit rate than his masters. Where Spectrum are able to foil Mysteron plots for most of the series, Captain Black never fails to target an unsuspecting victim and violently transform them into a Mysteron operative. On that level alone, he is easily the Mysterons' greatest asset in the fight against Spectrum, emphasising his reflective relationship with Captain Scarlet. David Upshal suggests that Captain Black's role within the series is made 'all the more convincing by the fact that Black succeeds in his mission as often as he is foiled.'[58] It's a summary of Black's character that does him a disservice when you consider that it's the Mysterons that succumb to Spectrum's heroic might, not Captain Black. Where other Mysteron agents are dealt with in deadly fashion, Black always manages to slip back into the shadows.

Captain Black's presence is often the highlight of any given episode, because it means that the latest prolonged method of Mysteron-induced death was about to commence. His appearance signals that the episode was about to be shot forward into bloodthirsty levels of action. What manner of death might befall our victim this week? Will they get run over? Buried under a mountain of snow? Encased in a fiery explosion? Captain Black is semi-regularly responsible for these action set pieces being put in motion. Mirroring Captain Scarlet still further, where Scarlet's indestructible prowess allows the weekly narrative to conclude in a satisfactorily explosive manner, Black's destructive means ignites that narrative in the first place.

Black Heart

For all of this menacing wielding of power, it's executed with a mostly dead silence on Black's part. If any character encapsulates how rigid *Captain Scarlet* could be in its characterisation, then it's Captain Black. He speaks only when it's demanded of him, rarely matching the jovial interactions of Captain Scarlet, Captain Blue and Lieutenant Green. Black's muteness is an audible confirmation of his tragic situation. He has nothing to say because he has no personality to speak of. It's been taken by the Mysterons. Captain Black's lack of any discernible character makes it difficult to gauge any sense of personality, but it helps to reinforce his stance as a stoic monolith of death. Captain Black treads a fine line between being a silent threat and a lost soul. When separated from his Mysteron masters, he's utterly unable to communicate with the human beings that he's forced to share a world with, displaying only slight body movements when conversation is thrust upon him.

---

[58] Upshal, D. (1988) 'Captain Black: A Subject for Sympathy?' *Supermarionation Is Go* (ed Nightingale, D). No. 20, pp. 22-23.

Intriguingly, 'Manhunt' shows us just how lost Captain Black becomes without the watchful eyes of the Mysterons guiding him. One of several episodes from *Captain Scarlet*'s first half devoted to a single character, Captain Black's episode features a curious absence of the Mysterons themselves. Black's attempted invasion of the Culver Atomic Centre goes awry when he exposes himself to radiation and allows himself be traced by Geiger counters. A furious cat-and-mouse game ensues as Spectrum attempt to track him down. It's a rare insight into how vulnerable Captain Black could be and that he was capable of making mistakes, just as his masters are prone to doing.

This culminates in his capturing of Symphony Angel within the atomic centre itself. Rather than allow a quick and painless death for his former Spectrum colleague, Black subjects Symphony to a style of death that's characteristic of the Mysterons by exposing her to extreme radiation. Without warning, he ceases his execution before it can be realised. Without his Mysteron masters hanging over his conscious, Black's concern for Symphony allows her a chance to escape. Where this scrap of sympathy originates from is left unspoken, but it remains a fascinating curio of what could be Conrad Turner's original human feelings and emotions attempting to pierce through Captain Black's mental programming.

Spectrum Spin-offs

Throughout the surrounding spin-off media for *Captain Scarlet*, a different kind of Captain Black emerges, one with a much firmer grip on his own identity. *Captain Scarlet*'s adventures in *TV21*, the *Spectrum File* novels, the annuals and the audio stories fashion a far more ruthless approach to Captain Black's character. Throughout these secondary stories, Black fills the same role as he did in the series itself as the Mysterons' main agent on Earth, but what differs between the two is the execution.

In this supplementary material, Captain Black here is no longer a wayward soul who lacks any sense of character. Instead, he's a gleefully sadistic individual who's fully capable of functioning under his own control as much as the orders of the Mysterons. Unwilling to conceal himself in the shadows as he does in the TV series, he's more than happy to run the risk of being spotted in broad daylight by Spectrum or even members of the public. This brazen attitude spreads to his Mysteron missions, as the *Spectrum Files* in particular show his tendency to proactively engage with human beings, either to use them as pawns to further his Mysteron goals or relinquishing them to the powers of the Mysterons themselves for them to become agents. During the events of the first *Spectrum File*, Captain Scarlet travels to San Jose on the hunt for scientist Doctor Standahl. There, he discovers Captain Black already nestled within the town, manipulating the town's mayor to suit the Mysteron cause, even going so far as to catch Black having a meal with the Mayor, embedding a calm terror into the situation.

Throughout every form of spin-off media that accompanies *Captain Scarlet*, a rivalry exists between Scarlet and Black. In the comics and novels in particular, Captain Black is prone to dispensing with the Mysteron plan at hand in order to pursue Captain Scarlet. It's as if a blinding sense of rage towards Scarlet overwhelms Black, feeling the need to violently engage with Scarlet whenever the opportunity arises. It's particularly jarring to hear Black speak so extrovertly in the audio adventure *Captain Scarlet versus Captain Black*. Black's more regular appearances throughout the spin-off media gains welcome context through this aggressive relationship he has with Scarlet, though he remains lurking unseen when his master command him to.

Whilst the spin-off media advanced Captain Black as a character, he can't entirely escape his tragic trappings. Despite a potted biography of Captain Black proving elusive alongside the other members of Spectrum in the 1967 *Captain Scarlet* annual, its follow-up a year later did much to rectify that absence. A two-page spread detailing Captain Black's pre-Spectrum life is found in the 1968 *Captain Scarlet* annual, revealing him to have been orphaned when he was seven months old, his parents killed in The Great Atomic War, an event found throughout various TV21-related literature. His life was defined by academic and military achievements, and whilst maintaining an aloof persona, he chose not to forge any close relationships with those around him. It's an emotionally distant precursor to his eventual succumbing to the Mysterons.

Captain Black's grotesque facial features have become one of the most visually recognisable elements of *Captain Scarlet* itself, ensuring that he's a much remembered player within the war of nerves. Considering our explorations in this chapter of *Captain Scarlet*'s lopsided approach to character development, this is a welcome achievement that's topped with a pinch of black comedy – the character who speaks the least throughout the series is one of the most fondly remembered characters themselves. Captain Black's stalking presence in the series gives the otherwise invisible Mysterons a physical pinpoint within their unseen vengeance against the Earth. It's impossible to take your eyes off-screen once he emerges from the darkness. His unnatural state borders on disgusting surrealism – a corpse removed from its coffin, stripped of its natural state and not allowed to rest in peace. Ironically, it's this undead appearance that ensured Captain Black enjoyed a long lifespan in the series. Puppeteer Christine Glanville recalls how the character was meant to meet his end during the first episode, but it was only after she'd 'painted him up to look gaunt and pallid, Gerry took one look and decided to keep him on as a regular.'[59] It would have been a desperate misfire to have restricted Captain Black to a singular appearance so early on in the series, as he stands as a formidable, evocatively anti-human addition to the series.

---

[59] Drake, C. Bassett, G. (1993) "The Finger is on the Trigger" *Captain Scarlet and the Mysterons*. p. 14. Boxtree. 1st edition.

'BEYOND THE COMPREHENSION OF MAN': THE MYSTERONS

'The Mysterons ... Sworn enemies of Earth ...' One of *Captain Scarlet and the Mysterons*' most recognisable utterances is tailor-made to stab total fear into its audience. Always heard but rarely seen, the Mysterons' omniscient, omnipotent, marauding nature enables a tenacious attitude to froth at their mechanised mouths. Their hatred for humanity is easily provoked and violently prolonged. The Mysterons' invisible appearance and indefinitely defined powers lends themselves to, at times, painfully convenient story-telling as their capabilities warp from one extreme to the other, depending on whatever the weekly story demanded of them to reach a satisfactory conclusion. However, over the course of *Captain Scarlet*, a richly structured picture is painted of them with enough mystery sustained to entice the imaginations. Indeed, there's few villains in Gerry and Sylvia's filmography that elicit such imaginative speculation as the Mysterons.

Architecture and Symbolism

In comparison to the villains we've previously seen in Anderson shows up until *Captain Scarlet*, the Mysterons present frightening intrigue from their first appearance. Enemies such as Titan or the Hood are presented as threatening characters right from their introductions. We're shown to be fearful of them, and their respective conquests for undersea domination and the secrets of advanced rescue technology galvanise their frightening appearance by being coupled with an immediate incentive for their villainous goals. By comparisons, the Mysterons aren't presented as being instantly hostile, friendly even, and yet provoke a tense sensation of something beyond our comprehension.

Their debut appearance in 'The Mysterons' remains one of the most evocatively constructed pieces of film-making from any of Gerry and Sylvia's works. Following on swiftly from the imposing, noir-horror tones of *Captain Scarlet*'s jarringly brief title sequence, we change in locations from some godforsaken metropolitan alleyway to the surface of Mars, following Captain Black's Martian Exploration Vehicle in its mission to uncover the origin of strange radio signals emanating from the planet. Pausing at a steeply inclined ridge, Lieutenant Dean prizes Captain Black's gaze away from his control panel to witness something no human has ever before experienced – the Mysterons' Mars complex.

Where Titanica's ramshackle makeshift stylings and the Hood's majestic temple blend into their respective environments, the unnatural, sickly, neon-coated glow of the Mysteron complex radiates like an atomic explosion amidst the barren Mars landscape. This wide-shot of the Mysteron complex is the closest we come to ever seeing the Mysterons' city in full, a selection of silent buildings interconnected, as if an exposed mechanical body. Zooming in closer, individual buildings throb as if they're alive, their distorted structures sprouting from the planet's surface like artificial woodland, all accompanied by Barry Gray's stupendous, riveting electronic soundtrack that violently tumbles over the scene, as if tripping over itself.

We proceed to melt into the innards of the city itself. It's never clarified which part of the city this Mysterons hub is housed in and perhaps that's the point. The mystery is maintained. Within the city, we bear witness to an interior structure not meant for human eyes to experience. Electronic sounds pulsate as indecipherable shapes and colour appear filtered through the same glow as before, intricate details hidden from our view. Within the centre stands a swollen, circular orb, beating like a cyberpunk heart, curved tubes spiralling out of it like arteries. The first instance of the Mysterons' speaking does well to continue that purveying sense of mystery, as their collective voice radiates from nowhere in particular and yet fills the structure. The low-slung panning of the camera, one unhurried, continuous shot from within, creeps around these structures, enforcing the sensation that this is a place no human should be near. Both the exterior and interior of the Mysterons' complex are meticulously-produced sets and a masterclass of production design, oddly enlivened by its genesis of converted household objects, as model maker Alan Shubrook recalls: 'There was much more of a futuristic approach to the complexes that were constructed for the Mysteron sets on Mars. I can remember that we used a range of 1960s' lamps and cooking bowls from Woolworths to build one set on Mars. The trouble was, looking back at it now, it just looks like a collection of Woolworths' lamps and bowls!'[60]

The emphasis on the look of the Mysteron complex throughout this sequence is a testament to the tenacity of Century 21's visual effects and surprisingly how being given free reign worked in their favour, as Mike Trim recalls: 'Everything started from the script and usually involved ignoring any descriptions therein. What would shape the final design was what the craft or vehicle had to do and what mission was it undertaking. Did it need tracks or wheels, did it fly or go underwater? How many crew

---

[60] Interview with author.

were involved, did it have weapons or equipment that needed to pop out of hatch? All these sort of things would give a basic idea from which one had to evolve a design that would meet all the requirements and, hopefully, be a pleasing, exciting look. Some thought needed to be given also to exactly how things were to be built and sometimes time constraints and ease of manufacture would be reflected in the final concept.'[61]

What these scenes tell us then is that so much of the Mysterons' initial personality is conjured through visual identity. The terror of the Mysterons is presented as initially being found in their appearance. Ironically, the one structural feature of the Mysterons' complex that doesn't share in the city's neon-baked vibrancy is the retrometabolism rays that stretch into life from a nearby cliff immediately following Captain Black's orders to destroy the complex. Their initial greetings of companionship misinterpreted, the Mysterons are now justifiable outraged, fully embracing their roles as the series' antagonists, their colossal voice now a weapon of fear rather than a tool of friendship.

Even if the Mysterons may be sterile in their development over the course of *Captain Scarlet*, they clearly show an evolution away from what had defined the Supermarionation villain prior to them. Even someone as menacing as the Hood was subjected to comical downfalls whenever he fails to acquire the secrets of International Rescue. The Mysterons aren't subjected to such comedy. An integral component of *Captain Scarlet*'s grim soul, the Mysterons are a serious enemy for a serious world.

Invisible Genesis

The downfall of such visual emphasis placed on the Mysterons so early on in the series comes with a surface level approach to development. We come to know so little of the Mysterons' backstory over the course of the series that we're forced to scour the spin-off media for details. The 1967 *Captain Scarlet* annual comes with a legitimate and substantial chapter detailing some proposed background detail of the Mysterons. Documented by Spectrum Intelligence, the two-page 'We The Mysterons' bursts with speculation, deductive reasoning and much teasing. Out of thin air, Spectrum Intelligence have been able to pull together disparate details that reveals more about the Mysterons than the television series ever did whilst retaining that welcoming sense of mystery that's hardwired into the Mysterons persona.

The report suggests that the Mysterons we come to fear over the course of the series are, in fact, not the real Mysterons at all. They are instead their computerised remains or counterparts, left to keep the complex in a secure

---

[61] Interview with author.

state whilst the real Mysterons evacuated Mars for reasons unknown. 'Where the Mysterons originally came from no-one will ever know,' the report summarises. The report proposes the idea that the real Mysterons settled on Mars after much travelling across the stars in search of a new home after leaving their original home world. The report goes onto expand on the Mysterons' computerised physicality, which is only ever visually hinted at within the television series. Supposedly, the Mysterons were a race of intelligent creatures whose entire existence was built around highly advanced computers, so much so that these machines had mastered the ability to reanimate destroyed matter.

More concrete links to how the Mysterons are presented in the television series itself arise when the report details of how the Mysterons first settled on Mars; 'Here, we think, they set up a thriving community, self-sufficient amidst its huge computer complex with the computer brains planning, constructing and running their city for them.' This is evidenced by what we see in 'Lunarville 7' and 'Crater 101', in which Captain Scarlet, Captain Blue and Lieutenant Green witness the construction of a Mysteron complex on the far side of the moon. The building of the complex, carried out by unmanned vehicles, is a subtle link to this report, even more subtle given that 'Crater 101' wouldn't be broadcast until early 1968 when the annual was published in time to coincide with the series' September 1967 launch.

'We The Mysterons' aids in enhancing the ethereal identity of the Mysterons. Much is speculated but little is confirmed. It's striking how *Captain Scarlet*'s spin-off media regularly goes to great lengths in adding additional depth to areas where the television series leaves shallow, including character biographies, vehicle cross-sections and a detailed history on the formation of Spectrum, and yet the secrets of the Mysterons remain hidden in the darkness. Still, 'We The Mysterons' provides some context at the Mysterons' collective consciousness, speaking as if a shared community collated into one being through computer-controlled brain, heart and soul. We can't be certain where the original incarnation of the Mysterons begins and where their computerised form ends.

Technological Violence

Through the Mysterons' mechanical embodiment come links to impossibly high intelligence. The Mysterons' previously held knowledge of mankind implies that they had kept a watchful eye over the Earth long before Captain Black arrived. With that intelligence comes a perverse approach to the Mysterons' weaponry – they target the Earth and its population by using the Earth's population itself as their armoury. The Mysterons regularly target figures of authoritative power across politics and technology, opting to assassinate these significant figures one by one in a prolonged effort to wear down people of importance to humanity. It's as if script editor Tony Barwick, alongside Gerry and Sylvia, were keen to twist the technological utopia tropes of their past works on their head by having aliens desire to kill those responsible for that utopia's construction.

Beyond these figures, the Mysterons also remain keen to cripple the world of 2068 by subverting its technological advances. Humanity is often at the mercy of the Mysterons because of man-made technology falling into the Mysterons' unseen hands. 'Renegade Rocket' and 'Point 783' for instance both feature advanced examples of military vehicles not necessarily destroyed and reconstructed by the Mysterons, but rather hijacked against their human masters by Mysteron agents. Acquiring machinery in this way without having to pursue the traditional Mysteron route of destruction and replication reads like the Mysterons extending their computer-defined reach to Earth's own technological marvels. Humanity's militantly technological decadence is a prime target for Mysteron impact. The possibility of Mysteronised Frost Line maintenance man Eddie driving his truck full of Liquid Oxygen into Frost Line Outer Space Defence System's command centre in 'Avalanche' feels like the Mysterons are regularly punishing humanity for its reliance on weaponised defence. Taking this a step further, the three human casualties seen in 'Shadow of Fear' when the Mysterons destroy the K14 Observatory are overshadowed by the enormity of the observatory's size crushing down on them. This can be taken to its most logical extreme by the Mysterons' ultimate intended victim is the world's most advanced security organisation.

The violence employed by the Mysterons, whether focused on technological ensnaring or the slaughter of individual humans, bolts a kinetic propulsion into *Captain Scarlet*, something noted by the series' writers. 'There was plenty of violence and menace in the Mysterons' lust for power to crush Spectrum – and from a writer's perspective, it was rousing, exciting and kept the juices flowing!' recalls Shane Rimmer[62]. Leo Eaton holds a similar view: 'Maybe they (the Mysterons) were going to sink a plane, blow up Cloudbase, kill the World President. That's the kind of cool thing, it could be whatever the writer's wanted to imagine.'[63] It's in instances like these that the aforementioned uncertainty in the Mysterons' capabilities works in the series' favour.

These calculated moves on the Mysterons' part come across as a failsafe switch being triggered, pre-programmed orders stirring into destructive life, and another shard of the Mysterons' identity having a light shone upon it. The end result is an insatiable appetite for global destruction, something that grounds *Captain Scarlet* into its core genre fusion of action/adventure-styled

---

[62] Interview with author.
[63] Interview with author.

science fiction. Susan Sontag (2017) notes how science fiction films are 'not about science, but about disaster.'[64] Whilst *Captain Scarlet* inhabits a different medium to film, it's a transferable summary and somehow even more applicable when Sontag explains how the spectacle of disaster seen 'in the wide-screen of Technicolour films ... does raise the matter to another level.' The Technicolour blockbusters of the era were the very sorts of entertainment that Gerry and Sylvia were hoping to emulate with their Supermarionation empire. The devastating quality of the Mysterons does much to argue that the Anderson not only matched those films, but surpassed them.

Psycho Killers

Hints of the Mysterons perhaps being more humane dripped through, episode by episode. The Mysterons' computerised nature remains prevalent throughout the series, but several episodes show that their fascination with subverting technology was keen to take a step back in favour of making things far more personal. 'The Heart of New York' sees the ambitions of a trio crooks to rob the Second National Bank in New York backfire when they become entangled in the Mysterons' plan to destroy the so-called heart of New York. This transpires to be the bank itself, but the episode lands with increased poignancy when Captain Black ensures that the three criminals are trapped inside the bank prior to its destruction, with Black declaring that their greed is their own downfall. The destruction of the bank becomes a symbol of the Mysterons attacking humanity's material lust.

'Traitor' is another example of the Mysterons shifting their goals to something more internal than external, its distinction aided by the Mysterons themselves taking an unexpected backseat during the episode. A malfunction within the hovercraft at Spectrum's Koala Base training centre in Australia is exploited by the Mysterons, who warn of a traitor within Spectrum is causing the hovercrafts to go haywire. The Mysterons spend much of the episode away from the action, content to stoke the fires of speculation as fears of a genuine traitor become rampant. The themes of 'Traitor' enable it to feel like a sequel of sorts to 'White as Snow', in which the Mysterons' attempts on Colonel White's life causes severe friction between the Colonel and Captain Scarlet, another example of how the Mysterons fuelled paranoia within Spectrum's own ranks.

The paranoid encroaches itself further by the apparent lack of acknowledgement within the world of *Captain Scarlet* that people are actually aware of the Mysterons. Just how well known the war of nerves is

---

[64] Sontag, S. (2017) 'The imagination of disaster' *Science Fiction Criticism* (ed Latham, B). p. 191. Bloomsbury Academic. 1st edition.

to anyone outside of Spectrum isn't entirely clarified. The Supreme Commander of Earth Forces from 'Point 783', General Ward from 'Avalanche' and the American President from 'The Launching' respond to the threats the Mysterons place upon themselves with a passive ignorance. Doctor Brodski from the audio drama 'Captain Scarlet is Indestructible' cements this ignorance by proclaiming she doesn't even believe they exist. The comic book prequel 'The Mark of the Mysterons' adopts this attitude further, pitting reporter John Marsh not just against the invading Mysterons, but against an ignorant world who refuse to accept Marsh's claims that the Earth is under threat from them.

Powers We Cannot Hope To Understand

The understandable frustration surrounding the Mysterons is one that can be applied to all of *Captain Scarlet*'s characters – we come to know so little of them. However, in the context of the Mysterons, such a detachment adds to their allure. Their inability to progress as characters is effective in lending them a continual menacing aura. The Mysterons stand as a constant, unshakable presence of murderous evil for *Captain Scarlet*. This often manifests itself into Mysteron agents, who are shorn of the less villainous aspect of the Mysterons we briefly see in 'The Mysterons' and are born, live and die with murder in their eyes.

The Mysterons' most effective contribution to *Captain Scarlet* is their violent upsetting of the bourgeois aspects of *Captain Scarlet*'s world, a world that's socially unified by technological advancement to better societal standards. Visually, there's nothing out of place in *Captain Scarlet*, something that can be attributed to the focused quality of the series' design. 'Although the show may appear cohesive, there were never any decisions taken that set to style for the series,' Mike Trim recalls. 'Both Derek's and my own default design style was a "near future" one that built upon and stretched the technology of the day, and they sat quite happily alongside one another.'[65] Alan Shubrook's perspective on working on *Captain Scarlet* gives credence to the model department's focus due to the Mysterons' savagery. 'Most models had to be built to be blown to pieces at one point or another during filming each episode. The reconstruction process of the Mysterons meant that a plane, car or truck would be destroyed and replicated at the start of each show. Whenever there was an explosive scene, which was practically every day, it inevitably meant that a large amount of the set dressing, such as trees and bushes, fences and buildings were all also destroyed.'[66]

The Mysterons' unprejudiced assaults on people, machinery, buildings

---

[65] Interview with author.
[66] Interview with author.

and more taps into how Rebecca Feasey (2008) describes *Captain Scarlet* as 'exploit(ing) the fears of 1960s America by presenting civil disobedience and the potentially negative impact of new technologies.'[67] The Mysterons can therefore be seen as the ultimate in new technologies, their ability to recreate life itself is summarised often throughout the series as 'powers we cannot hope to understand.' The ultimate appeal of the Mysterons lies in our inability to comprehend them.

---

[67] Feasey, R. (2008) 'Science fiction and fantasy television: challenging dominant gender roles'. *Masculinity and Popular Television*. p. 57. Edinburgh University Press. 1st edition.

MARINEVILLE CONTROL TOWER: 21ST CENTURY STRUCTURES

STAND BY FOR STARDUST: *STINGRAY'S* BLOSSOMING FROM *FIREBALL XL5*

Placing the original Supermarionation era under a cynical gaze, one can argue that Gerry and Sylvia Anderson and their team of puppeteers were at least partially responsible for parents' wallet-fearing nightmares about continually buying merchandise from TV franchises in where each entry was, in their eyes, indistinguishable from the other. On close inspection however, each of the eight Supermarionation television series from 1960's *Four Feather Falls* to 1969's *The Secret Service* clearly boasts their own distinctive characteristics. *Captain Scarlet and the Mysterons* is not the same series as *The Secret Service*. *Thunderbirds* flies miles beyond *Supercar*. Yet two contenders for Supermarionation series that really do blur into each other are 1963's *Fireball XL5* and 1964's *Stingray*.

They share the exact same premise, an aspect of both series that's been noted elsewhere. 'The series, in essence, only differs slightly from its predecessor,' Stephen La Riviere comments, 'mainly transposing the space setting to an underwater one.'[68] Both *Stingray* and *Fireball XL5* complement each other's bare essentials: A World Security Patrol outfit is in place to keep the peace, spearheaded by a starring craft that's piloted by a handsome daredevil of a hero, protecting Earth from alien attackers, aided by a love interest and led by a grouchy commanding officer. However, taking this comparison a stage further, *Stingray* is far more than simply *Fireball XL5* Mk II. *Stingray* not only cherry-picks at *Fireball XL5*'s concepts and characters, it vastly improves upon them, evolving the general premise into something more extravagant, more sophisticated and more watchable than *Fireball XL5*.

The Fastest Characters Alive

The similarities between the two series are firstly apparent in the immediate caricatured charm of their characters, and therefore it's most evident how *Stingray* betters *Fireball XL5* here, and further evidence of how Sylvia Anderson was making her presence felt in Century 21's output in her role as

---

[68] La Riviere, S. (2009) 'Stand By for Action' *Filmed in Supermarionation: A History of the Future*. Hermes Press. p. 96. 1st edition.

supervisor of characters and dialogue. Given the tendency to delegate Sylvia's role in hers and Gerry's work to a footnote, it's always worth remembering that she was responsible for injecting the human presence into his hardware. *Fireball XL5*'s cast are transplanted into *Stingray* in varying combinations – sometimes the same, sometimes different, but always with more care taken in crafting colourful personalities to match the equally engaging sculpted visuals of their faces. Commander Zero and Lieutenant Ninety very much become Commander Shore and Lieutenant Fisher, not just in their military ranks but also in their tempestuous relationship of commander versus subordinate. Doctor Venus becomes split into two distinct types when the archetypal female co-lead evolved in *Stingray*; the otherworldly lure of Marina and the tomboyish, down-to-earth vibes of Atlanta. The technologically-inclined male character in Professor Matthew Matic, with his quirky persona and technological knowhow, manifests into Phones. Colonel Steve Zodiac has the most distinct transformation, as the handsome, action-ready heroic lead is easily found in Troy Tempest, yet where Steve maintained an uncomplicated coolness about him, Troy is a much more tempestuous personality.

The changing dynamics of the two series' casts, whilst featuring the same stereotypes of characters themselves, elevates *Stingray* to creative heights *Fireball XL5* otherwise couldn't achieve. Both Commander Shore and Commander Zero have family members shown within the series, often becoming embroiled in adventures. Where Zero's wife and son mostly stay away from the action and provide some comedy relief, *Stingray*'s savvy character development meant that Shore's daughter, Atlanta, was firmly part of the core Marineville set-up and therefore more involved in the action. Emotional connections to Troy and Shore give her a welcome if melodramatic depth, emphasised whenever she becomes in danger, triggering Shore's gruff exterior to fall away and reveal a more sensitive, desperate side, something rarely seen in Zero, who spent much of his time berating Lieutenant Ninety. The icing on the cake is the broken down status of Shore and Atlanta's family set-up. With no mother figure present, all they have is each other, unlike *Fireball XL5*'s traditional nuclear family with the Zeros. Whilst no direct references are made to Atlanta's mother during the course of the series, Shore lets slip in 'Invisible Enemy' that Atlanta is all he has in terms of family.

Shore and Fisher's relationship is carried over from the bickering styles of Zero and Ninety, yet Fisher is far more meek and reserved than the comparatively exuberant Ninety, and doesn't endure a horrific dream episode in which he imagines he single-handedly destroys Marineville. Whilst Fisher may be the least developed and least interesting character in *Stingray*, lacking the spontaneous energy of Ninety, he remains a capable and willing addition to the WASP crew, evidenced best in 'Rescue From the

Skies', in which Fisher trains to become a genuine WASP submarine aquanaut, entrusted with piloting *Stingray* as part of his training. Even when *Stingray* falls victim to an attack from Agent X20, Fisher doesn't succumb to the hysteria that Ninety would surely crumble into. He remains calm and collected throughout, but also remains the punching bag of Shore's cigar-chomping barks. Phones, meanwhile, isn't as scientifically minded as Professor Matic, yet he fills the role of being the secondary main male lead in *Stingray* comfortably and exhibits a more natural friendship with Troy than Steve and Mat. His Southern drawl and occasional dim-wittedness made him a well-rounded foil to Troy's otherwise firm captaining of *Stingray*.

Alongside Phones, Troy's prickly personality, prone to outbursts of jealously, anger, humour and more enables him to be the greatest example of how *Stingray* evolves the stock personalities seen in *Fireball XL5*. Zodiac's unshakeable coolness clashes with the eccentric personalities around him – the stereotypically ditzy female, the quirky man of science, the thuggish commander, the bumbling lieutenant, the talking robot and the pet alien. What makes the *Stingray* crew more believable as a family unit than, say, the Tracy family, is the fact that no one pretends to be as perfect as Zodiac, especially Troy. The fully formed nature of *Stingray*'s cast comes from their strengths and weaknesses alike, often interacting with each other to both reveal and solve those weaknesses.

The transition from Venus to the joint females of Atlanta and Marina is another muscular example of how *Stingray* betters the characters of *Fireball XL5*. Atlanta is a far more determined and confident female character than Venus. All too often, Venus is the butt of sexist gags from her World Space Patrol colleagues. Atlanta rebukes any prejudice thrown against her, aided by her being one of the few people in Marineville able to challenge Commander Shore's strict, militant leadership, but also given substance by Lois Maxwell's commanding performance, a far cry from Sylvia Anderson's dozy-sounding Venus. However, the sexualisation of the women don't entirely evaporate with *Stingray*. Marina is presented as being utterly alluring, seen almost entirely through the male gaze, a luring siren to the terranean men of *Stingray*. Her mute nature gives way to the occasional and utterly eye-rolling comments from a variety of jocular men who suggest that a silent woman is the best kind of woman. Being the alien of the *Stingray* crew, Marina's underwater biological make-up often gets trotted out as an inexact, wave-away explanation for how she occasionally rescues Troy and Phones from various natural or unnatural phenomena under the oceans. It's not the most sophisticated way of inclusion, but it's gratifying to see Marina's usefulness played straight as the series progresses.

Stingray's most obvious approach to a more careful handling of its characters compared to past Supermarionation productions arguably comes in the introduction and rapid exclusion of Oink, the friendly seal who follows in the comically destructive footsteps of *Fireball XL5*'s Zoonie the Lazoon and *Supercar*'s Chip the monkey. Initially introduced as the standard animal pet character for this particular series in the episode 'Sea of Oil', Oink appears for only a handful of episodes before being quietly written out, their disappearance going without explanation or protest. Perhaps it was hurriedly deduced that the animal sidekick had run their course.

The addition of underwater dictator Titan and his primary lackey Agent X20 as regular villains adds another layer of character growth for the series. *Fireball XL5* had its own semi-regular villains in the form of the space spies, Boris and Griselda, but they would suffer a similar fate to Oink. Introduced early on in *Fireball XL5*, they would gradually be forgotten about as more one-off villains populated *Fireball XL5*'s episodes. Indeed, the one-off villains come off as entirely disposable, almost none of them appearing from one episode to the next, the exception being the villainous Subterraneans, who make several attempts to destroy Steve Zodiac and XL5. Titan and X20's more continual presence gives *Stingray* a lingering danger, predating how *Thunderbirds* and *Captain Scarlet* made use of the Hood and Captain Black only in sparse amounts, rather than overexpose them in every episode. These performances are strengthened through new additions to the cast. Whilst Sylvia and David Graham would appear in minor guest roles throughout *Stingray*, the extraordinarily diverse vocal talents of Ray Barrett (Shore, Fisher, Titan) and the enjoyably distinctive Robert Easton (Phones, X20) livened things up. Titan and X20 are shown to be menacing and slapstick in equal measure, their danger counteracted by their humorous back-and-forths whenever their latest plan to capture *Stingray* goes awry.

The Worlds' Security Patrols

The manners in which each of these two universes are erected results in another firm suggestion that, despite the similarities, *Stingray* was able to pull concepts established in *Fireball XL5* towards heightened and more imaginative levels. The endless cosmos of *Fireball XL5* and the sprawling oceans of *Stingray* are both littered with alien civilisations, some antagonistic, some friendly, some monstrous and some passive. A key differing tactic employed by both shows is that a great deal of alien cultures are known to the World Space Patrol and come under a vaguely defined galactic alliance of shared planets and civilisations. *Stingray* however injects a credible punch of mystery into its relationship between Terraneans and sea creatures. Much of the underwater cultures that populate *Stingray* exist in a detached manner to humanity – they exist beyond the reach or knowledge of the World Aquanaut Security Patrol, often becoming known in explosive fashion whenever the alien race of the week attempts to overthrow *Stingray* and Captain Troy Tempest.

In a clever thematic move, this sense of mystery is galvanised by the diversity in the motives of *Stingray*'s villains. Whilst *Stingray* shares a varied approach to how friendly or unfriendly alien races may be, sometimes starting off as enemies but finishing the episode as allies, *Fireball XL5* relies all too often on its aliens being menacing groups, all out to overthrow either the World Security Patrol or other planets, a firm reflection of *Fireball XL5*'s focus on appealing to a youthful audience who were on the lookout for some space-age action, regardless of any deeper ideas at work. Despite working to that same demographic, *Stingray* paints a far more complex picture of the underwater landscapes that Marineville patrols. As we previously explored in Marine Morales, not only are races portrayed in positive and negative stances, but some races enter the episode in question as antagonistic before becoming friendlier (such as in the episodes 'Sea of Oil' and 'The Ghost of the Sea'), and vice versa ('Deep Heat'). This isn't to say that *Fireball XL5* was completely bereft of an enlightened approach to giving its alien creatures morally complex personas. We're led to believe that the gnome-like creatures seen in 'Ghosts of Space' are the enemies, but the real reason blossoms into a simple misunderstanding between various parties. 'The Last of the Zanadus' paints a tragic image of the final survivor of a doomed alien race, destroyed by their own insanity. By comparison, *Stingray* is more confident, better equipped and more far-reaching in delivering these diverse creatures, resulting in the distinct impression that two entirely different yet focused worlds exist, one above the ocean's surface and one beneath it.

An emphasis on the mechanics of the security organisation to which the star vehicle and its intrepid pilot work under also ensures that *Stingray* is a more considered affair than *Fireball XL5*. Both craft are the star vehicles of their outfit respectively, but the chain of command goes higher. In *Fireball XL5*, 'Prisoner on the Lost Planet' makes reference to the United Planets Organisation, an outfit whose meaning and purpose is never quite fully explained, but somewhat confirmed that it's the official body networking Earth with other inhabited planets throughout the cosmos. The *Stingray* equivalent of this is the World Security Patrol. Far more regularly seen than the UPO, the World Security Patrol is positioned as a backdrop of *Stingray* to contextualise the existence of Marineville and the World Aquanaut Security Patrol, creating a lived-in atmosphere for *Stingray*'s world. No higher outfit is ever mentioned for the World Space Patrol.

The increased presence of a commanding power occasionally delivering orders to Marineville helps to make *Stingray*'s world feel more fleshed out and fully formed. On the antagonistic side, there are loose implications that a hierarchy amongst the villainous underwater races also exist. Whilst many civilisations appear to exist independent of each other, scatterings of references to various conquests Titan has made help to ensure his dictator characteristics are intact. A more direct hint at a collective of underwater communities comes in 'The Ghost Ship', when the anonymous, silver-bearded villain, with skin glistening like fish scales, lays a trap to capture Troy Tempest by hijacking Commander Shore and Phones. When Troy inevitably attempts to rescue his colleagues (against Shore's orders), the creature declares his motives for wanting Troy, to place him under arrest for crimes against the advancement of the underwater peoples. Numerous alien groups are named by race in *Stingray*, making this key reference to 'peoples' come across as a collective attempt to target Tempest, who is seen as an oppressor of underwater civilisations. *Fireball XL5* was averse to dropping such hints and nudges within its own villainous factions, although Steve Zodiac was a primary target for more than few villainous space invaders. Such droplets of information spoken from *Stingray*'s characters can't help but advance the series out of the restrictive narrative landscapes *Fireball XL5* was working within.

A Wonderland Of Production Values

What would have passed audiences by in 1964 but is readily apparent by today's standards is the juxtaposition between the monochromatic *Fireball XL5* and the Videcolor *Stingray*. Whilst both series were originally broadcast in black and white, *Stingray* holds the proud distinction of being the first British television series to be filmed in colour, which is naturally how we view it today. *Stingray* therefore holds an inevitable advantage over *Fireball XL5* of being a far more rewarding and stimulating watch when viewed back by more contemporary generations, as *Fireball XL5* remains trapped in its monochrome wonderland.

Aiding these heightened electrifying visuals, which ironically wouldn't be truly enjoyed until the series' release on home video, *Stingray* evolves the production values of AP Films thanks to Lew Grade's purchasing of the company and bringing the Supermarionation crew under his commercial wing. Having financially backed *Supercar* and *Fireball XL5* and impressed with their continuing success, Grade's sinking of his financial teeth into Gerry, Sylvia, Reg Hill and John Read's puppet empire enabled the crew to up sticks from their then-current premises in Slough to newly built industrial complex based on Stirling Road. This was a time of huge advancement for Gerry and his team, no longer forced to produce under low budgets and the creative glare of Roberta Leigh. Grade catered to their every production whim, his faith in the company absolute. Nowhere is the advanced production techniques now available to AP Films more apparent than how the vibrantly unusual visuals of *Stingray* blast off to more enthralling heights than the worlds *Fireball XL5* attempted to conjure up. Interior and exterior locations, from Marineville to Titanica, burst with eye-catching personality, a playground for art director Bob Bell to unleash his imaginative mind.

The alluring underwater landscapes *Stingray* regularly traverses through are infinitely more mesmerising than the two-dimensional star-speckled black backdrops of *Fireball XL5*. Soaring rock faces and jungle-like plantations create otherworldly atmospheres littered in intricate detail, some of which permanently hidden by the tall water tank placed in-between the model sets and the cameras to give the complete illusion of being underwater, adding a sense of enchanting vagueness. The inside and outside of Marineville is more architecturally complex than that of Space City. Marineville consists of numerous outbuildings, all of which possess the ability to sink below ground in case of an incoming missile attack, to be replaced by a rising bombardment of nuclear missiles on the base's front lawn. A world of imagination is built into Marineville. Indeed, we appear to only ever see half of Marineville in action, given the endless array of missiles and complexes nestled beneath the surface.

The concealed nature of Marineville's defences, with its domestic mod-cons living in relative harmony above atomic firepower, leaves Space City in the dust, even if the revolving tower and the elongated runaway for Fireball craft still easily captured young imaginations, so much so that a Space City playset was produced during *Fireball XL5*'s original broadcast run. *Stingray* fans would have to wait until the early 1990s for their own Marineville playset. Whilst both nerve centres lent themselves effortlessly well to merchandise opportunities, Marineville has the imaginative thrust over the more disparate, undefined Space City, much of which can be boiled down to the enhanced production values and larger budget *Stingray* was privileged to have going for it over *Fireball XL5*.

Anything Did Happen In the Next Half Hour

Considering both of these series on a purely surface level analysis alone, it makes little sense that they should be so different, given the interchangeable nature of their premises and stereotypical characters. But aided by renewed financial backing from Lew Grade, a more focused approach to scriptwriting on the parts of regular contributors Alan Fennell and Dennis Spooner (who had cut their teeth writing on *Fireball XL5* and had therefore surely become more acquainted with writing for puppets as production on *Stingray* commenced), more sophisticated visual effects and the general continuing evolution the AP Films crew were conscious to as each series progressed, the end results speak for themselves. Alongside Fennell and Spooner, regular directors David Elliott and Alan Pattillo, who had served AP Films as far back as *Four Feather Falls* (Elliot had served even longer as an editor on *The Adventures of Twizzle*) continue to shepherd the series' visuals into something magnificently slick. The Supermarionation series remain incredibly well-edited productions.

Stingray goes in every direction *Fireball XL5* either only ever hinted at or simply didn't peruse, either through lack of sophistication from writers and directors or a less expansive budget. It's as if with AP Films' earlier efforts under their belt and having tested the waters in expanding their brand of science-fiction adventure, it made perfect sense to go under those waters and to take advantage of the fascinatingly inscrutable fantasies that thrive throughout the oceans. The evolution would continue with the cinematic scale of *Thunderbirds* and the dark heart of *Captain Scarlet*, further proof that AP Films, and eventually Century 21 (as the company's productions bettered, so too did its name), weren't just aware that each production had to be better than before, they encouraged and insisted upon that working mind-set, too. With its colourful characters, attention to detail in practical effects, exuberant scripts that were keen to balance humour and adventure and subtle yet welcome hints in world-building, *Stingray* proves that AP Films leapt from series to series, rather than simply strolled from one to the other, otherwise allowing themselves to get comfortable in their work. The end result is that whilst *Fireball XL5* is aged, *Stingray* is ageless.

FAILURE TO LAUNCH: WHY THE *THUNDERBIRDS* MOVIES MISUNDERSTOOD THEIR AUDIENCES

It's difficult to imagine a more crushing blow to Century 21 Productions' creative ego than the damp reception the two Supermarionation *Thunderbirds* films received on their respective releases. Premiering in December 1966 and July 1968 respectively, *Thunderbirds Are Go* and *Thunderbird 6*, the former especially, were touted as being the crowning jewels of Century 21 Productions' output at that point. Long-standing comparisons to being the British Walt Disney would now be surely justified as Gerry and Sylvia Anderson and their marionette masters made the leap from domestic TV screens to the glittery world of cinema. This pair of cinematic offerings were clearly stylised as more than mere extensions than the TV show, again *Thunderbirds Are Go* all the more so. With enlarged production values, celebrity voice roles and the first Anderson production to bear the famous Century 21 sting and to actually be titled as a Century 21 production (after discarding the company's former title of AP Films), they were designed as dramatic, confident statements of intent. Instead of launching *Thunderbirds* to the cinematic heights Gerry Anderson clearly wanted them to soar, both films instead opted to crash-land into dismal critical and box office reception.

Various reasons have been speculated over the years as to why neither film took off in popularity, ranging from Gerry himself suggesting that audiences were so accustomed to viewing *Thunderbirds* on TV that it seemed pointless to venture out to an entirely different location to see the series, to a genuine lack of interest on audiences' part in *Thunderbirds* on either the small screen or the big screen by the time *Thunderbird 6* blasted off. 'The only thing we could think was that at that time the audience was not used to seeing a feature film version of a television show,' Gerry reasoned in 2009.[69] What's striking about this perspective of Gerry's is his view that both films were quality productions that he held in high regard. Speaking in 1996, a time of

---

[69] La Riviere, S. (2007) 'Now On the BIG Screen' *Filmed in Supermarionation.* p. 144. Hermes Press. 1st edition.

greatly renewed love for his work, Gerry spoke of the films fondly; 'Today those two *Thunderbirds* feature films are having huge success on television, video and specialised screenings around the world. It seems that some of my shows are like vintage port; they need time to mature.'[70] Reading between the lines, Gerry gives a pleasantly damning encapsulation of *Thunderbirds Are Go* and *Thunderbird 6*; that they're both curios rather than substantial productions. His words on the films' continued 'success' on TV, given his earlier perspective, is bitterly ironic. Those words ring true to this day, as *Thunderbirds Are Go* continues to have sporadic screenings on Film4, presumably when there are gaps that need filling in their Sunday afternoon slot.

At least the films look the part. Indeed, both *Thunderbirds* films are meticulously produced forays into an advanced and truly cinematic form of Supermarionation. But probing the production qualities deeper and examining the handlings of plot and character, whatever the true reason may be for why neither of these films succeeded, they display a misunderstanding of what audiences may have expected and wanted from a large-scale version of *Thunderbirds*.

Neither *Thunderbirds* films emphasise the wrong elements necessarily, but they don't translate enough of the core premise of *Thunderbirds* to the big screen. Reviewing *Thunderbird 6* for Film4, the website suggests that *Thunderbird 6* suffers from similar problems to *Thunderbirds Are Go*, in that 'We don't get to see anywhere near enough of the very cool Thunderbird 2.'[71] Whilst the website's spellings of such words as 'Tracey' and 'Captain Scarlett' suggests the writer in question, uncredited, didn't entirely do their research, it does bring up one significant element missing from these films – International Rescue. They're secondary characters in their own films. It's not unfeasible to determine that the reason neither *Thunderbirds* films succeeded was because they disregard the heroes that audiences had come to love in favour of unnecessary celebrity cameos, illogical story-telling and tedious emphasis on non-Thunderbird vehicles. These two *Thunderbirds* films are about many things. They're about *Zero-X*, Cliff Richard, Rock Snakes, Black Phantom, Lady Penelope and Skyship 1. They're just not about *Thunderbirds*. Audiences going to see the *Thunderbirds* on the big screen would have undoubtedly been disappointed to find that entirely different aspects take priority in these films.

---

[70] Archer, S. Nicholls, S. (1996) 'Chapter 17' *Gerry Anderson: The Authorised Biography*. p. 134. Legend Books. 1st edition.
[71] 'Thunderbird 6' *Film4*. (2010) Available from – https://www.webcitation.org/5qmcC3OCT?url=http://www.film4.com/reviews/1968/thunderbird-6.

'You will be the first men to land on Mars'

Viewed in retrospect, *Thunderbirds Are Go*'s title is downright mocking. The title sequence is the closest we get to seeing all five Thunderbird craft in collective flight. Whilst the technical superiority of the film should be lauded, it's also been written and discussed about extensively in other publications. What's less discussed are the film's lesser qualities, themselves a sure-fire sign of the film's damp reception on its original release. A cinematic edition of one of the most popular TV shows of its time, released during the Christmas market, justifies what *Kine Weekly* described as 'certain money maker' in their enthusiastic review of the film. It must have taken something spectacular then for that to all go up in supersonic smoke. The main problem at work in *Thunderbirds Are Go* is the lack of linear story. No amount of incredible model and miniature work, an aspect noted by critics past and present, can disguise a poor script. In *Thunderbirds Are Go*'s case, they enhance and enable that poor script to be all the more obvious.

Thunderbirds Are Go's story is so disparate, so inconsequential from one scene to the next, that it has little ability to grip its audience. The elaborate model sequences, mostly devoted to *Zero-X*, are used as the glue to hold these loosely connected events together, and it shows. *Thunderbirds Are Go*'s plot consists of a series of events casually interlinked by the first manned mission to Mars in the form of *Zero-X*, the colossal space exploration craft that provides the film with as much of a blessing as it does a curse. *Zero-X* has remained a popular stalwart of Anderson mecha for good reason, but *Thunderbirds Are Go* drowns in the gluttonous screen time that's devoted to the craft, and its achingly long assembly sequence. The five-man *Zero-X* crew are the true main characters of the film, and are little more than carbon-copies of the Tracy brothers in their set-up, only without the distinguishable personalities. Their square-jawed, fair-haired all-American nature sees them as a hangover of 1950s sci-fi films, out of place for productions that purposefully looked ahead to the future.

Adding insult to injury, despite International Rescue only performing one single rescue during the entirety of the film (their security escort of *Zero-X* early on the film hardly counts), *Zero-X* gives the outfit ample opportunity to deploy their full resources on multiple occasions throughout the film. From beginning to end, *Zero-X* runs into gargantuan trouble in the skies, in outer space, on land and in the oceans, but it's really only Thunderbird 2 that performs the most rescuing. Thunderbirds 1 and 3's roles are skeletal, Thunderbird 5 has a mere cameo and Thunderbird 4 technically isn't seen within the film itself, but instead relegated to a cursory appearance during the film's opening titles. It's not as of *Thunderbirds Are Go* is lacking in visual splendour and scale, it's just that it's applied to all the wrong elements, namely giving non-Thunderbird craft the spotlight.

Another example of incredible production design and miniature work overpowering anything else is Alan Tracy's dream sequence involving himself and Lady Penelope partaking of the intoxicating pleasures of the Shooting Star nightclub, imagined as a literal planet amongst the stars. It's meticulously realised and utterly ridiculous. Sylvia Anderson herself would later describe the entire sequence as 'sheer indulgence' (2007).[72] It's during this sequence that *Thunderbirds Are Go* stops being *Thunderbirds Are Go* and succumbs to being an interminable Cliff Richard and the Shadows music video for a few merciless yet brief minutes. Placing a pop star within your film may be an understandable marketing move to get more bums on seats, but it unforgivingly dates *Thunderbirds Are Go*, trapping a movie that blends the retro-futuristic sensibilities together but then forcefully reminds you that this is 1966. Ironically, it's this entire sequence that has any deeper meaning, namely a reflection of Alan's anguished state at being treated like a kid by his elders and his desire to be treated like one of the men, eventually validated when Jeff tasks him with boarding the *Zero-X* on its re-entry to Earth after it disastrous encounter with the Rock Snakes on Mars to fix its escape hatch. It's not the most sophisticated subplot in cinematic history, nor does it neatly compliment the wider technologically-themed adventure of *Zero-X*'s constant stream of malfunctions or coming under attack, but it's the closest the film gets to injecting personal dilemma into its characters. Writing in the *Thunderbirds*' 50th anniversary bookazine, Marcus Hearn (2015) similarly suggests that 'it might have been better spent exploring the film's characters.'[73]

Thunderbirds Are Go's misplaced visual adventure and detached sense of adventure does it no favours. The message the film seems to say is that it doesn't matter if International Rescue barely have a substantial presence in their own film. If it's filmed in Supermarionation, it doesn't matter what exactly it is that's being filmed. The spectacle provides the riches the audiences came to enjoy. What the film misunderstands then is that by flinging that perspective on compelling disaster-action to pop stars and spaceship pilots devoid of character, the audience won't feel compelled to engage with the material. Without the substance of genuine character or plot, the spectacle lands with a bang, but without an impact. A visualisation of this summary comes in the film's final climactic moments, when *Zero-X* crash-lands in the city of Craigston. The trapped *Zero-X* crew have successfully launched their escape capsule prior to the craft's descent and the town itself has been evacuated. All that's left is a lot of sound and fury

---

[72] Anderson, S. (2007) 'Technical Wizardry' *My FAB Years*. p. 67. Hermes Press. 1st edition.

[73] Hearn, M. (2015) *Thunderbirds: A Complete Guide to the Classic Series*. p. 112. ITV Studios/Panini Magazines.

signifying nothing as *Zero-X* demolishes the city. There's no human life at stake, just a lot of bangs and crashes. This is the film's most direct assault on our senses and its most direct confirmation of the ill-founded belief that Supermarionation can win audiences over when it's presented as an entirely surface level art form with no attachment to substantial character or plot development. On the much larger screens of the cinema, *Thunderbirds Are Go* displays these shortcomings all too well.

'And I'm telling you Brains, in no uncertain terms ...'

In the wake of *Thunderbirds Are Go*'s unfortunate commercial reception however, a curious thing happened: a second *Thunderbirds* film was approved for launch. Gerry explained that *Thunderbird 6* was greenlit owing to the confusion surrounding the failure of *Thunderbirds Are Go* (2002): 'None of us could understand why the film hadn't succeeded, so it was decided we would make another.'[74] It's a limp if understandable move. If you can't determine why one film failed, you can't offer a satisfactory reason why a follow-up shouldn't go ahead. However, Stephen La Riviere notes in *Filmed in Supermarionation* that, in December of 1966, *The Daily Mail* had suggested that two *Thunderbirds* films had been approved simultaneously (a further reflection of the faith broadcasters and investors had in the franchise), with a second film possibly being focused on a 'Russo-American space project' (2009, p. 173).[75] Whilst that idea would be abandoned, it does offer a more substantial explanation for how *Thunderbird 6* came to be, even if Gerry makes it sound like one film was decided after the other. It also clashes with Gerry's earlier thoughts as to why *Thunderbirds Are Go* didn't succeed, ie that audiences weren't used to seeing cinematic extensions of TV shows. If Gerry's thoughts held weight, why would work allowed to proceed on a second *Thunderbirds* film otherwise?

Ironically, whilst the unenthusiastic response that greeted *Thunderbird 6* on its release confirmed to Lew Grade at least that *Thunderbirds* was no longer a profitable endeavour and that newer productions from the Century 21 stables were the way forward, it's the better of the two films with its strengthened approach to characters and story-telling. Whilst it remains the more cohesive of the two films, it demonstrates that the momentum that had propelled *Thunderbirds* to early success had long since dwindled by this point.

Thunderbird 6 dispenses with overly-large spaceship crews and

---

[74] Hearn, M. Archer, S. (2002) 'Spectrum Is Green' *What Made Thunderbirds Go! The Authorised Biography of Gerry Anderson.* p. 159. BBC Books. 2nd edition.
[75] La Riviere, S. (2009) 'Tiger in the Tank' *Filmed in Supermarionation.* p. 173. Hermes Press. 1st edition.

awkwardly-placed pop stars and positions Lady Penelope and Brains as the joint lead characters with its premise of Penelope, Parker, Tin-Tin and Alan enjoying the maiden flight of Brains' latest invention: Skyship One. Their peaceful holiday is sabotaged by spies after Lady Penelope and International Rescue, led by the mysterious Black Phantom. Only Brains' further invention of a new Thunderbird craft has any hope of saving the day. This is one of the quirky strengths the film has going for it. Despite there being even less Thunderbird action in *Thunderbird 6* than *Thunderbirds Are Go*, the film does at least focus on some established characters within International Rescue's ranks. If *Thunderbirds Are Go* can be seen as a backdoor pilot for a *Zero-X* spin-off (which did occur in the form of its *TV21* strip), then *Thunderbird 6* may reasonably be interpreted as a showcase for Lady Penelope. Well, showcase may be a strong word. It's more of a case of the action happens around her.

Much like *Thunderbirds Are Go*, barely any genuine rescuing occurs, though this is something of a deliberate move. Director David Lane (2007) recalls how where *Thunderbirds Are Go* focused on the hardware, a more light-hearted approach was taken for Thunderbird 6. "'It was felt that we'd done the one with the hardware," Lane recalls. "And that now we wanted to do something amusing"'.[76] For a series so engrained in the appeal of the hardware, this was an audacious choice to make with the film that had the pressure of securing the future of *Thunderbirds* as a viable media property. The lighter nature of *Thunderbird 6* is found within it titular craft. The laughter that greets Brains' grand unveiling of the Tiger Moth on Thunderbird 2's runway, almost mocking and scornful, is entirely justified. The film can't even muster the confidence from its characters to confirm that this diminutive, ancient craft is worthy of being a Thunderbird. Audiences expecting to see a new and awesome craft become Thunderbird 6, one with entirely new capabilities that no other Thunderbird could boast off, would have surely been left utterly deflated to see this anti-Thunderbird drag itself along Thunderbird 2's runway.

Alienating its audience further, *Thunderbird 6* feels like it's actively trying to work against the *Thunderbirds* formula. Any good faith *Thunderbirds Are Go* managed to sustain from its youthful target audience by being the first *Thunderbirds* production fans would have seen in colour must have been crushed by the sight of *Thunderbird 6*'s two starring guest vehicles being so against the usual formula. Skyship One is a lumbering, uninteresting thing, so bland in its appearance that it can't help but blend into the clouds it floats against. Its interior decoration remains a masterclass in production design, but its inability to *do* anything, compared to *Zero-X*, was decidedly

---

[76] La Riviere, S. (2009) 'Tiger in the Tank' *Filmed in Supermarionation*. p. 171. Hermes Press. 1st edition.

unappealing to the all-important merchandise concerns. A flabbergasting move by this point, as Century 21 Productions had bought an entire separate toy company to handle such matters. Far less people are saved than they are rescued in this film, as the crew of Skyship One are horrifically murdered and their bodies disposed of by Captain Paul Foster and his villainous gang of spies by being tossed into the oceans, but there's little in the *Thunderbirds* canon quite as shocking as Scott and Virgil using Thunderbirds 1 and 2's array of deadly machine guns to slaughter Black Phantom and his forces. *Thunderbird 6* so desperately wants to be a *James Bond* film rather than a *Thunderbirds* film that it's happy to eschew the bare ingredients of the International Rescue ethos. Kids must surely have felt disappointed to see Thunderbird 6 crawling along Tracy Island, but how did they feel when seeing their beloved heroes reduced to murderers?

Distributor United Artists appeared to see the writing on the wall before anyone else, ironically being the ones who greenlit the film in the first place. Chris Bentley (2000) notes that despite *Thunderbird 6* being completed in January 1968, the film wouldn't premier until July of that year, gathering dust as audiences grew even more distant from a television series that had already cancelled by that point.[77]

'Now, on the big screen'

The passage of time has cemented a key set of appealing aspects of Gerry and Sylvia's work. In *Thunderbirds'* case, the action and adventure so commonplace in the worlds of Supermarionation is balanced with a humanist approach to saving life. Every time someone is saved in either *Thunderbirds Are Go* or *Thunderbird 6*, it feels like an afterthought, a reaction on the part of the film-makers that their indulgences needed to be checked by incorporating some form of rescue. By not making International Rescue the focus of their own films, so too is the act of rescuing itself no longer the focus of the films, when that itself is what defines *Thunderbirds*.

However, the speculative nature of this reasoning means that the above thoughts could very well be unfounded, and that any number of reasons could contribute to the failure of these two films. But Gerry's thoughts of audiences being perplexed by the idea of going to the cinema to see *Thunderbirds* when they could just stay at home remains a curious interpretation, given that cinematic expansions of science fiction and spy-fi TV shows were a thing before and long after *Thunderbirds*. Eleven years before *Thunderbirds Are Go*, Hammer Film Productions had transplanted the BBC's sci-fi TV series *The Quatermass Experiment* from TV to film, with *The*

---

[77] Bentley, C. (2000) 'The Making of *Thunderbirds*' *The Complete Book of Thunderbirds*. p. 41. Carlton Books. 1st edition.

Quatermass Xperiment debuting to instant critical and commercial success, spawning several more feature film adaptations of further *Quatermass* TV productions and making Hammer celebrated architects of British horror films.

Elsewhere, by the time *Thunderbirds Are Go* debuted in December of 1966, *The Man From U.N.C.L.E.* had released *One of Our Spies is Missing*, its fourth cinematic feature, earlier that year based on the TV series of the same name. Mere weeks before *One of Our Spies is Missing* debuted in August, July saw the release of *Batman: The Movie*, spun out of the popular 1960s *Batman* series, which *The Man From U.N.C.L.E.* would eventually succumb to in its style in an attempt to equal that show's popularity. August 1966 also saw the release of *Daleks' Invasion Earth 2150 A.D.*, the second of the two *Doctor Who* films directed by Gordon Flemying adapted from two of *Doctor Who*'s Dalek-based TV serials. Clearly, the demand was there to see movie interpretations of science fiction previously restricted to the comparatively low-budget, monochromatic nature of television, but these various films weren't on an equal footing as the two *Thunderbirds* films, and had different goal posts to contend with. Nevertheless, the need to satisfy audiences remained palpable.

Quatermass wasn't an ongoing TV series like *Thunderbirds*. The franchise consists of a handful of serials, mostly made up of six episodes. Seeing *Quatermass* on the big screen was a chance for audiences to relive the horrors that had gripped the UK back in 1953. *The Man From U.N.C.L.E.*'s films, eight overall released between 1964 and 1968, were in fact versions of some of the TV episodes, with newly filmed footage slotted in as conveniently as possible to create the illusion of them being fully fledged movies. *Batman* came along two months after the series had actually drawn to a close, sedating any lingering demand to see more of Adam West and Burt Ward's take on the Dynamic Duo. *Dr. Who and the Daleks* and *Daleks' Invasion Earth 2150 A.D.* were both adapted from the two earliest *Doctor Who* serials involving the infamous creatures that are so often mistaken for robots. This was a time when science fiction entertainment in television and film was enveloping audiences, constantly quenching a thirst for speculative adventure that was out of this world.

With the exception of *Batman*, *Thunderbirds Are Go* and *Thunderbird 6* wisely made themselves more valuable than the cinematic translations of *Quatermass*, *The Man From U.N.C.L.E.* and *Doctor Who* by bypassing past material reserved for television and instead told entirely original stories. This added a fantastic amount of worth to the films, distinguishing them from most of the competition and making them the events they wanted to be. There's a delightful irony in that where these other franchise turned TV stories into blockbusters, *Thunderbirds*' own TV stories were already blockbusters, movies in TV form. Perhaps that points to where the

Thunderbirds movies really failed to take off. Having perfected the series' format on the small screen, maybe Gerry and Sylvia saw fit to treat the films as experiments to push new concepts into the *Thunderbirds* world. The lesson to be learnt here then is that once you have perfected that format, where are you meant to go from there?

Fast forward nearly 40 years on from *Thunderbird 6* to 1997 and screenwriters Karey Kirkpatrick and Peter Hewitt are suffering from a similar case of creative frustration in nailing down the basics of *Thunderbirds* into a concise script. In 1995, PolyGram had acquired ITC Entertainment, thereby owning Gerry and Sylvia's Supermarionation back catalogue at that time. Working under PolyGram-owned company Working Title, a live-action *Thunderbirds* movie would enter a long-gestating period of script rewrites as numerous concepts were thrown around. Writing about the ill-fated reboot in his book *The Greatest Sci-fi Movies Never Made* (2008), David Hughes notes how Kirkpatrick and Hewitt were struck by the difficulty in writing a script that could give ample screen time five leading characters, ie the five Tracy brothers. This in turn leads to the problematic issue of writing a satisfactory single story that ensures all five Thunderbird craft and leads receive an equal amount of screen time, something neither *Thunderbirds Are Go* nor *Thunderbird 6* achieves. This is made all the more obvious when the later tries to fashion an entirely new additional craft to the line-up.[78]

The eventual movie that did occur, directed by Jonathan Frakes and written by William Osbourne, neatly solves this tricky little issue by popping Scott, Virgil, Gordon and John on-board a damaged Thunderbird 5, trapping them for the majority of the film, thus making them irrelevant to the story as it focuses squarely on Alan. The message all three *Thunderbirds* films seem to say, amplified by each successive entry, is that *Thunderbirds* cannot function on the big screen. Century 21 attempted to appease their audiences by giving them the overindulgent aspects of Supermarionation, all but stripped of the bare essentials that make *Thunderbirds* so endearing. Gerry and Sylvia appeared to both hold sincere, genuine beliefs that both *Thunderbirds* films are decent outings. Whilst their respective production values have stood the test of time, in the context of what makes *Thunderbirds* to enjoyably memorable, *Thunderbirds Are Go* and *Thunderbird 6* misjudge the expectations of their audience to mammoth proportions.

---

[78] Hughes, D. (2008) '*Thunderbirds* Are No' *The Greatest Sci-Fi Films Never Made*. p. 251. Titan Books.

LIFE AS WE DON'T KNOW IT: *ZERO-X* ON THE SMALL SCREEN

Few Anderson productions provoke such imaginative speculation as the *Zero-X* television series. This is precisely because there isn't a *Zero-X* TV series. *Intergalactic Rescue*, *Five Star Five* and *Thunderhawks* account for some of Gerry Anderson's works that failed to venture past the pre-production stage (even though *Thunderhawks* was extensively retooled into *Terrahawks*), but in the fan's minds, *Zero-X* is the greatest *what if* that got away from the Anderson and Century 21 Productions. The idea of a spin-off production focusing on the colossal starship that features in *Thunderbirds Are Go* and *Captain Scarlet* remains a rich source of feverish debate, its skeletal appearances throughout various productions aiding speculation for what might have been. The craft boasts a starring role in the first *Thunderbirds* movie, but features in a limited yet vital capacity in the first episode of *Captain Scarlet* as the craft that transports Captain Black and his crew to Mars to unwittingly discover the Mysterons. Aside from a long-running comic strip in *TV21* (*Zero-X* is the only property in *TV21* to have its run illustrated entirely in colour), the craft made no other appearances, but where then might a television or film spin-off of the starship blasted off to?

In the interests of objectivity within this largely subjective book, it's worth settling the score, here and now; a *Zero-X* TV series was never something that was planned during Century 21 Productions' lifespan. Script editor Tony Barwick was probed this very question (1986) and confirmed as such; 'As far as I know there were no plans.'[79] By the time *Captain Scarlet and the Mysterons* arrived, Barwick had made his presence felt in Century 21, aiding in the integration of additional story material for *Thunderbirds* and its two movies, but now promoted to the role of script editor for *Captain Scarlet*. If a *Zero-X* television spin-off was ever on the cards, it naturally would have fallen to Barwick to steer the series in the correct direction. It's likely that the company would have struggled to venture into making another television series when multiple arms of the company were making both TV series and movies.

However, it remains fun to envision this cottage industry perusing such a venture, particularly at a time when Gerry and Sylvia were focusing on the

---

[79] Drake, C. Howard, A. Barwick, T. (1986) 'Solenoid Spotlight Part 1: The S.I.G. Interview: Tony Barwick' *Supermarionation Is Go* (ed Nightingale, D). No. 16, p. 26.

company's film division. By the time *The Secret Service* went into production, the day-to-day running of the company was in the hands of executive producer and long-time colleague Reg Hill. At a time when much of Century 21's television output was drifting away from techno-fantasy adventure and more towards low-key spy-fi and becoming more formalised in its appearance, a *Zero-X* series could very well have maintained the caricatured vibrancy of Supermarionation's earlier years.

'Assembly Control calling all *Zero-X* units...'

Before we speculate on what a *Zero-X* series could have entailed, it's best to contextualise these perspectives as realistically as possible by determining *when* a *Zero-X* series could have begun. If *Thunderbirds Are Go* had been the bigger box office draw it desired to be, then a justifiable reaction to the movie's success could have been the birth of a production focusing on *Zero-X*. A TV series of *Zero-X* then may well have been produced either alongside or in place of *Captain Scarlet and the Mysterons*, *Joe 90* or *The Secret Service*. As if to avoid disrupting the flow of the established Century 21 output, it's more pleasant to envision that *Zero-X* would have been made alongside these productions. After all, it's not as if Century 21 hadn't already dabbled in making numerous productions at the same time.

Two versions of *Thunderbirds* had been forced into life when the series was being extended from its initial 25-minute run time to 50 minutes. A failed sister series of *Fireball XL5* didn't move past the concept stage which, despite never being produced, suggests that there was enthusiasm and resources for Century 21 to produce multiple productions simultaneously. This is something enforced by an article from *Television Mail* in 1963, and preserved in *Filmed in Supermarionation*, which reported that ATV was preparing Century 21 (then operating under its former title of AP Films) to produce further series of *Supercar* and *Fireball XL5*, alongside their then newest production *Stingray*[80]. Whilst further adventures for the World Space Patrol appeared to go no further than this article, a new series of *Supercar*, a smash ratings hit in the key American markets, had been toyed with for some time at this point. Advertising restrictions ultimately forbade allowing a potential third series of *Supercar* to go into production, the biggest takeaway from this intriguing nugget of information is that simultaneous productions were pulled due to circumstances beyond Century 21's control, not because they weren't skilled or equipped to handle making multiple series at once. This is further evidenced in how one side of the company busied itself with its television division and another side focused on films.

---

[80] La Riviere, S. (2009) "Stand By for Action" *Filmed in Supermarionation: A History of the Future*. p. 93. Hermes Press. 1st edition.

A *Zero-X* TV series would obviously have spun out of the craft's debut appearance in *Thunderbirds Are Go*, bringing to mind the idea of just what a *Zero-X* series could have been about. It would surely have been caught amidst the shift from caricatured to realistically proportioned marionettes and the letting go of the hard-nosed sci-fi after *Captain Scarlet and the Mysterons* into the lighter hearts of *Joe 90* and *The Secret Service*. The premise of such a series can remain intrinsically linked with the craft's function of exploring new and strange worlds for the betterment of mankind's understanding of the universe, discover regions of space untouched by humanity and the ensuing cosmic chaos the *Zero-X* crew would inevitably chance upon. At a time when Supermarionation's new physical form of super-proportioned miniature humans was filtering itself into the storytelling becoming more formalised, one can imagine how *Zero-X*'s premise would lend itself well to tapping into the more colourful, less sterile stylings of *Fireball XL5* and *Stingray*. Where those two series detailed each of their respective heroic crews becoming entangled in otherworldly characters and awesome phenomena unknown to human science, if *Zero-X*'s *TV21* strips is anything to go by, one can easily envision *Zero-X* pursuing a similar path.

However, a couple of bumps in the road are felt here. *TV21* was such a creative success partly because of the freedom allowed by its medium. A comic doesn't encounter the same practical struggles that a TV or film production may have. As such, the sequential nature of *Zero-X*'s *TV21* stories easily resulted in extravagant, space-based adventures that could never be quite pulled off in Supermarionation. Also, re-treading former ground wasn't entirely common for the ever-inventive and forward thinking Century 21 Productions. Whilst it's easy to imagine that *a Zero-X* TV series could succeed simply for being a vastly improved version of *Fireball XL5*, *Zero-X* surely had to be more than that. A space-faring adventure series in which the craft encounters cosmic threats alien and antagonistic to mankind is a solid enough premise with which to sell *Zero-X* on, but ideas are cheap. That's why everyone has them. The value comes in the execution of the ideas.

Consider the two fleeting on-screen appearances *Zero-X* makes in the Century 21 worlds. The two trips *Zero-X* makes to Mars and drenched in horror. The scene in *Thunderbirds Are Go* in which the MEV traverses the uninviting landscape of Mars, with its tense camera work and half-caught Barry Gray soundtrack that pierces into jittering life at various points, stands as the closest Century 21 came to producing pure space horror in puppet form. The entire scene doesn't so much predict *Captain Scarlet*, but rather calls out to it, as if imploring that darker attitudes were the right movement at the right time for Century 21 make, with the opening scene of *Captain Scarlet*'s first episode eventually calling back in delayed response, echo-like.

You could almost argue that *Captain Scarlet* reorganised the Rock Snakes scene for its own benefit in order for the series to pursue its own path, leaving *Zero-X* stranded.

The craft's further trip to discovering the Mysterons doesn't quite have the same power, but the fearful vibes remain regardless. A cosmic space horror tone for a *Zero-X* TV series wouldn't just give the series its own bespoke identity but would also be a handsome compliment to the similarly darker atmosphere of *Captain Scarlet and the Mysterons*. Horror is also a key thematic component of *Zero-X*'s TV21 adventures, which manifested into such threats as dangerous cosmic intelligences to Captain Paul Travers, space navigator Brad Newman, Doctor Ray Pierce and space captain Brad Newman (Doctor Tony Grant didn't appear in the *TV21* strip) regularly being subjected to grim physical experimentations. That style of body horror may be difficult to pull off on a Supermarionation puppet, but all available evidence point to *Zero-X*'s longing for embracing the fear of the unknown. After all, *Captain Scarlet* had little trouble in producing scenes of violence with its own puppets. Further time spent with Paul, Greg, Brad and Ray allows for a firmer grip on the characterisations of the core foursome, whose personalities aren't given a huge chance to shine in *Thunderbirds Are Go*. It's an area where Sylvia Anderson would have been assigned to sharpen up the personas in her role as character developer and readjust them into more likeable and watchable people, although the all-male crew of *Zero-X* would likely have been a limited palette for her talents to work with.

For *Zero-X*'s own adventures then, such horror stylings, which could range from further alien jeopardy beyond the wonderfully grotesque Rock Snakes to intangible cosmic experiences, had every chance of being successfully and convincingly crafted thanks to the leaps the special effects department had made since those early days of *Fireball XL5*. From painting background sets of *The Adventures of Twizzle* to the dazzling attention to detail in *Thunderbirds Are Go*, by 1966, the likes of Derek Meddings, Shaun Whittacker-Cook, Mike Trim, Bob Bell and the rest of the special effects units and art departments were well equipped and experienced to produce fantastical exterior and interior that stretched far beyond the mostly Earth-bound cityscapes we see throughout *Captain Scarlet*, *Joe 90* and *The Secret Service*. More imaginative, more ambitious, more three-dimensional than the monochrome era of Supermarionation, the worlds they could have crafted for *Zero-X* could have been a masterclass in miniature, post-psychedelic wonder. Additionally, the aforementioned senior staff at Century 21 were leaving the demands of the television departments in the hands of younger staff, who were being promoted whilst the more experienced and learned crew members were focusing on movies. It's nice to envision that these comparatively newer ranks to Century 21 would have relished the chance to produce something worthy of their mentors.

At this stage it's worth noting which marionette style a *Zero-X* TV series would have stuck with: the caricatured look that the crew first appear as or stay in keeping with the uniformed look as marionettes graduated to more realistic proportions from *Captain Scarlet* onwards? In truth, the most sensible answer would be to just continue with the puppets as they appeared in *Thunderbirds Are Go*, even when the better proportioned style of marionettes were becoming the norm. There would have been little sense in reproducing an entirely new form of the same cast when they're ready and waiting for further adventures (much of the *Zero-X* crew marionettes returned as new characters for *Thunderbird 6*). It's also worth remembering that doing so wouldn't have been entirely clashing with the *Captain Scarlet*-style marionettes. The truth is that from *Supercar* to *Thunderbirds*, the physical style of the marionettes became less extroverted with each series. This culminated in *Thunderbirds Are Go*, when the characteristically large heads maintained their colourful expressions but advances in Supermarionation technology meant that their heads could now be reduced in size, making their bodies appear fully proportioned whilst maintaining that same look that would be eradicate entirely from *Captain Scarlet* onwards.

Scriptwriting As We Don't Know It

All of the above then gives reason to think of not just what kind of stories *Zero-X* could tell, but how exactly they would be told. Century 21's productions always strove to be bigger and better than the previous production (at least from a commercial standpoint), suggesting that *Zero-X*'s starry-eyed premise would have encouraged the company's writing and directing staff to build on what had come before. Long-time Anderson scribe Tony Barwick, who Gerry always had a kind word for, would no doubt have served as head writer and script editor for the series, a role he had shared at first with Gerry and Sylvia on *Captain Scarlet*, but eventually took on single-handedly with *Joe 90*, *The Secret Service* and *UFO*. Gerry (2009) always spoke of Barwick in positive terms, once describing him as 'one of my favourite writers.'[81]

Barwick's unassuming, easy-going style of script management lent itself well to various writers delivering a wide variety of scenarios being played out in the Earth-based settings for *Captain Scarlet* and *Joe 90*. Biological warfare, planetary invasion, political power struggles, fashion-themed spies and dubious businessmen are just some of the episodic concepts these series dabbled in. Would the comparatively space-based setting of *Zero-X* reduced the possibility for such varied scenarios? The imaginative scope of *Zero-X*'s

---

[81] (2009) 'Interview: Gerry Anderson' Den of Geek. Available from – https://www.denofgeek.com/tv/the-den-of-geek-interview-gerry-anderson/.

TV21 adventures would suggest not. If the craft's comic strip adventures are anything to go by, the hypothetical TV series could well have thrown forward to *Space: 1999*'s themes of embarking on a strange and unpredictable galactic odyssey where the promise of experiencing new worlds lures *Zero-X* into constantly terrifying and action-packed adventures. There's the feeling that Barwick and the new stable of directors Leo Eaton, Alan Perry and Ken Turner would have relished the opportunity to bring to life darkly-minded space adventure after the mostly Earth-bound scenarios of Supermarionation's then-current output.

A further indication of what kinds of stories a *Zero-X* series may have told can be interpretated through the craft's inclusion in the *Project SWORD* franchise. *Project SWORD* was one of Century 21 Production's greatest gambles. The company had taken stewardship of a line of space exploration toys and the decision was made to fashion a multi-media brand out of them, using the toys as a jumping off point ala *Transformers*. The logic was that Century 21 Productions has grown in such stature that it might just be possible to conjure up a series that had the success of something like *Thunderbirds* without the need for an accompanying television series. *Zero-X* ended up playing a small but intriguing role in this ill-fated venture.

After a false start in the pages of *Solo* in 1967, (one of numerous comics within Century 21 Publishing's stable), *Project SWORD* found greater success as a text story in the pages of *TV21* a year later. The ongoing narrative focused on the adventures of the Space World Organisation for Research and Development (SWORD), which had been previously tasked with mining alien worlds for their natural resources, only to have been drastically reformatted. The destructive arrival of a colossal meteorite triggers a deluge of natural disasters on Earth, prompting SWORD to be reorganised to salvage the last remnants of society and repopulate other worlds. A *Zero-X* toy became part of the line-up of merchandise available, even if the starship didn't entirely fit into the aesthetic of the toys. This is perhaps more of an indication of leftover stock from *Thunderbirds Are Go* not being a worldwide hit rather than any concrete indication that a *Zero-X* series was ever on the cards. Nevertheless, Zero-X's integration into the *Project SWORD* mythology was embellished further. A two-page cross-section of *Zero-X* was featured in the *Project SWORD* annual from 1969, with an accompanying biography explaining that the *Zero-X* Mark 101 (*Project SWORD* was set in the far-flung 3020s) was being utilised as something of an intergalactic bus. Zero-X was now part of SWORD's colossal evacuation fleet, redesigned to fit 500 people from the dying Earth to SWORD's pre-existing off-world colonies. Admittedly, it's a stretch to suggest that *Zero-X*'s relatively inconsequential inclusion in *Project SWORD*'s *Mad Max*-esque post-apocalyptic scenario is any firm signposting of how a *Zero-X* TV series may have evolved (*Zero-X* wasn't woven into much else of *Project SWORD*'s media), but this and the craft's fiercely compelling *TV21* adventures offer some glimmers into the kinds of stories a *Zero-X* TV series may have told when prized away from the world of *Thunderbirds*.

How *Zero-X* may have told its adventures is open to equally intriguing possibilities. Until *Captain Scarlet*, much of Century 21's television series had been episodic in nature, standalone stories being the order of the day. *Captain Scarlet* evolves the status quo by introducing multi-episode stories, with actions and consequences on Spectrum and the Mysterons' part spiralling from one episode into the next. You can't watch 'Spectrum Strikes Back' without having watched 'Operation Time', for example, and the same goes for 'Winged Assassin' flowing directly from the events of 'The Mysterons'. The three-part 'Lunarville' trilogy, as it's unofficially known, presents the peak of *Captain Scarlet*'s multi-episode ambitions. Given that this series evolves from the episodic nature of *Thunderbirds* and *Stingray* (which themselves had dabbled in some multi-part adventures), a *Zero-X* TV series could have been one further leap forward in its story-telling ambitions. In an effort to maintain the cinematic grandeur of its debut and harking back to the series' base concept sharing slight similarities with swashbuckling space adventurers *Flash Gordon* and *Buck Rogers*, a *Zero-X* TV serial presents equally creative possibilities as a *Zero-X* TV series. Single adventures stretched out to prolonged structures over several episodes, something not attempted throughout Supermarionation, yet arguably a logical extension towards the direction that *Captain Scarlet* was suggesting. It's also a format audiences were accustomed to, with *Doctor Who* and *Quatermass* proving that science fiction serials were experiencing a high demand for viewership.

How marketable such a format for a *Zero-X* TV series would be could also be seen as being at odds with ITC's commercial output of productions. Serialised television production within ITC's catalogue weren't commonplace, with the majority of the company's sci-fi and spy-fi themed series maintaining that episodic, standalone nature. Not even Century 21 could sustain the multi-episode story-telling mechanics of *Captain Scarlet* as *Joe 90* would revert back to individual stories for its own episodes. A return to *Thunderbirds*' lengthily 50-minute running time perhaps functions as the happy middle ground, providing a wide canvas from which Century 21's newly honed space explorations could truly take flight whilst still enabling that commercial angle, short enough to function as primarily standalone adventures, but long enough to provide a sense of scale and grandeur.

Grounding the above explorations in the context of how Century 21 Productions was progressing during the late 1960s benefits us with at least some plausible indication for how a *Zero-X* television series may have developed, but in creative worlds, several courses of action are always possible. Whilst the television department of Century 21 Productions was straying into curious and effervescent spy-fi after *Captain Scarlet*, its cinematic endeavours remained fixated on outer space drama, namely the Andersons'

1969 effort *Doppelgänger*, a film detailing the perilous consequences of travelling into the darkest recesses of the stars. Space clearly remained on their minds and a *Zero-X* television outing could have been one of the most visually spectacular productions of the company. Stripped of the flippant leanings of *Fireball XL5* and *Stingray* and cribbing from the darker, more sophisticated *Captain Scarlet* and taking a pinch of inspiration from the comic, *Zero-X*'s small-screen adventures could have grappled with electrifying space horrors beyond the comprehension of man. If *Captain Scarlet* can be taken as a prototype *UFO*, then *Zero-X* should have been the forerunner to *Space: 1999*; a hazardous, unpredictable adventure into the great, cosmic unknown.

SPECTRUM IS CANON: CONTINUITY IN *CAPTAIN SCARLET*

Captain Scarlet and the Mysterons is a rare instance in Supermarionation in which to understand the events of the series, you have to start from the first episode. That may seem like a strikingly obvious place to start, but the vast majority of Supermarionation series are produced in such a way that they function perfectly well by being dipped in and out of from any given episode, coupled with the fact that they're much more episodic in nature. 'Trapped in the Sky' may establish itself as the first episode of *Thunderbirds*, but there's little serialised story in *Thunderbirds*, meaning that there's no great detriment to the audience's enjoyment if they were to start with 'Sun Probe' or 'City of Fire'.

In the case of *Captain Scarlet*, one must begin firmly at the beginning with 'The Mysterons', the episode that sets the war of nerves into motion. From there, *Captain Scarlet* shows itself to be a series reliant on a linear sense of continuity, as events from key episodes ripple into further episodes later on in the series and multi-part stories arise. The series does much to align itself with how the Oxford English Dictionary defines continuity: '1. The fact of not stopping or changing. 2. An unbroken connection of line or development. 3. Organisation of a film or television programme so that the plot makes sense and clothing, scenery etc. remain the same in different scenes.' That second definition of the word feels best suited to how *Captain Scarlet* executes its own story. Curiously, around halfway through the series, the focus on the series' canon buckles, and any adhering to sensible continuity is unexpectedly tossed aside. As an overall package, *Captain Scarlet* has a troublesome relationship to continuity, sometimes confident and carefully considered and other times ... not.

Televised Spectrum

Throughout roughly the first fifteen episodes, the seeds of *Captain Scarlet*'s continuity are firmly sown and confidently grow as a sense of escalation swells throughout these episodes. Advances and setbacks alike are presented for Spectrum and the Mysterons as the war of nerves is declared. Weaknesses are found within the Mysterons and weapons are developed to exploit those weaknesses. Spectrum loose at several instances to the Mysteron might. The Mysterons themselves gradually shift tactics as the series progresses, initially delivering precise threats against individuals, places and more, before learning to adopt a more cryptic style of threat that leaves Spectrum in the dark.

As a source of continuity analysis, the Mysterons themselves present much to untangle as the series develops. Their reconstructive powers remain reliably fear-inducing, able to recreate anything or anyone. As a sign of extension of the Mysterons' abilities or the need for story-convenient escape routes to race an episode to its conclusion, the Mysterons acquire other capabilities. 'The Trap' shows that Mysteron agents have the ability to replicate the vocal patterns of human beings. 'The Heart of New York' marks the first instance of Captain Black being able to teleport himself away from situations too dangerous for him to be in physical contact with. These supplemental powers hang loosely onto the Mysterons, with the scripts demanding that the audience accepts these as additional powers that should make the Mysterons more terrifying, when the more obvious answer is that the inherent imprecision in the Mysterons as a concept lends itself well to instances such as these.

The Mysterons continue to present *Captain Scarlet* with much of its continuity wrangling in other aspects too. In 'Operation Time', it's accidentally discovered that the Mysterons are impervious to x-rays and that electricity is the one weapon that can murder a Mysteron, their agents otherwise as indestructible as their masters. Following on from this, 'Spectrum Strikes Back' sees the implementation of the Mysteron Gun and the Mysteron Detector, two vital pieces of kit added to Spectrum's arsenal. *Captain Scarlet*'s freewheeling approach to continuity rears its head once again, as we have another instance of fact being established early on in the series, only to be disregarded as the series continued. Where the Mysteron Detector is mentioned and utilised in several episodes after its introduction, the Mysteron Gun is never seen or heard of again, whilst the idea of electricity being the sole effective weapon against Mysteron agents is thrown aside when regular bullets or blazing destructions within vehicles or buildings being detonated prove to be enough to take down a Mysteron agent. The latter-day gem 'Noose of Ice' is the only other episode of *Captain Scarlet* to show how merciless electricity is in defeating a Mysteron and also the only instance in the entire series in which it's acknowledged that high voltage electricity could also kill Captain Scarlet himself. Equally guilty of sporadic usage is Captain Scarlet's sixth sense to detect any nearby Mysteron agent, coming and going whenever the script felt it necessary.

These examples display how *Captain Scarlet*'s world-building flirted between somehow both more complicated than *Stingray* or *Thunderbirds* and yet awkwardly executed in how that world-building was maintained. It's always worth remembering that Century 21 Productions could never have envisioned that we would be examining their works in such detail over half a century later, but should that be waved away as an acceptable excuse for poor continuity management, particularly for a series that placed a great deal of its foundations on a carefully maintained linear set of actions and consequences? This loose-handed manner of delivering on continuity is reflected further in the varying viewing orders. The broadcast order of *Captain Scarlet*, which itself transitioned into the ordering of episodes on DVD and Blu-ray, markedly different to ITC's official recommended ordering of the series.

Where world-building in *Captain Scarlet* is a decidedly mixed affair in terms of quality control, the episodic running order of the series brings to mind the various strands of multi-episode stories that are scattered throughout *Captain Scarlet*. Multi-episode arcs were commonplace for Century 21 at this point, but they mostly consisted of guest characters reappearing in otherwise standalone adventures. Captain Scarlet succeeds in progressing past this mind-set, breaking free to create some gripping arcs across the series. The aforementioned duo of 'Operation Time' and 'Spectrum Strikes Back' is a fine example of how consequences would ripple from episode to episode whilst the episode's actual stories remain relatively solitary from each other. More effective is the so-called Lunarville trilogy, the unofficial designation given to the story found between 'Lunarville 7', 'Crater 101' and 'Dangerous Rendezvous'. The fact that no official name exists to bridge the gap between these episodes together and that their titles avoid hinting at their interlinked nature is a sign of how unassuming *Captain Scarlet* could be in its continuity ambitions.

This three-episode arc concerns the discovery of the Mysterons constructing a new Mysteron complex on the far side of the moon ('Lunarville 7'), Spectrum's retaliations against its construction ('Crater 101') and the consequences of doing so ('Dangerous Rendezvous'). It's a definite highlight of the series, presenting the idea of the Mysterons being able to slowly encroach themselves closer to the Earth under Spectrum's very nose whilst maintaining the status quo of the series through the destruction of the base and the rescuing of Cloudbase when the cryptic, throbbing artefact alien pulsator, retrieved from the complex before its destruction, is used in an attempt to destroy Cloudbase.

A further multi-episode story can possibly be found in the linkage of 'Noose of Ice' and 'Flight 104'. 'Noose of Ice' details the Mysterons' attempts to sabotage the discovery of a new type of rocket material to be used in spacecraft, whilst 'Flight 104' sees the Mysterons try to disrupt a Spectrum conference by world leaders to determine the best course of action to return to Mars, having not done so since the ill-fated *Zero-X* mission led by Captain Black. Chris Bentley (2017) claims that 'Noose of Ice' is meant to naturally flow into the events of 'Flight 104', due to the material extracted in 'Noose of Ice' and used to construct a new fleet of space vehicles being determined as the best method of returning to Mars, the conference of which forms the premise of 'Flight 104'. According to Bentley, the original script for 'Flight 104' contained suitable references to 'Noose of Ice' that would have tied the episode's subplots together, but was cut from the final draft, ensuring that both episodes don't acknowledge each other, enforced by their switched positioning on home release boxsets.[82]

It's undoubtedly a frustrating move to cut the already paper-thin bond between these two episodes which, when viewed in their intended meaning, provide an intriguing insight into how Spectrum attempt to advance the war of nerves in their favour, their efforts hitting with more impact given how these episodes occur so late in the series. These smaller stories running in the background of more immediate, action-focused tales enable *Captain Scarlet* to be a much more rewarding watch with their determined efforts to push the status quo along, only to be halted in their efforts by whichever higher powers demanded so, and for whatever reason.

Even with this set-back hampering what could have been a delectable confirmed link between these two episodes, *Captain Scarlet* still took some extraordinary leaps in pushing the boundaries of Supermarionation's narrative conventions, presenting not just a series, but an actual story, one with distinct chapters that demand being experienced in a certain order to maximise viewer's enjoyment when engaging with the narrative. Surely the biggest offender to *Captain Scarlet*'s sophisticated approach to continuity comes in the presence of *Zero-X* in 'The Mysterons', which many interpret as a sure-fire confirmation that *Captain Scarlet* is set in the same world as *Thunderbirds*. What was more likely an understandable and economical case of prop reuse continues to excite and confound fans who are desperate to track down confirmation of continuity links between the two series when no such thing appears to exist. However, if the *Captain Scarlet* TV series comes off as ambitious in its handling of continuity, then the series' spin-off media took things to another level entirely.

Supplemental Spectrum

Like *Thunderbirds* prior, *Captain Scarlet* was accompanied by a vast nirvana of supplementary media in the form of comics, novels, annuals, story books and audio dramas that stretched the war of nerves into different mediums. Like much sci-fi media of *Captain Scarlet*'s era, the canonicity between spin-off media and the television series, the central piece of media by which all

---

[82] Bentley, C. (2017) 'Flight 104' *Captain Scarlet: The Vault*. p. 171. Signum Books. 1st edition.

other incarnations are often judged by, is questionable, with no official sources confirming or denying any definite links.

However, the continuity maintained throughout *Captain Scarlet*'s extended universe is meticulous and often breath-taking. Much of this extended universe came from Century 21 Publishing, the arm of Century 21 Productions responsible for all literature-based material. As such, the same pool of writers, editors and artists found themselves working on the same publications, the end result being that cross-pollination of continuity between comics, novels and annuals in particular was fairly regular. Author John Theydon, who wrote numerous paperback adventures for *Stingray*, *Thunderbirds*, *Captain Scarlet* and *The Secret Service*, was a particular fan of this approach. The events of his debut *Stingray* novel, simply titled *Stingray*, makes reference to *Stingray*'s very first *TV21* comic strip adventure. He applies much of the same shared universe enthusiasm to his Captain Scarlet novels, the first of his three *Spectrum File* novels featuring a prolonged sequence involving the Mysterons hijacking a Fireball XL craft in an attempt to catapult Captain Scarlet into the sun. The second *Spectrum File* novel, *Captain Scarlet and the Silent Saboteur*, makes reference to Bereznik, the enemy nation who exists outside of the World Government's harmonious existence and who regularly featured throughout *TV21*.

Through instances such as these, *Captain Scarlet*'s extended universe did much to colour in details that the television series otherwise left relatively blank. In doing so, the extended universe does much to make *Captain Scarlet*'s world feel vastly more lived in, but in doing so, forcing that world to come into contact with the other Anderson worlds, bringing with it inevitable clashes of established fact. The main nagging issue the bulk of this spin-off media presents is how *Captain Scarlet* places itself as a focal point in Century 21's extended universe that *TV21* had been busily crafting long before Captain Scarlet's arrival in 1967. *TV21* had already spent two years building on the idea that *Fireball XL5*, *Stingray* and *Thunderbirds*, alongside *Lady Penelope* and *Zero-X*, were not singular sagas but in fact each cohabited in an overall world of danger and excitement. When *Captain Scarlet and the Mysterons* landed however, it wasn't content with simply being another piece of the *TV21* puzzle. It became a unifying centre in this ongoing multiverse. The 1967 *Captain Scarlet* annual, released in September 1967, united the television world together by explaining that Spectrum was an outfit purposefully designed to have more authority than any of the various World Security Patrol organisations. Created to rise above the red tape experienced by these other outfits, Spectrum would clash with no-one and answer only to the World President.

There's little inherently wrong with this backstory for Spectrum, because within the events of the television series, we never actually learn what Spectrum's function was prior to them discovering the Mysterons, and thus there's no prior information to clash with. However, if one does accept this reason, then one must devalue the status quo of each Gerry and Sylvia Anderson series, in which all these shows exist in their own individual universes and don't overlap each other in anyway. These worlds all existed side by side, reinforced by character biographies revealing that the various characters of Spectrum had previously served in the World Space Patrol and World Aquanaut Security Patrol. *TV21* built up the shared world argument for *Captain Scarlet* too, with numerous front covers teasing the imminent arrival of Spectrum in the form of speculative reports in the run up to its TV debut. The first *Captain Scarlet* strip in *TV21*, the nine-part operatic epic 'Unity City', features cameos from the World Space Patrol and the World Aquanaut Security Patrol, furthering *Captain Scarlet*'s ties with the other Century 21 worlds.

Captain Scarlet's integration into the shared world of *TV21* and other Century 21 publications is particularly fraught when viewed in the context of the Earth Space Empire, the planet-spanning region in which much of *TV21*'s adventures were set against. As the name suggests, it's a network of planets throughout our Solar System, with humanised colonies existing throughout the empire. This includes the planet Mars, the human colony of which is called Kahra and had been humanity's home on the Red Planet for decades by the time the events of *Captain Scarlet* commence. The head-scratching issue this brings up then is how this weaves itself with the Mysterons, given that they declare Captain Black's *Zero-X* mission to be the first instance of humankind setting foot on Mars.

A workaround to this perplexing matter of multi-media stories not entirely complimenting each other comes in the joint *Captain Scarlet* and *Thunderbirds* annual from 1969. In this publication, a three-page spread details a map and timeline of Mars as defined by the worlds of Century 21, cleverly explaining that Mars is only *partially* colonised and that the Mysterons, along with the Rock Snakes from *Thunderbirds Are Go*, inhabit a restricted area of Mars, far beyond Kahra. It's not a perfect answer, but it's gratifying to have some kind of answer at all.

The colourful depths that *Captain Scarlet*'s extended universe ventured to in an effort to include the series as comfortably as possible alongside the long-established shared universe found throughout Century 21 Publishing's output is valiant and often yields entertaining story results that go beyond what the television counterpart could offer. It's also readily apparent through these bump-in-the-road instances that the puppet studios weren't in any great consultation with Century 21 Publishing in any semblance of effort to ensure that strict continuity was being upheld. Though jumbled and imperfect, the continuity littered throughout *Captain Scarlet*'s multimedia formats shows a passionate throw of the dice to establish a riveting and convincing world for the war of nerves to take place in.

SUPERSONIC FANTASIES: CELEBRATING THE MECHA OF SUPERMARIONATION

The sci-fi Supermarionation shows produced by AP Films/Century 21 Productions offer something for every generation, and contemporary celebrations of them focus on what made them popular in the first place: the painstaking and glorious depiction of futuristic, wildly imaginative mecha — space rockets, supersonic jets, submarines, tunnelers, all capable of breathtaking manoeuvres and armed with explosive firepower — that effortlessly tapped into the minds of a generation rapidly being turned on to the visual thrills of science fiction in mainstream media.

These magnificent machines often walked a fine line between accuracy and fantasy. Much has been written, for instance, about the physics of the Thunderbirds and whether or not they could actually fly, reflecting the real-world influence these shows have. Young fans at the time, however, probably didn't concern themselves with such thoughts but simply marvelled at the aesthetic joy of the models — chiefly designed by Reg Hill, Derek Meddings, and Mike Trim—being flung across rolling backdrops or back-screen projections of otherworldly landscapes. These fiery machines are a large part of the ongoing appeal of *Thunderbirds, Stingray, Captain Scarlet and the Mysterons*, and Gerry Anderson's other productions, so let's examine their attributes in further detail.

A Wonderland of Monochrome

Despite the wonders that would explode onto our screens when the likes of *Thunderbirds* and *Captain Scarlet* came along, the mecha of Century 21 had fairly primitive beginnings. Their first show to be promoted as being filmed in Supermarionation, *Supercar* (1961-1962), furnished the rough blueprint of all that would follow. With compact yet gaudy design by series producer Reg Hill, the titular vehicle's abilities reflected the ambitions of Century 21 Productions, then known as AP Films, to create first-class entertainment. Though it was predominantly used as a form of aerial transport, Supercar possessed the ability to journey through the sky, outer space, on land, and under the oceans. Its quirky exterior appearance and cramped interior cockpit were less imaginative than later designs like Thunderbird 2 and the SPV, but the machine still plays an indispensable role in Supermarionation's history. It paved the groundwork for what would follow.

Fireball XL5 was as much a leap in premise as it was in aesthetic. A bold, imposing design courtesy of Derek Meddings, *Fireball* has a degree of realism instilled into it via the craft's detachable, Space Shuttle-esque component *Fireball Junior*, which both complemented the series' sense of adventure and, inevitably, augmented its merchandising potential. With its imposing cylindrical length enabling it to shoot across the stars like a dart, the craft looks infinitely more robust and evocative than *Supercar*, and, perhaps most important, it looked like it could actually fly. Enhanced by the outer space setting, the powerful aesthetic of *Fireball XL5* captured young fans' imaginations with cosmic aplomb. After all, the flagship security, rescue, and combat vessel of the World Space Patrol *needs* to look like it can do the job.

Stand By for Rescue

Stingray, from the 1964 series of the same name, marked a progressive step forward for the chief mecha of Supermarionation. Designed by Hill, the craft's perfectly formed amphibious appeal lay not just in its exterior, but in its interior too. The increased budget furnished by financial backer Lew Grade allowed AP Films to fashion an extremely chic, futuristic style for *Stingray*'s control decks, sleeping quarters, and relaxation areas, an aesthetic firmly entrenched in 1960s fashions. And *Stingray* was filmed in colour. The swirling blue, yellow, and grey of *Stingray*'s exterior and its smooth, contoured shape give the craft a wonderfully distinctive vibe, effortlessly tapping into the aquatic themes of the show. The guest vehicles in the show also impressed. Some of the submarines themselves were clearly kit-bashed from other sources, such as the Big Gun from 'The Big Gun,' clearly modelled on a tank, and the craft from 'Sea of Oil' was quite obviously taken from a jet. With these vehicles often making an appearance in only a single episode, their interior designs were often redressed from craft to craft, with props culled from previous models.

Thunderbirds marked the point where Derek Meddings and cohort Mike Trim started working in tandem: Meddings designed much of International Rescue's core craft, prioritizing sharp bulk and heft, while Trim took care of secondary/guest vehicles, producing more streamlined and sinuous craft. The aerial gymnastics of the sleek, supersonic first responder Thunderbird 1 starts the action of each episode, complemented by the lumbering, powerful Thunderbird 2, the most recognizable of all of the Andersons' mecha and a craft that fills the screen whenever it takes off, soars through the skies, or lands in some danger zone. Thunderbird 3 is more of a curiosity, since we only ever see it in a handful of episodes, yet it remains another of Meddings' fascinatingly gargantuan designs. The trim, squat Thunderbird 4 is everything

Supercar should have been, while the immobility of space station Thunderbird 5 is at odds with its sophisticated, complex design and exposed mechanics.

The separate functions of each of the five Thunderbirds gives the show a visual depth and sense of scale. No one Thunderbird performs the same function, and that specialization enables International Rescue's daring and eye-catching missions to be fully realized. *Thunderbirds* distinguished itself from past Supermarionation fare by not placing all of its toys in one sandbox: the aerodynamics of Thunderbirds 1 and 2, the space-based Thunderbird 3, the sub-aquatic Thunderbird 4, and the watchful, sentinel-esque role of Thunderbird 5 gave the series its panoramic sense of adventure.

Most Special Mecha

The post-*Thunderbirds* shows marked the rise of Mike Trim as the main designer of the vehicles tasked with communicating the action and energy of Supermarionation. With the more senior figures of Century 21 Productions chiefly concerned with expanding the company's cinematic division, it fell chiefly to the younger staff to handle production of the TV series. By the time *The Secret Service* (1969) went into production, day-to-day operations were being supervised by Hill, with Gerry and Sylvia Anderson focusing their efforts on 1969 science-fiction film *Doppelgänger*.

With *Captain Scarlet*, for which Meddings produced Cloudbase, the SPV (Spectrum Pursuit Vehicle), and the Angel Interceptors, it was Trim's responsibility to design the remainder of Spectrum's wide variety of vehicles and guest mecha. Spectrum's mecha reflect the military aesthetic of the series: gone are the vibrant colours and evocative names of the Thunderbird machines. In their place are stern, sombre colours, chiefly greys and cold blues, with acronyms mainly used for naming conventions. The monolithic presence of Cloudbase, the grandest mecha of any Supermarionation show, now serves as a ubiquitous reminder of Spectrum's watchful presence over the world.

Elsewhere, Spectrum's core mecha veer between the bulky and the nimble. The tank-like SPV and the sorely underused MSV (Maximum Security Vehicle) further underline Spectrum's hawkish vocation, yet even though the SPC (Spectrum Patrol Car), SPJ (Spectrum Passenger Jet), and the Angel Interceptors are far slicker, more agile vehicles, all evoke perfectly the darker attitude of the show, especially when compared to *Thunderbirds*. Like the guest vehicles he designed for *Thunderbirds*, Trim's other mecha for *Captain Scarlet* continue the streamlined shapes from before, helping to give the futuristic setting of the series a visual immediacy.

Compared to the fleets of vehicles found in *Thunderbirds* and *Stingray*, *Joe 90* (1968-1969) boasted a far more limited array of core mecha, Professor Mac's car and Sam Loover's saloon being the only vehicles that regularly appeared in the show. Mac's car is a marked departure from past designs. Here, Meddings takes a significantly experimental approach, producing a vehicle that harks back to the days of *Supercar*: a cumbersome mecha characterized by exposed components, easily the least elegant thing he ever produced. Professor Mac's car is either delightfully quirky or off-puttingly clunky, depending on your point of view. Fortunately, Trim delivers a further batch of handsome companion vehicles throughout the series that are very similar in flavour to the mecha of *Captain Scarlet*.

The Secret Service (1969) took things to extremes by not featuring a core vehicle of a futuristic design at all. A re-fashioned 1917 Ford Model T, Gabriel is the furthest departure from the retro-futuristic visions the Andersons were famous for producing. Again, more companion vehicles do appear scattered throughout, but the limited number of episodes for the series—a grand total of 13—meant that the blade fell prematurely on the reign of Supermarionation, and with it the eye-popping display of ingenuity and creativity of the company's vehicle department. The Century 21 team would continue to entertain viewers with the live-action productions *Doppelgänger* and *UFO* (1970-1973), but the evocative, sometimes nearly anthropomorphic designs that had defined the visual action of the puppet shows would end here.

Tomorrow's Cross-sections Today

Beyond the style of the craft, then, what exactly has been written about their functionality? Some basic details of the craft's capabilities and mechanics had been mapped out by Anderson, but it would fall to those at Century 21 Publishing to flesh these details out. One of the many arms that Century 21 Productions grew as the company blossomed in commercial success, the publishing division's in-depth cross-sections were produced to delight readers and published in both the TV21 comic and annuals produced to tie-in with each series.

Fascination with these mecha remains strong 50 years on, and book-length collections of cross-sections exist almost as a distinct subculture within Anderson fandom. As revivals of *Stingray*, *Thunderbirds*, and *Captain Scarlet* have come and gone since the 1990s, fresh interpretations of Anderson mecha have been produced, and books that collect past material continue to sell, as do original works, such as the pair of ever-popular Haynes Manuals written and drawn for *Thunderbirds* and *Captain Scarlet*. Packed with in-depth examinations of the functionality and interior of the shows' respective craft, these books are testament to the imaginative response the vehicles of Supermarionation continue to inspire.

IRONMONGERY VS. AGONY: WHEN WAS *UFO* AT ITS BEST?

Like so much of Gerry and Sylvia Anderson's output, *UFO* makes a lot more sense when it's viewed in the context of what came before and after it. With that purposefully framed positioning in mind, it's little wonder that many consider *UFO* to be a peak of the Andersons' filmography, if not *the* peak. *UFO* knows that it's time to evolve from the earlier days of Supermarionation. It's a series that's packed with the pyrotechnic energy perfected by Century 21 Productions throughout the 1960s, but it marries that energy with a grim introspection. As we explored in **A Question of Survival**, *UFO* doesn't just make plenty of room for exploring the human fallout of the war between SHADO and the anonymous aliens – such explorations are part of the series' very fabric. *UFO* is a series where technological alchemy is fused with the agony of those who pilot these fantastic machines that do battle against the never-ending invasion of aliens. Rather than embrace this newfound mentality, freed from the shackles of kidult entertainment (as described by Sylvia Anderson), *UFO* cautiously implements this balance to varying degrees of creative success throughout its run. When then was *UFO* at its best? When the agony overpowered the ironmongery, or when the ironmongery was in control of the agony?

UFO clearly marked the point where Gerry and Sylvia Anderson sought after new and older audiences, desperate to leave their marionette marvels behind. With its scenes of human death being in equal aplomb as scenes of techno-destruction, *UFO* had its eyes on an audience capable of accepting these darker moods. Ironically, that audience would have been the same ones who initially grew up enjoying *Thunderbirds* and *Captain Scarlet* as they were now surely of a suitable age to enjoy *UFO*'s grimmer palette. As such, *UFO* strives to explore themes the Supermarionation series otherwise couldn't accommodate.

It was Ed Bishop (1991) who defined *UFO*'s greatest strengths as when focusing on the vehicular side of things; 'I had always felt that the main interest in the series existed best when we were dealing with hardware. All the actors saying "I'd like to do more with the human relationships" – I don't think that was the format ... Where I think the series breaks new ground, as is still challenging to people to a certain extent today, is in the ironmongering of it, the nuts and bolts of it.' [83] There's no denying that after *Joe 90*, *Thunderbird 6* and *The Secret Service*'s distancing of reliance on hardware that *UFO* boasted a renewed vigour in depicting models and miniatures with a visually impressive swagger. Watching your average episode of the series, it's hard not to see why Bishop would take that stance. *UFO* harks back to Century 21's merchandise-friendly golden age of *Thunderbirds* and *Captain Scarlet* via SHADO's multi-purpose fleet of vehicles designed to defend the Earth from marauding invaders. Rockets, interceptors, submarines, aircraft and ground vehicles make up the core arsenal of SHADO, and surely provided a key reason why audiences remained hooked to the series. Guest vehicles of varying purposes and abilities had always been a mainstay in Supermarionation, but post-*Thunderbirds*, they hadn't formed part of the main line-up of vehicles.

With vehicles that can travel under the oceans, in outer space, through the skies and along the ground, *UFO* displays an animated attitude in its reinvested focus on the visual exhilaration of varied combat sequences that enabled Derek Meddings' special effects and Mike Trim's designs to find a new lease of energetic life in a live-action setting. *UFO* succeeds in marrying the visual stimulus of *Thunderbirds*' multi-purpose rescue vehicle with the context of *Captain Scarlet*'s war weary rage, moulding them into *UFO*'s own identity. This ironmongering then forms the visual basis for much of the series, as Commander Ed Straker continually leads desperate action against the alien invaders. How the agony of the characters weaves itself around the techno-militant aesthetic of *UFO* is what gives the series its emotional depth. The actions of the episodes are propelled not by the technology, but by the characters. Technological mishap is the key event that launches much of *Thunderbirds*' episodic stories into action, but in *UFO*, the technology served as a backdrop to the character-driven plots.

UFO routinely shows its dexterous nature in showing the human fallout of SHADO's invisible war. 'A Question of Priorities' for example remains one of the most striking episodes of the series. The mecha action never intrudes upon the tense drama. It's an episode whose heartbreak is fashioned out of failure to communicate. Ed and Mary barely on speaking terms. Mary forbidding further contact between Ed and John. Ed, Mary and her new husband unable to talk in the hospital waiting room. Ed unwilling to disclose his family troubles to his SHADO personnel, and still unable to explain to Mary why his abrupt departures continue to plague their already fractured relationship. The alien unable to speak to the blind woman and whose only way to communicate is via an electronic device. The episode can't even bring itself to verbally tell us that John has passed away. It's only

---

[83] Drake, C. Bishop, E. (1991) 'CD21: Voices From The Twenty First Century, Vol. 1: Gerry Anderson and Ed Bishop.' Blast From The Past Productions.

ever shown, not told.

For an episode famed for its anguish, it managed to pack in scenes of the mecha-tinged action that gives *UFO* its commercial edge. Interceptors, Mobile Controls, Skydivers, UFOs themselves and the lesser-seen Shad-air craft all make appearances, yet the action set pieces they appear in are directed in a suitably restrained manner. They never intrude upon the pair of trauma-focused plots of Straker losing his son and the blind, elderly woman having her peaceful routine quietly shattered by an alien invasion. The alien themselves appear willing to communicate and be found by SHADO, possibly in an effort to engage with them, yet that never comes to pass. A further UFO murders the alien in cold blood, seemingly confirming the alien's desire to move to the other side of the conflict. Again, communication breakdowns help to pronounce the anguish of the episode further. Nobody in this episode achieves their outcome, humans or alien. The action set pieces curl themselves around the human anguish in this episode even more thanks to the tense, night-time setting that the climax occurs in, with Sky-1 and SHADO Mobiles churning around desolate, midnight countryside. It's not what the characters say in 'A Question of Priorities' that makes their respective dramas stand out, it's what they don't, or can't, say. For all of the hustle and bustle of SHADO's arsenal, it's rendered mute when placed against the human element.

Whilst 'A Question of Priorities' handles its tragic elements in a finely-tuned balance, other episodes embraced friction between characters whilst pushing the hardware to the background. 'The Psychobombs' never manages to acknowledge the ritual-like sacrifice of the trio of humans who become mentally ensnared by the aliens and sent to infiltrate SHADO defences in the most violent manners possible, but its undertones of psychological imprisonment are riveting to watch. Even Straker's acknowledgement of the aliens psychological burrowing into individual human minds to control them at the very end of 'Destruction' comes across like an afterthought to ensure the episode ends on a downbeat note. 'E.S.P.' and 'Flight Path' are more of a success with their focus on individual victims of the aliens. 'Flight Path' has the drama of a SHADO operative forced to work for the aliens like an undercover spy, placing the organisation in jeopardy whilst the human drama unravels itself as the episode progresses, revealing a desperate state of affairs for all involved. 'E.S.P.' pits its human victim already suffering from the internal strain of possessing psychic abilities, with its core threat blooming out of the aliens' choice to exploit this, eventually communicating with Straker directly through this person, no longer a living, thinking human being, but devolved into a biological transmitter. The thrill is witnessing the aliens talk directly to Straker for the first time. The drama is by having to manipulate a human to do, an extension of their probing and deconstruction of the human body itself.

'The Square Triangle' is the episode that comes closest to the dramatic thrust of 'A Question of Priorities', but it's a more disconnected affair. Here, there's no complimentary interplay between dramatic events and SHADO and alien combat. A plot by a pair of lovers to murder the woman's husband falls foul when they accidentally murder an arriving and invading alien, initially believing it to be the husband. SHADO intervene using their standard mind wipe capabilities, but are forced to consider the moral conundrum of either maintaining their secrecy by allowing their murderous plot to play out or stopping the pair's actions by forcing to come out into the open. They ultimately decide on the former. The episode's ambiguous end, replacing the usual nightmarish drift through space, shows the wife walking away from an undisclosed grave to meet her lover. The grave she's visiting is never explicitly confirmed to be her husband's or not, but such is implied. What's being told here then is an adherence to character dramas to embellish the quality of the stories, rather than have the focus entirely on vehicular adventure.

In terms of attempting to master a coherent theme for itself, what *UFO* is also telling us then is two things simultaneously: Not every episode is as creatively successful as the ones discussed, suggesting that *UFO* either couldn't find focus on implementing mature, character-driven emotions into its high-tech mecha-powered stories and couldn't get a grip on a finely-tuned balance between the ironmongery and the agony, or else that the series plundered down an unpredictable path in just how much that human drama would form the basis of each episode, ensuring further viewership by keeping the audience on their toes and refusing to be tied down to a set series of tropes. Whichever view you may subscribe to depends on your interpretation of the series. However, a previously discussed aspect of 'A Question of Priorities' can signpost towards the reasoning behind *UFO*'s jagged thematic push-and-pull. ITC's American branch's decidedly cool treating of the episode suggests that instead of *UFO* not being able to manage itself thematically, the episode's controversial courtship with the higher powers implies that it knew exactly how it wanted to position the iron-mongering and the agony, giving them an equal level of attention.

However, from ITC's perspective, a sci-fi adventure series bristling with vehicles of all shapes and sizes that regularly go into battle against imaginatively-designed aliens was surely an easier sell than intimate human dramas. As such, *UFO* succeeds in delivering on this visually commercial edge, demonstrating from a purely action-centred perspective alone why it's so fondly remembered within the Andersons' back catalogue of productions. In terms of iron-mongering value alone, *UFO*'s importance to Century 21 cannot be underestimated. Whether it's the cerebral *Space: 1999* or the downbeat *UFO*, one element that makes bums sit on seats is the incredibly sophisticated special effects. An inescapable viewing habit of Andersons' output is having viewed past productions when witnessing a new one. In *UFO*'s case, that becomes integral to appreciating the special effects. Having attempted to widen Century 21's cinematic division with mixed results, *UFO* sees Derek Meddings return his attentions to the small screen, having left vehicle designs and other elements to Mike Trim. Here, Meddings and Trim's designs are in sync with one another, having been more of a sort of master and apprentice level during the winding down of Supermarionation. Trim's sleek constructions collide with Medding's brawny bulk in a visually arresting fashion. *UFO* abandons the two-dimensional approach to stock footage of craft soaring through the skies and outer space by filming them in profile, a tactic used to increasingly dull effect post-*Thunderbirds*. More tilted camera angles are used throughout to illuminate these creations in action, creating a much more three-dimensional impression of the action sequences. In *UFO*, special effects sequences come alive by a more cinematic approach, made all the more engaging by the aforementioned diversity in the craft themselves.

That aesthetic dressing gave ITC confidence in the series, so much so that the proposed *UFO 2* would enhance the special effects further by stripping away the recognisable backdrop of Earth and being set mostly on the moon with an enlarged SHADO Moonbase. The enthralling special effects understandably held more exciting prospects when fixated in an outer space setting, enabled due to ITC's findings that the more space-based episodes of *UFO* achieved higher ratings.

UFO 2 never came to pass, but if it did, how might it have shifted the thematic status quo the series had already established for itself? The moon-based setting implies that any further adventures for the series would have learned more towards the iron-mongering side of things, or at least episodes with a more speculative edge to them in place of grounded drama. 'Mindbender' and 'Kill Straker!' are evident of the non-Earth location almost being used as an excuse to dabble in more surreal story-telling in which character arcs are mostly eschewed, though such irregular gems as 'Timelash' and 'The Long Sleep' occur primarily on Earth. Any moon-based series would have robbed us of the likes of Skydiver, but given more room for SHADO Interceptors to take flight, as well as the possibility of new and more adventuresome space-based vehicles too. Presumably then, this would have been less of a second series, but a total reinvention of the series itself.

Pre-production work being scuppered on *UFO*'s second series and quickly turned around to become *Space: 1999* may be a blessing in disguise for those who admire *UFO*'s balance of drama and technology. *Space: 1999*'s debut season is crowded in dense philosophical analogies, as if to wash over the dour attitude of *UFO* that make it a unique viewing experience. *Space: 1999*'s own mind-bending themes are somehow both preposterous and awe-inspiring, continuing to split opinion to this day. *Space: 1999* often made room for its own engaging character dramas, but these are often caught in the crossfire of cosmic phenomenon outside of Moonbase Alpha's understanding. By comparison, *UFO* is down to Earth, in every sense of word.

But energetic, well-crafted special effects can't mask over the cracks that come when there are no characters to draw you in. What makes UFO function so well and so often is the traumatic context given to these special effects. Spin-off media aside, *UFO* consists only of a single series of 26 episodes, during which *UFO* often felt like it struggled to assert itself creatively and fine a genuinely well-cut thematic core. The ideas are undoubtedly there, but the execution sometimes wobbled. *UFO* remains at its most captivating when the agony is enlivened by the ironmongery and when the ironmongery artfully slices into the agony. Some episodes prioritise one or the other, but the series is at its best when the two are treated the same. With its second series unexpectedly forced to morph into an entirely different production, *UFO* had its wings clipped before it could fully embark towards its destination, but the journey it was on is clearly visible and remains one of the most mesmerising, dramatically inclined and mechanically colourful journeys Gerry and Sylvia ever took.

THE UNSOLVABLE MYSTERY OF *THE INVESTIGATOR*

Gerry and Sylvia Anderson's output is so voluminous and has been subject to numerous fan-made and professional reference guides, publications and interpretations over the years that fans have inevitably cast an equally curious eye over their productions that never quite made it off the ground. There's a fascination with pop culture media that never made it past the concept or scripting stage. It has no physical form, but only exists in hushed tones; a film, television series, novel, comic book or album that was never fully completed but whose unfinished state of existence becomes legendary. The out-of-reach nature of these forms of media enables wild speculation to catch fire. What are these works? What could they have been like? What do they currently consist of? How could they have been different from the creator's other works? The thrill is in the guessing, the not knowing. In the case of *The Investigator*, it's a case of not wanting to know.

In the run-up to the autumn debut of *Terrahawks* in 1983, Anderson Burr Pictures issued a press pack dispatched to the world, detailing the premise, characters and vehicles of the series to drum up interest. The back pages of the press pack include a brief professional timeline of Gerry and Christopher Burr's careers to date. Gerry's timeline lists key events in his career, such as *Stingray* being the first UK TV series to be made in colour and the rise of Century 21 Productions as a multifaceted company. Curiously, in-between detailing key factors of *UFO*, *The Protectors* and *Space: 1999*, the timeline mentions, of all things, *The Investigator*, at that point still a relatively unknown property. The timeline has the confidence (or should that be nerve?) to describe *The Investigator* as an 'experimental puppet film'. At that point in time, *The Investigator* remained an unseen venture, highlighting its value as a mystery production, one in whose appeal remained in its invisible nature.

Produced in 1972 within the aftermath of *UFO* and *The Protectors* but during the period when *UFO*'s proposed second series was in pre-production, *The Investigator* was spontaneously conjured into life and almost culled just as quickly. A single pilot episode was made, and it's a pilot whose premise is utterly headache-inducing, with production hampered on almost all sides and ultimately elicits a sigh of relief when the credits roll. Commanding a mere three pages in his 2002 biography, Gerry recalled how the idea for a new children's television series arose from the friendly relationship he had with George Heinemann, vice president of the children's department at NBC. Hedging his bets on the idea that if he were to make a pilot for a proposed children's television series and brought it before Heinemann it would get greenlit, he and a modest film crew packed their bags for Malta to produce one of the lesser concepts to bear the name 'Gerry Anderson' on the credits.

Anderson describes *The Investigator* as many things – a 'gamble', 'a dull, uninspired piece of film-making' and 'a disaster'.[84] No-one involved has ever referred to it in positive tones and their disdain is really quite justified. *The Investigator* is one of those things that's fascinating in its awfulness, but like a lot of productions, its awfulness comes from a mixture of unfortunate circumstances and ill-founded creative choices. Fresh from working on the downbeat adult drama of *UFO* and the slick espionage of *The Protectors*, *The Investigator* sees Anderson take a step back in both medium and premise. Puppets are made use of again, specifically the ultra-proportioned style of *Captain Scarlet* onwards. The premise harks back to the quirky spy-fi of the kid-as-heroes mentality of *Joe 90* and the novelty shrinking abilities seen in *The Secret Service*. Even if the making of the pilot wasn't strewn with problems for the production crew, it's difficult to envision how a full series might have developed.

The worst aspect of *The Investigator*'s story is that it's so incomplete. The Investigator itself is an omnipotent, omniscient alien who ventures to Earth from their own world, compelled to right the wrongs of our planet. To aid their efforts, the Investigator enlists the help of two Earth children, John and Julie. He miniaturises them to marionette-size (though it's never acknowledged that they go one step further and turns them into actual marionettes themselves), bequeaths them with a pair of supersonic vehicles, one of which has the ability to … go really fast, and the other … can go on water. The Investigator tasks them with stopping wealthy art thief Stavros Karanti from stealing a priceless painting. Using their newfound miniature forms and colourful vehicles, John and Julie embark on their first mission.

The more you poke at *The Investigator*'s premise, the more it crumbles. The pilot offers no genuine explanation for why John and Julie must be made smaller, why the Investigator requires outside help at all, what exactly they intend to do on Earth or who exactly the Investigator is. It's also difficult to ascertain who exactly *The Investigator* may be aimed at as a series. The Andersons' recent forays into live action were at least partly as a result of the dwindling popularity of their marionette productions, making *The Investigator* feel like a step back in every sense of the word. The exterior locations add a welcome sense of fun exoticism for the pilot, but still there

---

[84] Archer, S. Marcus, H. (2002) 'Stand By For Action' *What Made Thunderbirds Go! The Authorised Biography of Gerry Anderson*. pp. 208-210. BBC Books. 2nd edition.

still remains the unshakeable sensation that *The Investigator* doesn't entirely know how to make its own premise function. There's touches of spy-fi capers, puzzling cosmic fantasy and techno-action characteristic of past Anderson productions, but the finished pilot doesn't fully gel these genres together into a satisfying whole. Much of this disparity can be attributed to problems endured on all sides during overseas productions in Malta. Both the car and speedboat models were prone to malfunctioning, filming the delicate marionettes in outdoor conditions proved awkward, stormy weather stole entire days' worth of shooting from the production crew and the crew ended up returning home with a disparate amount of footage to piece together.

Watching the finished pilot gives little indication of these issues, however. Once you push past the daft premise, the story told is cohesive enough, but just doesn't strive to be as enjoyable as its odd cocktail of ingredients may suggest, which can equally be attributed to issues arisen from the pilot's production and the slap-dash attitude of the premise. It raises more questions than it answers, but not the sort to hook you into wanting a full series. They're the sort of questions, as laid out earlier, that makes you wonder how this series was meant to succeed at all. In a peculiar twist on an already peculiar premise that speaks volumes about either the lack of footage to edit or the sheer oddness of the script, the episode opens with a brief voiceover from the Investigator explaining their presence on Earth before opening in a cave in Malta with John and Julie not only having already made contact with the Investigator, but are already in their miniature form. We don't see their fully-grown counterparts at all, made even stranger by the lack of awareness on their part that they haven't simply been shrunk – they've been turned into puppets. Unless the pilot is telling us that John and Julie are still puppets in their fully grown state, of course.

The opening scene of the pair in their hideout establishes that they've been awaiting the Investigator's first mission for some time. As John and Julie converse on the weirdness of their situation, a fire keeps them warm, whilst slowly cooking a previously caught fish, gargantuan in size when compared to the miniscule duo. Is the Investigator essentially keeping them prisoner here? And how exactly did the pair manage to catch the fish? So many questions and so few answers. Our feelings of empathy which we're presumably meant to experience for our pint-sized heroes is squandered on hearing two familiar voices bring these characters to life – Sylvia Anderson and Shane Rimmer. Despite making sense from a production stand-point to have familiar faces making an already fraught production a smoother ride, having a pair of then-middle aged actors portray characters who are meant to be children only smothers the illusion the pilot's trying to make.

It's worth noting that *The Investigator*'s premise, whilst bizarre and unnourished, isn't strictly bad. *Joe 90* and *The Secret Service* made their curious ideas work to great effect, securing their places as endearing chapters in cult television. *The Investigator*'s execution of its own ideas is where the weakness lies. The novelty hook of John and Julie being miniaturised is underserved by the fact that their usefulness in being so small is barely made use of throughout the pilot. There's a skeletal amount of genuine action and adventure as well, climaxing in a moralistic manner in taking down your enemy. Secluding themselves within Karanti's private plane after his successful robbery of the painting, John demands that Karanti turn himself in to the authorities, masquerading as Karanti's subconscious. A petrified Karanti obliges, presumably now scarred for life by this mysterious voice that will haunt his dreams forever. Speaking of psychological implications, there's some strange dialogue that highlights the problematic nature of John and Julie being shrunk. Staking out the church where the painting is and where Karanti plans to strike, Julie brings up the subject of just how long she and John will remain in their miniature forms, implying they now live a cursed existence. Just before Julie can dive any further into the matter, John interrupts her as Karanti strikes.

This particular scene goes some way in highlighting the personalities of the pair, Julie appearing more reflective and self-aware whilst John is more concerned with being an Action Man hero brought to life. It also highlights how John gets much of the spotlight here and how Julie is left out in the cold. It's John who most often springs into action, John who pretends to be Karanti's subconscious and it's John who pilots the Investigator car. Both car and speedboat are a by-product of the Investigator's abilities, as well as subtly implanting the knowledge and experience into John's brain in order to pilot both vehicles, in true *Joe 90* style. Neither vehicles scale the heights of Thunderbird 2 or an SPV, but they're bright, blocky vehicles that give the scenes they're featured in bursts of energy.

Of course, this being *The Investigator*, it can't end without a last desperate thrust at mind-numbing confusion. With Karanti in the hands of the authorities and the painting back where it belongs, John and Julie return to their hideout to inform the Investigator of all that has happened. The Investigator, represented by a throbbing green light hidden within the rock walls of the hideout cave, states that there's no need for such a report, because he has been watching the events the whole time, once again raising far too many questions regarding where the Investigator's abilities begin and end and why therefore, given how omnipotent they appear to be, do they need the help of two children at all. It's a weird and vague end to a weird and vague story.

Unsurprisingly, *The Investigator* was not picked up for a full television series, but not because Heinemann shared Gerry Anderson's negative view of the pilot. The finished pilot was deemed to be so unwatchable that Gerry restricted its release and Heinemann never even saw it. *The Investigator* was discarded as a poor effort on everyone's part. Gerry spoke in not-so-positive tones about Reg Hill and Sylvia Anderson's contributions. Sylvia herself was responsible for the script writing (with story contributions from Shane Rimmer), a decision that Gerry regretted. *The Investigator* isn't even mentioned in Sylvia's own autobiography *My Fab Years*, further indication of how this was a production nobody involved wanted to remember.

Despite its reputation, or perhaps because of it, interest in *The Investigator* has commanded some substantial level of interest. The pilot's profile was raised thanks to its inclusion on Network's *The Lost Worlds of Gerry Anderson* DVD set. Placed alongside stronger lost gems such as *Into Infinity* and the 'Star Laws' pilot for *Space Police* (before it was refitted to become *Space Precinct*), *The Investigator* is as dwarfed as John and Julie are whenever they come into contact with the real world. Given the jumble of ideas at work here, perhaps the worst thing one can say about *The Investigator* is that it's ... dull. It simply doesn't make good use of its madcap ideas to be as hooky a production as it may want to be, but watching the episode, there's the distinct atmosphere that very few people's hearts are fully in it – lacklustre special effects, uncommitted performances, half-hearted story-telling bump into each other without much care or attention. If there's one positive aspect to *The Investigator* one can raise, it's that this pilot is, thankfully, all that exists of a creation that should never have come into existence.

CUBED HUMOUR: TRACKING *TERRAHAWKS'* COMEDIC EVOLUTION

Terrahawks is held in various regards within the Anderson fandom. It's a series that's well-known, but not in the same way that *Thunderbirds* or *Captain Scarlet* are well-known. *Terrahawks* is noted for its low production values in comparison to past Anderson works. It's noted for its humorous characters. It's noted for its imaginative, well-crafted special effects. It's also noted, infamous even, for its sense of humour. Comical characters and tongue-in-cheek storylines collide into each other like wrecking balls. It's as if *Terrahawks* casts a leering eye over Gerry Anderson's past efforts throughout the '60s and '70s and finds as much to parody about them as it does to celebrate them. An overall yet inaccurate portrait of the series perceives that it's a comedown from what Anderson had produced before. Many fans will inform you, frothing at the mouth, that *Terrahawks* is the worst series he created, dismissive of the fact that among the variety of failed or discarded concepts for films and TV shows Anderson had trailing around him during the late 1970s and early 1980s, it was *Terrahawks* that was given the green light, and ultimately reminded audiences of Gerry Anderson after several years away from the limelight, not so much as a person, but as a brand, a creator of sci-fi entertainment.

After the grim human drama of *UFO* and the philosophical musings of *Space: 1999*, a pair of series that had targeted a more adult audience than the child-focused Supermarionation era had done, *Terrahawks'* view as being a step backwards is encouraged by the fact that it didn't have those older Anderson fans in mind. It was focusing on a newer, younger audience. The older fans made their disdain for *Terrahawks* known early on by writing into *Supermarionation Is Go* (otherwise known as *SIG*), one of the earliest Anderson fanzines. In issue #10, published in the spring of 1984, fans liberally let their feelings on the series be known in *Lip-Sync*, the regular letters feature of the publication. 'I must say that I was quite astonished at how bad *Terrahawks* is,' wrote one disgruntled fan. 'Frankly, I think it is a disappointment,' wrote another[85]. In the interests of balance, a variety of

---

[85] 'Lip-Sync: S.I.G. Letters' *Supermarionation Is Go* (eds. Nightingale, D. Sheehan, B). No. 10, pp. 12-13.

other letters are included that commend the series' special effects, the characters, and acknowledge the unfair comparisons *Terrahawks* will inevitably incur to the Andersons' past work. Nevertheless, from the pages of vintage fan publications to the current digital landscape of fan forums, fans continue to be quickly dismissive of *Terrahawks'* less sophisticated attitude and how its humour compound scripts that were being perceived as ill-thought out. Like the majority of the Andersons' output however, *Terrahawks* rewards close inspection. For a series celebrated and ridiculed for its comedy in equal measure, and that Big Finish would take to gleeful extremes with its three-series audio continuation which started in 2015, it's intriguing to uncover that *Terrahawks'* comedic foundations were gradually built up rather than being fully formed from its launch.

Terrahawks never outright began as the action-comedy it's otherwise known for. It began as being more concerned with pushing violent, stern and sometimes horror aesthetics into the otherwise child-friendly storytelling and even then never quite let go of these early elements. 'Expect the Unexpected' forms the first two episodes of the series, but its fallout leads seamlessly into the events of 'Thunder-Roar', forming a loose three-part story that highlights the less comedic aspects that *Terrahawks* was exhibiting in its early days. Indeed, where episodes throughout the second and third series are littered with episodes purposefully made to break out the laughs, much of the first series is quite a different beast. The elements were all there for *Terrahawks* to be a comedy – the tempestuous relationships between Doctor 'Tiger' Ninestein and Sergeant Major Zero, along with Zelda and her dysfunctional family, but it would be a slow-burn for all of these elements to be fully embraced. Humour is also to be found in how script editor Tony Barwick wrote the majority of the episodes, but continually credited the episodes under pun-flavoured pseudonyms – T I Gerstein, Ivor Purstein and I C Bergstein are just some of the 'names' used to great effect. Given how readily the pieces were there, it's odd that those comedy vibes weren't taken to heart right away. At a time when Anderson had been away from the cameras for such a prolonged spell, perhaps he and his team were still getting used to making TV shows again.

Throughout these first three episodes, scenes of death and destruction fill the screens and are treated with severity rather than played for laughs. *Terrahawks'* opening credits feature of a digitally-constructed cutaway of Zelda, revealing her android interiors, a grotesque bio-robotic skeleton, before leaping on to her destruction of the NASA Mars geological space base as she arrives to claim her new territory. 'Expect the Unexpected' goes onto display Zelda's freakish telekinetic powers in full swing, whilst the eventual 'Thunder-Roar' depicts the monstrous Sram causing devastation wherever he roams and roars, his eventual confrontation with the Terrahawks resulting in his defeat, oozing out a green, clumpy substance as he succumbs to his strange death. In these early episodes, the absurdity of *Terrahawks'* premise is firmly locked in, but the series hadn't yet clocked onto the idea of surrealism as a conduit for comedy, which would be how much of *Terrahawks'* humour would be found throughout the course of the series. Instead, bodily deconstructions of alien menaces are the focus.

However, humour was still clearly on *Terrahawks'* mind early on, highlighted by such moments as the burial of Number 13, the first Zeroid to be destroyed by Zelda when she makes her presence known to the Terrahawks on Earth. A soldier's funeral is carried out by Zero in the aftermath of Zelda's initial invasion and only attended by the Zeroids themselves. The oddity of the scene is emphasised by another Zeroid revealing to his leader that he fails to understand the significance of the burial, enquiring if another Number 13 will eventually be reconstructed. Cementing his wry but soulful nature, Zero quips that Number 35 has no heart, a literal and mental reflection of the robotic nature of this subgroup of characters who dependably brought humour through their diverse personalities. What we have here in is a schizophrenic pull between the gruesome and the gaudy. This notion of *Terrahawks* being not entirely one or the other but a tangle of both is the legacy it leaves behind as its core, but during these earlier episodes, it was a case of confusion, the sense that *Terrahawks* was still lacking the confidence to assert what kind of series it wanted to be. As *Terrahawks* strolled on, it would find its identity in that confusion.

Comedic episodes were at the forefront of *Terrahawks* throughout the second and third series, but such gems as 'Play It Again, Sram' (in which Zelda and her family's latest plot against the Terrahawks is to thwart Kate Kestrel in the World Song Contest) and 'Runaway' (a starring adventure for the hapless Yung-Star, who runs away from his mother to the safety of … Earth?) are almost nowhere to be found in the first series. 'A Christmas Miracle', complete with Zelda in drag, wooing a reluctant 'Tiger', comes closest to the humour *Terrahawks* would eventually embrace, but that was a dream-induced episode, a clear-cut separation between reality and fantasy. The episode then tells us that far-out humour is relegated to fantasy and not the reality in which the series occurs.

The light-hearted 'The Ugliest Monster of All', featuring the first appearance of the furry Napoleon space bear Yuri, hints at the series-wide comedic tones to come. Zelda and her family repulsing at the sight of this cuddly cosmic creature is the initial source of humour, yet its positioning in official episode guides as next to the much more morose 'Close Call' highlights how *Terrahawks* was awkwardly still figuring out if it wanted to be serious or comedic, before it would go onto realise it was at its most entertaining when the two were in balance. There's little in *Terrahawks'* overall canon quite as sternly downbeat and morally righteous as 'Close

Call'. Even 'The Ultimate Menace' finds humour in Zero's interaction with the colossal, seemingly unstoppable computer entity Zyklon, a robotic force so powerful its presence commands a temporary truce between Ninestein and Zelda. The militant vibes of 'First Strike' finds its comedy value in the vastly oversized Great White One spacecraft sent to do the task the Terrahawks hadn't achieved at that point of wiping Zelda from the face of Mars. Clearly then, *Terrahawks* showed some focus in balancing grand threat with offbeat comedy, yet 'Close Call' encapsulates how the series was still heading towards that destination as the cameras were rolling, rather than its course set beforehand.

'Close Call' sees Zelda exploit the interest in Terrahawks' secretive nature by targeting obsessive reporter Mark Darrel, commandeering his services to invade and destroy Hawknest. The episode's emotional core sees the ever-present clash between the righteous, iron-fisted Ninestein and the more humanist Mary Falconer, whose ability to cool 'Tiger''s temper always gives the pair a harmonized juxtaposition. During the episode, Mary questions 'Tiger''s totalitarian view in maintaining Hawknest's security from Darrel in what feels like a set-up for 'Tiger''s might-makes-right mentality to be put in its place by Mary, as it often is. However, the episode comes to an unexpected climax when it's revealed during Darrel's attempted destruction of the Terrahawks base that Darrel isn't only under Zelda's influence, but that he's become a full-blown android. 'Tiger' is the one who demands Mary shoot Darrel prior to the shock reveal, justifying his iron rule. Doing so exposes Darrel's inner circuitry, with Mary lamenting how 'Tiger' was right all along.

It's an episode with the darkest of hearts, the ambiguity in how Zelda constructed an android rendition of Darrel (unless this *is* the original Darrel, in which case Zelda must surely have gutted his innards to be replaced with a robotic make-up), which is never confirmed, is crushed under the weight of the episode's portrayal of the Terrahawks organisation as a law unto itself, with an innocent human life caught in the middle and ultimately lost, the death of Darrel taken as confirmation that one human life can't outweigh Terrahawks' secretive security set-up. Tragedy and morality would never quite meet on the same page again with *Terrahawks*. Despite the new production now underway, one that was markedly different in its style from what had come before, everyone involved clearly thought they were still making *UFO*.

The manner in which *Terrahawks'* humour really takes a firmer grip gradually occurs as the series evolved over time. Whilst the general premise of Zelda arriving on Mars and declaring war against the Earth as punishment for her people once being the slaves of humanoid creatures (initially described as humans themselves) is treated with a suitably grandiose amount of threat, menace and danger, it's also portrayed with appropriate surrealism, right from the off. This is primarily enhanced by the Supermacromation production standards. It's the surrealism that enables the humour to be pushed to the forefront as the series progresses. The sheer ludicrous attitude of so much of *Terrahawks* grants a natural occurring humour to settle into place.

It ranges from regular character fractures to more one-off moments. Zelda's family is one of abundant, continuous dysfunction, with much mirth to be found in this omnipotent, omniscient would-be ruler of the universe hampered at almost every turn by her slovenly, idiotic son and her vein, dim-witted sister. Interestingly, Yung-Star's caveman-esque mentality is saved for later on in the first series whilst Cy-Star isn't introduced immediately. The balance is restored and the chaos is furthered with the arrival of the scheming, fiercely intelligent, gender-fluid It-Star, the child of Cy-Star, the only immediate member of Zelda's family capable of being on her intellectual level. Zelda's own supernatural powers can't help but gain an absurd undertone in how ill-defined and plot-convenient they are, particularly on numerous occasions where instead of sending her ready-made monsters to Earth one by one, it's casually implied she could bring the Earth to its knees from the comfort of her Mars base.

Even more comically odd is the fact that the final scene of 'Expect the Unexpected' reveals that Zelda has brought not only herself but an entire army of deadly alien creatures, frozen in cryogenic storage, to aid her in her quest to destroy the Earth. Towering stacks of rectangular storage containers are housed in Zelda's complex as we see through the frosted glass of one such box that Sram, ruler of Felony, is Zelda's first choice. Most likely due to the budget constraints placed on the series throughout its existence, Zelda would ultimately end up making use of the same small handful of monsters she'd gradually unfreeze, rather than make use of the seemingly endless array of creatures she may cherry-pick from. Sram's multiple deaths, dying and reappearing inexplicably without explanation across 'Thunder-Roar', 'Thunder Path' and 'Play It Again, Sram', is a preposterous consequence of this.

The villains of Terrahawks are where much of the humour lies, their grotesque appearances and exaggerated personalities lending themselves well to comedic instances. Comedy is also found within the human and Zeroid heroes of the series, though less so when compared to the villains. The Zeroids strike up more comedy than their human masters, with their amusingly distinct personalities resulting in battles of wits between such characters as the jovial Sergeant Major Zero and the camp Space Sergeant 101, both of whom exhibit easily tempered personalities. Other allies of the heroes add to the outside sense of comedy being interjected in sporadic doses, as if to make sure they don't outstay their welcome alongside the more grounded personalities of 'Tiger', Mary, Kate, Hawkeye and Hiro.

NASA representative Colonel Johnson never quite puts two and two together when he routinely meets with 'Tiger' to assign new missions at what he thinks are secret locations, unaware that he often visits Hawknest itself, but it's the wonderfully over-the-top personality Stew Dapples that lent *Terrahawks* much of its early humour, confirming that the comedy wasn't going to be restricted to the villains. An entire episode devoted to him in the second with 'Cry UFO' and suggestions that a fourth series of *Terrahawks*, which ultimately went unmade, would have expanded upon his relationship with Kate Kestrel highlight how *Terrahawks* increasingly veered towards the comedic, taking advantage of its caricatured comedy.

Several key episodes from *Terrahawks*' second and third series revel in being amusingly exaggerated. 'Play It Again, Sram' quite happily throws caution to the wind and embraces the humour that had struggled for space amidst *Terrahawks*' other themes until now. After several campaigns of terror involving everything from distortion of physics, alien warships descending to Earth, armies of Cubes assaulting construction sights and terrifying monsters laying waste to Earth's natural landscape, Zelda concocts a plan to ruin the Terrahawks through the power of music.

Kate Kestrel's successful winning of the World Song Contest outrages Zelda, who argues that she has no right to move onto the Interstellar Song Contest when Zelda and her family represent Mars yet were not consulted on the competition. Intergalactic bureaucracy overrides Ninestein's astute observation that she invaded Mars by force, and thus Zelda and the Muzoids enter a battle-of-the-bands styled standoff between themselves and Kate on an abandoned mining complex within a large asteroid. The episode is rife with music industry parody, akin to *Stingray*'s own pop culture send-up 'Titan Goes Pop'. These include Kate initially going up against stiff competition such as Kay, Gee & Bee and Rod Stalwart, Sram being recruited on the drums for Zelda's group and a trio of Cubes providing backing vocals to Zelda's absurd performance. The greatest witty instance though comes in more subtle terms, specifically the fact that the existence of an Interstellar Song Contest in the first place casually confirms that humanity in the *Terrahawks* world co-exists peacefully with other alien lifeforms and are on good enough terms to initiate a friendly musical competition such as this. It's hard to imagine *Space: 1999* or *New Captain Scarlet* interjecting references to *Casablanca*, Rod Stewart and *Star Trek*, but only *Terrahawks* has the audacity to pull such a move off.

More substantial in its humour is the third series gem 'Cry UFO', an episode centred on the exploits of *Terrahawks*' ultimate comic relief character Stew Dapples. Having spent much of the series as a go-to source for one-liners, 'Cry UFO' prizes open Stew's troubled life away from Anderburr Records. It's revealed that he lives with his overprotective mother and that he harbours unrealised musical aspirations away from Anderburr Records.

His humdrum routine lifestyle is made all the more unbearable when his witnessing of a colossal alien spacecraft goes unbelieved by everyone around him. Only Kate believes his wild claims, even more odd comedy to be found in the fact that despite *Terrahawks* takes place in a world where space travel appears to be quite common, a UFO sighting is treated with mockery.

It's an episode that casts a self-aware gaze over a character who had been treated as almost a throwaway addition to the cast, a deliberate and well-worn punching bag of a gag of a character, one who only existed to spew forth amusing interjections and enable any situation he's in a humorous one. The life that Stew leads in 'Cry UFO' brings to mind elements of tragicomedy, a thoroughly suitable motif for a character whose sole function up until now was to be the funny one. His depressing existence gives the punchbag motif some welcome substance, whilst the episode itself ends on a note of redemption for Stew as the Terrahawks trace and obliterate the enemy craft, with Stew looking on in proud justification in front of those who refused to believe him earlier. 'Cry UFO' is an absolute highlight of *Terrahawks*, an unusual episode from a series famed for how unusual it is overall, because it balances the trashy with the savvy.

What's to be noted here then is that much of *Terrahawks* humour is drawn from its characters, with storylines used to enhance and highlight the oddity of the heroes and villains. The quirkiness of the premise effortlessly ripples into the bizarre story choices throughout the course of the series and with it the characters who bring those stories to life. Where the humour in *Terrahawks* takes its time to settle in and become comfortable, *Terrahawks* is always at ease to tell imaginatively strange stories that elicit a more amusing reaction than what had come before. After the space opera epics of *Space: 1999* and the cosmic Cold War drama of *UFO*, *Terrahawks* feels like a renewed burst of fresh air with the angst scrubbed clean, made even fresher by the humour that would grip the series as it progressed.

The constant tripwire balance of comedy, sci-fi, action and horror that's constantly at work within *Terrahawks'* individual episodes is an understandably perplexing experience. It points to either lack of cohesion in maintaining *Terrahawks'* tonal form or a rampant playfulness that gives the series plenty of rewatch value, depending on your perception of the series itself. It's unsurprising that older fans were keen to wash the bitter aftertaste the second series of *Space: 1999* had left with something more akin to *Space: 1999*'s first series or *UFO*, where the ingredients were in a more tasteful balance. *Terrahawks* remains utterly tasteless, and all the more distinctive and entertaining in the Andersons' back catalogue because of that.

INSTRUMENTS OF DESTRUCTION: HOW *NEW CAPTAIN SCARLET* EVOLVED ITS CHARACTERS

With *New Captain Scarlet*, Gerry Anderson's final television production to be fully realised before his death embraced modern production values with its CGI construction and contemporary world-building perspectives, packing in as much exuberance in shaping a believable, hyper-techno-futuristic world as its original incarnation had done so. Where 1967's *Captain Scarlet and the Mysterons*, like so many Anderson productions of its era, has come to be partially defined for its retro-futuristic appeal, 2005's *New Captain Scarlet* feels much closer to home in its tonal aesthetic. A totally fresh continuity allowed Anderson to apply genuine 21st century trends and values to the world of the war of nerves. The technology of Spectrum and the Mysterons is upgraded to digital standards and the Spectrum uniforms and vehicles fiercely modernised, amongst other obvious elements that demanded reinvention. In the story-telling department, *New Captain Scarlet* also clutched at contemporary audience expectations by implementing a more confident approach to carving out personalities for the men and women of Spectrum and far greater emotional development for its characters than the original series accomplished.

Children and young adult's television was still in its infancy in 1967. A mere 10 years had only passed since characters on kid's TV were no more sophisticated in personality than Bill and Ben or Andy Pandy. But where the likes of *Doctor Who* gave its youthful audience appreciable, complicated characters to engage with, the Supermarionation shows straddled an awkward balance between wanting to be treated like human actors and yet rarely investing in fully-rounded personality or character arcs. In terms of growth, the majority of the heroes and villains of Supermarionation exit their respective series as they entered it. This was something *New Captain Scarlet* rectifies immensely, with numerous characters forced to become entangled in personal conflicts within the far greater threat that the Mysterons pose to the world. By doing so, much more concrete personalities and arcs emerge throughout the series, some slower than others, some bubbling beneath the surface, but it creates an entirely new layer of emotional damage for the war of nerves.

Best of Enemies

Numerous episodes aren't focused solely on action and adventure; they're also focused on how the characters themselves animate that action and adventure, making the stakes feel all the more palpable by enwrapping the technologically-centred action around a very human heart. It's as if *New Captain Scarlet* doesn't take inspiration solely from its source material, but also from that other classic Anderson series that features human drama woven around a secretive outfit battling against omniscient aliens; *UFO*. Like the 1970 live-action sci-fi drama, *New Captain Scarlet* featured a bountiful handful of episodes and subplots devoted to exploring the human fallout of the war of nerves, rather than being content to focus squarely on the Mysteron threat of the week. This isn't to say that *New Captain Scarlet* is a total magnum opus in executing considered, astute character growth for its various players. Not every character gets their fair share of development. But in the context of how undernourished the heroes and villains unfortunately amounted to in the original series, *New Captain Scarlet* pulls on the strings of the original series, dragging the new incarnations of the original's characters into compelling directions.

At the centre of *New Captain Scarlet*'s invigorated emphasis on the characters is the love triangle between Captain Scarlet (Paul Metcalfe), Captain Black (Conrad Lefkon[86]) and Destiny Angel (Simone Giraudoux[87]). The opening two-part story 'Instruments of Destruction' shows us that Conrad and Simone were once in a loving relationship, but Conrad's conversion to the Mysteron cause tears into their formerly harmonious bond. Once the Mysterons establish themselves as the new status quo against Spectrum, Destiny and Scarlet's own romantic relationship begins to, always flirtatious yet never consummated. As if to enhance the dark heart of *New Captain Scarlet*, Black's transformation into a Mysteron early on in the series, much like in the original series, means that we only ever see the destructive remains of his and Destiny's relationship, and never witness them in happier, pre-war of nerves times. Likewise, we never see Scarlet and Destiny's own relationship advance beyond suggestive playfulness, despite a very real bond being struck up between the pair. The feeling is that *New Captain Scarlet* wants to maintain a sense of tragedy by making sure none of its characters are allowed a happy ending, with this very real sense of

---

[86] Black's name was changed for the series from 'Conrad Turner' to 'Conrad Lefkon'. (His new second name coming from *Space Precinct*'s associate producer, Roger Lefkon.)

[87] Changed from 'Juliette Pontoin'.

desperation enabling *New Captain Scarlet* to be more engaging than the disconnected atmosphere the original series so often succumbed to when delivering its take on the characters.

Then there's Scarlet and Black's own relationship, which has far more in common to its portrayal in the comics, novels, annuals and audio dramas that were spun off from the original TV series than the actual original series itself. Where the 1967 take on Captain Black remained a reclusive, mostly mute figure, the spin-off media portrayed him in a much more open manner and more than willing to engage verbally and violently with Captain Scarlet. This attitude is brought over into *New Captain Scarlet*, but with a key difference. Conrad loses his stiff, corpse-like mannerisms and embraces a more cunning, snarling persona, more intent on intimidating his enemies, more willing to crack a dark joke. He also harbours a more direct resentment of Captain Scarlet, making their relationship more confrontational, emphasized by not only the fact that Scarlet essentially steals the love of his life, but in how Black and Scarlet represent two sides of the same coin, one Spectrum and one Mysteron, blurring the lines between the definition of the hero and the villain, a reflection of *Captain Scarlet*'s anti-war attitude, whatever the incarnation.

'Enigma' catapults the paranoia surrounding these three characters into the open, manifesting these characters internal feelings for one another into sometime seemingly very real. A gargantuan Mysteron structure descends silently upon Earth. Spectrum investigates, only to be sucked into the entity and proceed to suffer psychological torture to varying extremes. Captain Scarlet finds himself trapped in a serene, snow-laden town just in time for Christmas, only to find Captain Black and Destiny enjoying a wholesome family Christmas. Despite the pair's insistence that Scarlet could possibly end the war and allow this once loving couple to reunite, it's all revealed to be a ruse, a distraction enabled by the Mysterons to inflict another threat elsewhere. The importance of this broken relationship was clearly something the Mysterons took note of, exploiting Scarlet's own feelings by targeting the guilt he feels towards embracing Destiny from Black's hands. A reformed Conrad who falls back to the love of his life proved to be nothing more than a lie, projected from Scarlet's own consciousness.

On occasion, the former human Captain Black does attempt to break through his newfound Mysteron identity in reality. 'Best of Enemies' sees Scarlet and Black trapped together in the confines of a Rhino that's collapsed beneath the surface of an icy Russian lake. Forced to cooperate if either of them are to escape alive, some intimate pathos is struck up between the pair as Scarlet surreptitiously probes Black about just how much of a Mysteron he has become. Slyly dodging the questions until the pair reach the surface, Conrad melts into the snow-ridden night, asking Scarlet to continue to take care of Destiny, an apparent acceptance on Conrad's part that he can never return to his former life. The series finale, 'Dominion', takes a cheaper shot at Conrad regaining his former personality. The episode sees Conrad claim to have freed himself from the Mysteron conscience, and he and Paul venture back to Mars to destroy the Mysterons once and for all. The episode and series ends overall on the cliffhanger of the two Mysteron rings remaining active, suggesting that Black's return to humanity may have been a lie, but it's a handsome reversal of fortunes that Paul and Conrad, the ones who accidentally started this war, should be the ones to end it. It's also refreshing to see how, on more than once occasion, Conrad attempts to pierce through the Mysterons' stranglehold. Overall Scarlet, Black and Destiny are at the centre of *New Captain Scarlet*'s keen eye on its characters.

Touch of the (Invisible) Reaper

The Mysterons themselves arguably have a far less developed moral stance than they did in the original series. Where the original series initially portrayed the Mars aliens as a welcoming race who viewed Captain Black's *Zero-X* mission with welcoming interest, they're only provoked into anger by Black's trigger-happy yet mistaken destruction of the Mysteron complex. Whilst the same set of events triggers the story for *New Captain Scarlet* into motion, albeit with Scarlet being the one who accompanies Black to Mars, *New Captain Scarlet* portrays the Mysterons as an inherently angry, destructive force, with no apparent semblance of calm or compassion. Their murderous nature is justified by the Mysterons proclaiming to Scarlet and Black, just prior to their reconstructions, that humanity's violence disgusts the Mysterons. From there, the war of nerves is declared, though 'Storm At The End of the World' would suggest that the Mysterons once looked upon humanity with nothing more than curiosity, their hatred for the race brewing over time.

On the opposite end of the spectrum (*ehem*), Captain Scarlet makes a determined and consistent attempt to break back into his human side. Captain Scarlet's manner of recreation from human to Mysteron is itself recreated for *New Captain Scarlet*, rather than copied and pasted. The premise remains much the same, but its execution differs. Scarlet, along with Black, are murdered and replicated by the Mysterons to become their Earth-based operatives. A failed attack on Scarlet's part to destroy Skybase sends him falling through Skybase's electrical power conduits, knocking the Mysterons' hold from him and allowing the original Scarlet's memory and personality to be regained – in a rather perverse reversal then, where the original series deemed that electricity was the only thing that could kill a Mysteron, and thus Scarlet, this event sees Scarlet reborn as his human self. Electricity frees him from the Mysterons' clutches.

A pair of episodes prize open the psychological impact that being transformed into a Mysteron appears to have on Paul, and in far greater depth than the original series was brave enough to venture into. In the series one finale 'The Achilles Messenger', a rogue Mysteron agent, intent on convincing Spectrum that there are factions within the Mysterons that despise the war of nerves and want to see it end, quizzes to Paul how he lives being a sub-Mysteron. Paul, as if in disbelief at her suggestions, states that he isn't a Mysteron, but remains a fully-fledged human being, albeit with a few Mysteron enhancements. However, the renegade agent clarifies that Captain Scarlet's body is still the work of the Mysterons, and that Scarlet overall is some unnatural amalgamation of Mysteron and human form. Scarlet doesn't react to this new and truer perspective of his identity, most likely because of the episode's running time, but perhaps also because he simply can't suitably comprehend this revelation.

This notion of Captain Scarlet being not fully aware of his mutated form comes to the surface in the next episode, 'Touch of the Reaper', the opening episode to the second series. CCTV footage captures a Mysteron reconstruction take place in a science laboratory, resulting in Spectrum being able to actually witness the Mysterons at work for the first time. Whilst other Spectrum personnel look on in mild shock or apparent disbelief, Scarlet undergoes a full-blown crisis in his sense of self, prompting the episode's sub-plot of Scarlet needing to regain his confidence. Whilst 'The Achilles Messenger' and 'Touch of the Reaper' are standalone episodes, story-wise, they contain something of a mini-arc for Captain Scarlet to confront, acknowledge and make peace with the fact that he's neither totally human or totally a Mysteron, aided by his friendship with Captain Blue, which itself feels warmer and more genuine than it did in the original series. This level of self-awareness that the series has for addressing the fact that Paul is a fusion of Mysteron and human components wasn't something the original series appeared invested in, a further sign of how *New Captain Scarlet* was willing and able to divert into directions that weren't fully traversed back in 1967.

Fallen Angels

Beyond the core set-up of characters in *New Captain Scarlet*, the series' other players are granted a mixed execution of character expansions from their original counterparts. Whilst Simone had a more definable personality than the original series' Juliette as a romantically-inclined action heroine, the remainder of the Angels come off as undeveloped as their original versions. A single episode, 'Fallen Angels', devoted to them doesn't go to any great strides to expand on their characters. They remain the action-ready fighter pilot heroines they were 40 years ago, their interchangeable personalities reflected by actress Jules de Jongh providing the voices for three of the five Angels.

Lieutenant Green however is another and better story. An entirely new character who dons the position of Colonel White's invaluable aide who doubles as an electronics expert (and not simply a gender-swap of the original character, as many fans fail to acknowledge), the routine presence of a black female character in semi-command of Skybase's operations provides a fresh angle to the set-up. Unlike Seymour's tenure on Cloudbase, Serena Lewis was often involved in the action and not restricted to Colonel White's side, whether it was on Skybase or off. The grim loss of her estranged father to Mysteron hands in 'Homecoming' initially paints her as a tragic figure, but it's resolved by the gradual surrogate father/daughter bond struck up between her and Colonel White, culminating in the episode 'Proteus'. Accompanying the Colonel on an inspection of a new, digitally controlled stealth warship whose computer systems are hijacked by the Mysterons, Lewis' gun-toting defence of the Colonel from the ship's rampaging robotic drones is second-to-none, resulting in their eventual safe escape from the vessel and the Colonel's offer of the rank of Captain for Lewis' actions. She rejects the offer, choosing instead to remain by the Colonel's side, with the episode ending with Colonel White saying that he'd rather hoped she'd say that. Serena's loss of her father and Charles' self-imposed rejection of his own family, including his daughter, to protect them from his work fighting against the Mysterons (a very *UFO*-esque motif) leads to the pair forming a genuine and heartfelt non-romantic connection that's outright acknowledged with 'Proteus'.

Not every character transplanted from *Captain Scarlet and the Mysterons* to *New Captain Scarlet* receives an improvement on their personality, identity and level of engagement in connecting to the audience. Captain Blue's more aggressive persona compared to his original incarnation is a decent foil to Scarlet's level-headedness, but the likes of Captain Ochre, Doctor Gold and Captain Grey are relatively background characters. Still, the majority of players in *New Captain Scarlet* were granted with a greater focus on how their own lives, relationships and personalities became a part of the war of nerves. Whilst Lieutenant Green and Captain Black receive the most drastic makeover, the remaining characters who are transformed from one incarnation to the other don't actually undergo any earth-shattering changes. Their personas are simply strengthened, rather than altered, with more palpable personalities both radiating through the stories and engraining themselves within the stories too, enhancing their dramatic appeal.

A much stronger focus on the characters makes them far more interesting to see interact with one another and act individually on their own intuitions, whilst providing a welcome touch of humanity to a story about the folly of humanity's trigger-happy nature. In the character department alone, *New Captain Scarlet* hits most of the right notes in hugely improving on the source material, rather than passively replicating it. By doing so, the dark heart of the war of nerves beats with a more assured rhythm.

RECREATING THE FUTURE: HOW *THUNDERBIRDS: THE ANNIVERSARY EPISODES* COLLIDES PAST, PRESENT AND FUTURE

Thunderbirds has a curious relationship with its longevity. Since the original series' end in December 1966, repeated broadcasts of the original series across the decades have seen the series accumulate new fans and reignite the interests of older ones. However, unlike other science fiction franchises of its ilk, the series has spawned few reincarnations. Failed remakes of *Thunderbirds* are littered all over the series' history – *Intergalactic Rescue*, *T-Force*, *Thunderbirds: International Rescue* and numerous attempts to create a live-action movie throughout the 1990s which eventually became the much-maligned effort directed by Jonathan Frakes. In the run-up to *Thunderbirds'* 50th anniversary in 2015, the series finally became reincarnated in the manner many undoubtedly preferred – a trilogy of 'new' episodes of the classic series.

At the time, *Thunderbirds'* was already enjoying a revival thanks to *Thunderbirds Are Go*, but seemingly out of the blue, a Kickstarter campaign was launched by Century 21 Films (then operating under the moniker of Pod 4 Films), makers of the much celebrated *Filmed in Supermarionation* documentary, to raise funds for the production of three episodes adapted from three 21-minute long original audio stories ('Introducing Thunderbirds' (October 1965), 'F.A.B.' (April 1966) and 'The Stately Homes Robberies Featuring Lady Penelope And Parker' (June 1966)), and utilising Supermarionation techniques. Whilst the basic campaign had hoped to raise enough funds to produce a single episode (at a cost of £75,000), it went on to raise £218,412 from 3378 backers. The delivered result was a handful of episodes made in the 21st century, but which looked, sounded and felt as if they had miraculously dropped out of 1965.

The episodes filled a void that had formed in response to *Thunderbirds Are Go*'s semi-CGI nature. Many see *Thunderbirds* as sacred ground, its production techniques capturing an artistry that some sections of the fandom deem inferior in comparison to more modern digital advances. If you don't want *Thunderbirds* to be remade, you do the next best thing; you don't remake the series from the ground up – you simply make more episodes of the original series. This is reflected in the fact that whilst the project began under the banner title of *Thunderbirds: 1965*, the trio have since been referred to as *Thunderbirds: The Anniversary Episodes*, readily placed alongside the classic series and fully accepted as extensions worthy of being a part of the original series.

The episodes themselves, 'Introducing Thunderbirds', 'The Abominable Snowman' (renamed from 'F.A.B.') and 'The Stately Homes Robberies', are painstakingly and lovingly made recreations of the original series' aesthetic. They blend together uniquely made visualisations of the original audio stories with archive footage and audio taken from pre-existing *Thunderbirds* episodes to bulk out the episodes, even going so far as to have entire original scenes composed for them not featured in the original audio dramas. This then brings to mind how best to appreciate them – admire their visual artistry whilst sidestepping the admittedly sub-par nature of the stories themselves, or embrace all aspects of them as fully rounded episodes of the classic series? It's worth noting that these audio stories have never been as readily available as the original series, or even as widely known. For many, these episodes are the first time these audio stories will be experienced, a full experience on offer.

There's the undeniable sensation, then, that you may come away from these episodes feeling ... deflated. From a story-telling perspective alone, they're not the greatest *Thunderbirds* had to offer, and were never meant to be. Even so, there remains the equally undeniable sensation that the Pod 4 Films crew made the best out of middling efforts. The episodes prominently feature Lady Penelope and Parker as the main characters, to the point where they dominate the proceedings and International Rescue themselves are pushed out of the limelight. The nature of their source material also means that they don't clock in to the usually 50-minute format, but a more concise 20-25 minutes per episode, offering an intriguing insight into how *Thunderbirds* might have functioned had its own initial 25-minute format remained intact. This double-whammy of distinction the episodes gain over the original series helps to give them their own identity. Whilst the quality of the visuals is a sumptuous treat, the tedious nature of the stories themselves will test viewer's patience.

'Introducing Thunderbirds'

The first of the anniversary episodes feels the most light-hearted. Originally released in October of 1965, just as *Thunderbirds* had taken off on screens, 'Introducing Thunderbirds' sees Justin T Lee in the director's chair and has come to be regarded as the official prequel to the series, as its events occur directly prior to 'Trapped in the Sky'. The episode essentially sees Lady Penelope and Parker visit Tracy Island for the very first time and are given a guided tour of the International Rescue base by Jeff Tracy himself, as well as an itinerary of International Rescue's security set-up. This includes witnessing Thunderbirds 1, 2, 3 and 4 launching in what now can be technically considered their debut appearance.

With its scaled-back running time, absence of actual rescuing, limited cast and general low-key nature, 'Introducing Thunderbirds' feels much more akin to being a companion to 'Trapped in the Sky' than a full-blown prequel. 'Introducing Thunderbirds' also demonstrates the liberal way these anniversary episodes mine pre-existing *Thunderbirds* stories to colour in story aspects left blank by the audio material. Stock footage is used for the various launchings of the Thunderbirds, whilst much of the original footage comes from the interactions between Jeff, Penelope and Parker, which are splendid to watch unfold. Tracy Island's exteriors are made to look as evocative as the original series, whilst Tracy Lounge is recreated down to the finest details. The blending of archive footage and newly shot material is expertly seamless, right down to an originally composed shot of Thunderbird 2 lumbering down its runway surreptitiously slotted into its recognisable launch sequence.

Curiously, seeing Jeff, Penelope and Parker interact with each other is the episode's biggest highlight. From the carefully coordinated puppetry to the wonderfully retro wardrobes (Penelope brings multiple outfits for her stay on Tracy Island), these newly crafted marionettes lend the episode a warm naturality. It feels lived-in, setting a nostalgic mood that the other two episodes also deliver on. The cracks in the source material rear their head once more on close inspection of the character's dialogue. The audio-only nature of the material means that Jeff, Penelope and Parker spend sizeable chunks of the running time describing the actions happening before them for the benefit of the listener, which becomes rendered rather dulled when it's so expertly visualised before us.

'Introducing Thunderbirds' hardly risks stealing the title of greatest-ever-episode from the likes of 'Terror in New York City' or 'Attack of the Alligators'. It's a fun, charming affair in which the real pleasure is seeing an intimate group of much-loved characters reanimated as if the 50-year gap between these episodes and the original series never existed. The episode's heavy reliance on stock footage may test the good faith of those who backed the original Kickstarter project expecting the episodes to be entirely 100% original visualisations, but their placement here at least makes sense in the context of the story. The warmth of the episode arises from the character dynamics, even if Penelope's treatment of Parker veers towards the exploitive. Readers of *TV21* may have been better clued in here, as their relationship feels hugely in-tune with the pair's portrayal in their pre-*Thunderbirds* spin-off strip from the comic book. Lee's firm yet gentle direction makes 'Introducing Thunderbirds' a thoroughly pleasant episode to open this trilogy on, but the following episode would make things rather more invigorating.

The Abominable Snowman

The second anniversary episode is the most muscular of the three. This has the unusual credit of being written by two people intrinsically linked to *Thunderbirds*, but who never wrote other *Thunderbirds* material – original series director Desmond Saunders and voice artist David Graham himself. Ironically, whilst the remaining two episodes were penned by Anderson stalwart Alan Fennell, 'The Abominable Snowman' feels like the most natural episode of *Thunderbirds* out of the three anniversary stories. Perhaps Fennell wanted to divert from regular story structures with his two audio stories and had a fondness for writing Penelope and Parker, whilst Graham and Saunders focused their inexperienced writing efforts into a traditionally *Thunderbirds* style story in which rescuing is firmly in the story's sights.

The episode's opening scene involving Thunderbirds 1 and 2 preventing the Meddings Uranium plant from destruction is a sudden blast of classically built *Thunderbirds* action that pushes past the quiet vibes of 'Introducing Thunderbirds' into something that recalls 'Terror in New York City' and 'The Mighty Atom'. It's a brief scene, but it provides a grin-inducing burst of energy to open the episode with. It was also a totally original scene created especially for this adaptation that wasn't present in the original audio adventure.

From here, the episode swerves tonally into the seemingly unconnected plot of Penelope and Parker being assigned by Jeff to Everest to investigate numerous reports of abominable snowmen attacking explorers. Directed by Stephen La Riviere, 'The Abominable Snowman' is heavy in exotic locales, gorgeously rendered in Supermarionation form. Penelope and Parker's investigations are thrown into jeopardy when their tour guide is revealed to be none other than the Hood, who has been manipulating the legend of the abominable snowman to capture wandering explorers to mine for uranium deep in the Himalayan mountains whilst also putting pre-existing uranium plants out of action. The nature of the story not originally featuring the opening scenes of Meddings Uranium results in the viewer left scrambling to piece the two events together in an episode whose pace feels undoubtedly unwieldy in having entirely new scenes bolted onto a pre-existing story, but there's plenty of well-crafted adventure to be had all over the episode.

A rare confrontation between Penelope and the Hood, who captures her and subjects her to a laser beam James Bond-style, make the episode great fun to engage with. The mountainous locations where much of the episode takes place in are a superbly atmospheric springboard in giving Thunderbirds 1 and 2 some ample screen time in their most substantial usage of new footage throughout these episodes. Scott Tracy is even adorned in a snow-friendly variation of his traditional International Rescue suit, further emphasising how the attention these episodes paid to the style and detail of the original series wasn't limited to the special effects.

It's easy to see why 'The Abominable Snowman' was the initial target goal of the Kickstarter campaign should only enough funds be raised to produce a single episode. The original story is a neatly compacted *Thunderbirds* adventure, but the embellishments made by Pod 4 Films enhance its enjoyability enormously. The extensions themselves aid in making 'The Abominable Snowman' the episode least reliant on archive footage, something that the next episode struggles to conceal.

The Stately Homes Robberies

The anniversary episodes of *Thunderbirds* conclude with the ponderous 'The Stately Homes Robberies', an episode whose story involving aristocratic thieves targeting Creighton-Ward Mansion to avenge a disgraced family heritage feels like a plot more at home in *Supercar* than *Thunderbirds*. The episode is noteworthy for the return of David Elliott in the director's chair, a key figure in the history of Supermarionation. After serving on editorial duties for *Torchy the Battery Boy* and *Four Feather Falls*, he directed numerous episodes of the later before serving as a primary director from *Supercar* to *Thunderbirds*, leaving his mark as a vital artistic voice in shaping the style of Supermarionation. This additional component of authenticity embedded into a handful of episodes made to look as close to the original as possible is a masterstroke to end the anniversary episodes on.

Writing-wise, 'The Stately Homes Robberies' has some curious credits – the original EP release of the audio story states that Alan Fennell wrote the script, but that it was adapted from a story written by Jim Watson. Presumably this is the same Jim Watson who drew and coloured the *Captain Scarlet* and *Zero-X* strips for *TV21*. This would be the only instance of Watson putting down the storyboards and picking up the typewriter in his contributions to the worlds of Century 21. It also emphasises how the cottage industry of Century 21 Productions' spin-off division operated – all five of *Captain Scarlet*'s original audio stories were written by *TV21* alumni.

Like 'The Abominable Snowman', 'The Stately Homes Robberies' has several elements weaved into the narrative to bolster its quality and make it closer to being a substantial episode of *Thunderbirds*. The subplot of villains Dawkins and Charles laying explosives in the houses who they steal priceless riches from wasn't a narrative component of the original audio adventure. This allows a brief subplot of Thunderbirds 1, 2 and 4 called into action to stop the Tower of London from being destroyed when Penelope and Parker task themselves with catching the upper-class crooks. These scenes are brought to life through some welcome original sequences of Gordon Tracy and TB4 performing the main rescue but are otherwise mostly stitched together from pre-existing episodes in *Thunderbirds'* back catalogue. It's a masterclass of editorial craft, as classic stock footage and newly composed scenes are interlocked with ease, but it's also tiresome for the viewer when the learned *Thunderbirds* fan won't have a problem in pinpointing which episodes the stock footage is taken from. The result is your viewing experience being disrupted as you're pulled out of the action when you catch recognisable dialogue and visuals.

This feels like a laboured problem to dwell over, as it's an issue not exclusive to this episode and is an aspect that's ultimately out of the producers' hands. The fact that Pod 4 Films put the additional effort into enlivening the source material in the first place is a valiant effort. However, with its abundance of non-original footage to aid the story in making it feel like a *Thunderbirds* adventure, it's this episode in which the cracks really start to show. Elliott's care and attention to detail in the episode's direction injects a warm recognisability to the delivery of the puppets' actions, but the episode otherwise remains a sluggish affair to conclude this unique trilogy on.

'Thunderbirds are definitely go'

A defining aspect of *Thunderbirds: The Anniversary Episodes* is their striking duality. The exquisite artistry of the episodes' production values is often painfully forced to be juxtaposed by some undeniably tepid storytelling and characterisation. It's forgivable in 'Introducing Thunderbirds' and grating by the time we reach 'The Stately Homes Robberies'. The weakness in the source material is understandably justified. These three stories were written as supplementary material meant to accompany the main event of the television series and never intended to be blown-up to Supermarionation proportions. The fact that they have now done so has still produced something that's marvellously entertaining, despite their drawbacks.

Taken at face value, these episodes are enthusiastic extensions of the original series. Appreciating the context in which these episodes were made however, *Thunderbirds: The Anniversary Episodes* is a splendid celebration of the practical creativity of Supermarionation. The art form is in hearty momentum throughout these episodes, barely dusted off after all these years, because these episodes carry with them a visual confidence and tactile swagger that appears as if the art form never went away, enhanced further by the thrill of hearing the original voice cast and soundtrack in full swing. For the most part, *Thunderbirds: The Anniversary Episodes* excel in whisking you away back to the retrofuture of 2065 as 1965 imagined it would be.

NEBULA-75'S 33 MILLION-MILE ADVENTURE

The COVID-19 pandemic and ensuing lockdown conditions throughout 2020 and beyond have undeniably had a scarring effect. The anxiety felt of when we may ever return to normality, or attempt to improve upon the world that existed in pre-pandemic times, feels heavy and relentless. Art and creativity across many mediums have provided much needed reassurance as we look to the things that are comforting and recognisable in a world turned upside down. A group of people situated in a London flat took this emotional reassurance a stage further. Crafting a universe of possibilities by using the techniques of an art form not seen since 1969, *Nebula-75* has proved to be a nostalgic eruption of retro-futuristic adventure.

For some time now, Century 21 Films have been on a mission to revitalise the art form of Supermarionation, the sophisticated production method that involved electronically advanced marionettes and incredibly detailed miniatures and model sets. Primarily employed by AP Films/Century 21 Productions in the making of much of their classic output, Century 21 Films have been creating new ventures in Supermarionation for a contemporary audience. Over the past few years, several productions varying in scale have seen the puppet-based techniques been deployed, most notably *Thunderbirds: The Anniversary Episodes*. The result is a handful of episodes of *Thunderbirds* that feel like they've been discovered from the cutting room floor of the Slough Trading Estate. During lockdown conditions of 2020, Century 21 Films took their next and unexpected leap in reviving Supermarionarion with an entirely new series for television – *Nebula-75*, chiefly masterminded by Stephen La Riviere and Andrew T Smith.

Initially produced as a one-off, 10-minute special and using low-budget sets and pre-existing puppets from past Century 21 Films projects, *Nebula-75* gradually evolved into a seven-episode series made entirely free to watch on YouTube, with an additional eighth episode not included in the eventual DVD and Blu-ray release of the so-called 2120 series. The series rapidly gained a feverish fanbase, national media coverage and perhaps most importantly, a television sale, whilst new episodes continue to emerge online. *Nebula-75* tells the continuing story of Commander Ray Neptune and his civilian crew aboard the space rocket *Nebula-75*, which has been accidentally catapulted millions of miles away from home. Stranded in the darkest corners of the universe, the crew of *Nebula-75* encounter an unpredictable medley of cosmic adventures, all the while desperately attempting to navigate their way back home.

The greatest compliment one can pay *Nebula-75* is not only that it provides irrefutable proof that there is palpable demand for a new Supermarionation series, but that it's capable of acquiring sustained viewership without having to rely on the brand recognition of a pre-existing Supermarionation work. Despite much of *Nebula-75* being recycled from past productions, there remains something fresh about the series – 'a new series filmed in Supermarionation', as is proudly boasted on the DVD/Blu-ray cover. A rich irony remains drenched over this still undeniable feat – in production values, characterisation style and narrative scope, *Nebula-75* feels comfortingly recognisable, easily recalling much of Supermarionation's previous glories.

Either through the combining factors of lockdown circumstances and creative choices, the series plays like something of a greatest hits remix of Supermarionation tropes. The series employs puppets with the stylised, disproportionate heads of the earlier years of Century 21 Productions, yet stretches back even further into Supermarionation's past. Rather than pick up where 1969's *The Secret Service* left off, *Nebula-75* takes its cues from *Supercar* and *Fireball XL5*, living every day as if Supermarionation progressed no further than 1962. The tropes are all there – Commander Ray Neptune is the unshakable hero in the mould of Mike Mercury and Steve Zodiac. Professor Popkiss and Professor Matic can be found in the heavily-accented Doctor Asteroid. Elsewhere, the alluring space maiden Athena, who shows up whenever the plot requires her to, channels strong Marina-vibes. The best character of the series is the one who is neither human nor alien, but rather is robotic. Circuit is the series' break-out star, the snide, passive-aggressive robotic companion to the *Nebula-75* crew who often breaks the fourth wall with episode's introductions that sees him welcoming viewers to another episode of, what he calls, Circuit's *Nebula-75*.

The story of *Nebula-75* attempts to cram in a universe of possibilities into its restrictive format. In each episode, the crew encounters some new cosmic scenario, sometimes friendly, sometimes dangerous but always bewildering to the crew. The tonal zigzagging of *Nebula-75*'s creative choices become more apparent here, rather than blaming any shortcomings on its limited productions. *Nebula-75* wears its *Supercar* influences firmly on its sleeve when the manner of friends and foes the crew encounter are quirky but also antiquated. The cockney scrap-iron merchant Rusty and the aristocratic con artists Lord and Lady Menteur are taken entirely from the pre-*Thunderbirds* Supermarionation playbook, one whose villains were more rooted in Ealing comedies than science-fantasy. At first, they're amusingly out-of-place, but on closer inspection, somehow fit right into the universe *Nebula-75* is presenting to us, a universe meant to look and sound like it was made not in

2020 but in the 1960s, and thus follows the Supermarionation tradition of what the 1960s thought the future would look and sound like.

Elsewhere, other threats paint a different picture of the series entirely. 'No One I Think Is In My Tree' and 'Freighter Fright' sees the *Nebula-75* become entangled with villains of a far more cerebral nature that feel taken more from *Captain Scarlet and the Mysterons*, or even *Space: 1999*, which the series recalls on a more general level through its core premise. This either adds huge narrative diversity to *Nebula-75*'s storytelling capabilities or throws the series off balance, tonally. We primarily shift between modest dangers that rely more on comical character interactions or cosmic threats beyond the comprehension of mankind.

We can't talk about *Nebula-75* without drawing some attention to its format. As well as being filmed in Supermarionation, the series likes to remind us that its production qualities also consist of Superisolation and Lo-Budget Recording System. How much leeway then do we give the series in this regard, a series that has the universe in its eyes, but barely a penny in its pockets? The confining sets, recycled puppets, low-budget original set pieces, and occasionally limp voice acting can't help but remind you that you're watching something that clearly wants to be so much more than the circumstances of its making grants it. Justin T Lee shines as the put-upon yet confident and heroic Ray Neptune and a selection of guest characters later on in the series liven things up, but the regular secondary characters aren't as inspired.

Where the classic era of Supermarionation resulted in a string of productions hugely distinctive from each other, when watching *Nebula-75*, one can't shake the sensation that we've seen all of this before. It struggles to say anything new. In its current format, born out of lockdown restrictiveness, *Nebula-75* is a series that's content to lean on the history of Supermarionation, rather than continue it anew.

The series makes regular but creative use of close-ups of characters to compensate for the lack of expansive sets and armada of miniatures that regularly populated the classic Supermarionation works. In that regard, *Nebula-75*'s derivative yet dedicatedly earnest characterisation makes the series a warm, pleasant thing to enjoy. In the height of the aggressive unpredictability that COVID-19 continues to bring, the snug nostalgia that radiates from *Nebula-75* makes a lot more sense. We've understandably clung to the safety of familiarity in this current world, perhaps making the success of *Nebula-75* not entirely down to the nostalgic joy of seeing puppets come to life.

At over two hours of entertainment initially released entirely for free and with a television sale to Japan secured, *Nebula-75* is clearly intent achieving the sustained quality to keep Supermarionation alive. Whilst the quality of the series' production doesn't entirely prevent the perception that

Supermarionation was always a thing of novelty rather than a substantial method of storytelling, the focus on characterisation and nuanced storytelling aid in elevating *Nebula-75* to the creative substance that it's aspiring to have. The uneven narrative scope and strictly limited sets make *Nebula-75* an awkward thing to enjoy, but there remains a tangible determination at work in this almost bootleg Supermarionation venture to prove that Supermarionation is a legitimate art form. With new episodes continuing to be released, *Nebula-75* offers the exciting prospect that the story of Supermarionation, once a closed book for many decades, now remains an excitingly unfinished adventure as these new chapters blast off.

ATOMIC TOMORROWS: THE BLAST OFF, CRASH-LAND & RELAUNCH OF SUPERMARIONATION

There was a time when Supermarionation's retro-futuristic saga was little more than an historical artefact. The highs and lows endured by Century 21 Productions in creating a raft of film and television productions whose pioneering approach to special effects and meticulously action-heavy stories and characters captured countless imaginations and influenced numerous corners of the television and film industry across numerous genres, cultures and generations. When devising the concept for 1967's *Ultraseven*, the follow-up series to the enormously popular 1966 tokusatsu series *Ultraman* and the third entry in the long running *Ultra Series*, *Ultraman* creator Eiji Tsuburaya proposed a series that would combine elements of *Thunderbirds* and *Lost in Space*, both of which had enjoyed much success when broadcast in Japan. George Lucas and Stanley Kubrick both attempted to poach members of Century 21's special effects unit to work on *Star Wars* and *2001: A Space Odyssey*, respectively. The ever-lasting impact Supermarionation made as an art form is pretty good going for a company who made these works out of desperation to secure their own success.

When you credit the influence that any form of media can have is an acknowledgement that the media in question has achieved all it will ever achieved, that it's told all of the story that it's ever going to tell. In Supermarionation's case, this has been no different, but in recent years, the dust has been blown off and through a mixture of the passage of time and actions of various parties, Supermarionation is nowadays considered a continuing concern rather than a point of television frozen in time. Gerry and Sylvia's works are no strangers to experiencing revivals in popularity since their arrival, yet the recently passed spate of 50th anniversary celebrations for all of the original puppet-based television series they created feel poignantly different. Alongside these celebrations, the rekindled interest in these works has aided in maintaining an appreciation of Supermarionation to such an extent that two new Supermarionation-inspired series are being made – *Firestorm* and *Nebula-75*. *Firestorm* proclaims to take Supermarionation to the next level by being filmed in

Ultramarionation, whilst *Nebula-75* celebrates the art form's historic value. We're at a renewed chapter in the story of Supermarionation where it's no longer simply begun and ended – it's now begun, ended and has begun anew.

21ST Century Visions

Today, the various Supermarionation productions sit relatively comfortably alongside other cult science fiction entertainment produced throughout the 1960s and the 1970s. Streaming platform BritBox packages numerous Anderson productions alongside much-respected gems as *Doctor Who, Blake's 7, The Avengers, Quatermass, The Man Who Fell to Earth* and *The Prisoner*. The platform even currently positions more modern and dark cult favourites *Dog Soldiers* and *Under the Skin*. Anderson productions are finally rubbing shoulders with the adult market Gerry Anderson so often shot for. Critical acceptance wasn't always so easy to come by throughout the Andersons' career. The December 1966 edition of the *Observer* ran a feature detailing the influence children's television held over their young audiences and whether or not they were exerting positive values, in a time when media commentary was rife. In the feature titled *Good Uncle Or Bad Uncle*, Gerry and Sylvia Anderson's output is shunted alongside *Doctor Who, Blue Peter* and *Watch With Mother*.[88] At this time, the Andersons were high in their profile as being producers of commercially-manufactured entertainment along with a growing filmography. Even before *Captain Scarlet* came along, the *Observer* notes the list of works the pair had under their belt at that time. From *Twizzle* and *Torchy* to the then-current *Thunderbirds*, the *Observer* caps off their commentary with a dismissive send-off of the Andersons producing their work 'a remarkable discard rate.' What's to be taken from this comment then is how disposable Supermarionation was regarded, not in its technical qualities, but in its artistic value, that it wasn't worth remembering. This is evidenced further by the extreme lack of existing models, marionettes and miniature sets existing from these programmes, trashed or recycled to become newer objects which themselves eventually discarded to the scrapheap.

Beyond us appreciating how the eye-popping, supersonic splendour of Supermarionation evolved over the course of its original run between 1960's *Four Feather Falls* and 1969's *The Secret Service*, what these programmes and films told us remains as effective as what they showed us. Bookended by these two charming, low-key entries are stories of vigilante heroism, space exploration, Cold War anxieties, globe-trotting spies and underwater alien warfare, all wrapped up within the perspective of what the 1960s mostly

---

[88] 'Good Uncle Or Bad Uncle?' (1966) *The Observer*. No. 18, p. 21.

imagined the 2060s would look like, now morphing into that cool, retro-futuristic vibe that makes contemporary viewing of Supermarionation an added joy – it's always fun watching this era of works with the benefit of hindsight, to see how the past imagined the still distant future. And the most astonishing about these cohesive landscapes mapped out in marionette form is how they tumbled out of their creators by accident. 'Why am I in science fiction?' Gerry pondered in 1995. 'Simply because I found myself making action series with puppets, which is kind of a crazy situation if you think about it. When I made a show called *Supercar*, I thought "I know what I'll do, I'll put these puppets that can't walk into a car, whiz them around all over the place at high speed, and that'll pep up the show." When it went out, people said to me "Oh, you're in science fiction now." I thought, "Am I? Oh!"'[89]

Whilst Supermarionation had its production values upped during its original era, this enabled its imaginative staff to vastly embellish all of the art form's components into something more extravagant than what had come before with each passing entry. Models, miniatures and marionettes had their quality enhanced, but the scripts, directing, editing and vocal performances bettered, too. If the only elements that improved from each successive Supermarionation series to the next were the special effects, they wouldn't continue to be as memorable as they are today. The themes and tropes that these series exhibited were in as much flux as the mechanical make-up of the marionettes themselves. As we explored in **Failure to Launch**, it pays to have significantly more than solid special effects to ensure that you've got a quality production on your hands. The live-action *Doppelgänger*'s purposefully thematic swirl of numerous genres feels like a stab back at the unfocused quality of the two *Thunderbirds* films, further advancing the notion that the Andersons endeavoured to make each work better than the one before. The wealth of thematic material to pore over during the Supermarionation era gives plenty of indication that such a mind-set was what ensured the medium met with such success throughout the decade.

There's Always Magic in the Air

Nobody within AP Films could surely have envisioned the heights their marionettes would soar to during the making of *Four Feather Falls*. Where the history books will tell you that 1957's *The Adventures of Twizzle* and 1959's *Torchy the Battery Boy* is where Supermarionation's story begins, the technical soul of the art form didn't truly manifest itself until this modest,

---

[89] Richardson, D. Anderson, G. (1995) 'Anderson's Precinct: Cops in Space, Courtesy of Gerry Anderson' *Cult Times* (ed Vincent-Rudzki, J). No. 1, p. 12.

infinitely charming fantasy Western. The acorn from which the bulk of Supermarionation grew, *Four Feather Falls* marked numerous firsts for Supermarionation's history. It was the first of AP Films' productions to be made without the involvement of Roberta Leigh, signalling a change in the hierarchy at the time and a tentative step towards AP Films being a self-sufficient unit. Scriptwriter Martin Woodhouse contributed a pair of scripts before making his presence felt more alongside *Supercar*, laying the foundations for the rough, proto-techno-thrillers that would be bettered with *Thunderbirds* and *Captain Scarlet*. David Elliott and Alan Pattillo etched out their debit directorial contributions to Supermarionation with this series. *Four Feather Falls* as also the first AP Films production to be filmed on the Slough Trading Estate.

Whilst the premise of *Four Feather Falls* ensures that it sits oddly alongside the predominantly science fiction-based content that Supermarionation would conjure up (rather similar to how David Bowie's debut album's stylings of bizarre music hall pop sits embarrassingly next to the glam rock and electronic masterworks that he'd go onto be better known for), it shouldn't be dismissed. The whimsical spy-fi meanderings of *Joe 90* and the quaint, quiet politeness of *The Secret Service* find their roots here, as does much of the light-hearted side to Supermarionation, away from the explosions. From a technical viewpoint, *Four Feather Falls'* impact wasn't nearly as delayed. This is the first series to use uniquely made puppetry that featured electronics within the puppet's heads to stimulate them into life, allowing for more convincing and elaborate performances from the marionettes themselves. *Four Feather Falls* is the first true Supermarionation series.

Piece by piece, the Supermarionation puzzle continued to be slotted together. With the advanced puppet technology now firmly in their grasp, 1961's *Supercar*'s low-key status as falling to be as ambitious as *Thunderbirds*, exotic as *Stingray* or as bloodthirsty as *Captain Scarlet* look more understandable when viewed from the other side. *Supercar* is as triumphant a leap from *Four Feather Falls* as *Four Feather Falls* was from *Torchy* and *Twizzle*. *Supercar*'s characters and stories may not have been as sophisticated as what would come afterwards, but with the advanced puppetry in full swing, *Supercar* succeeds in adding more and more firsts that other Supermarionation productions wouldn't just merely continue, but be proactive in evolving. *Supercar* is another instrumental chapter in Supermarionation's history, presenting the world's first genuinely science fiction Supermarionation production which involved a star vehicle to command the series' name and the audience's attention. The series' contemporary setting compared to *Four Feather Falls'* Western setting reads like a comment on bringing AP Films' growing film-making prowess firmly into the modern era. *Supercar* presented a rather domesticated approach to the techno-disasters that *Thunderbirds* would eventually pursue, but it carries the charm and innocence of *Four Feather Falls* effortlessly into science fiction scenarios of a globe-trotting nature, something that would be somewhat lost in the brashness of *Supercar*'s follow-up.

The next great leap went from shifts in timelines to shifts in entire planets. 1962's *Fireball XL5*'s approach to imaginative alien menaces is a solid example of flinging concepts at the wall and seeing what would stick, but even if it's a series where the enthusiasm overrides quality control, then what enthusiasm it is. The cosy, aesthetic homeliness of *Supercar* isn't totally discarded with *Fireball XL5*. Instead, that homeliness becomes atomically charged to delirious extremes. The outer space threats in *Fireball XL5* violently swing from being cheerful to horrifying to farcical to the point of being whiplash-inducing for the viewer. Humanoid plants, pulsating brains, pilot fish assassins and pesky little goblin creatures suggests that imagination wasn't permitted much editorial control throughout the series. Nevertheless, the space-age wonder of *Fireball XL5* came along at precisely the right time for young audiences hungry for cosmic adventure. Even the smaller creative elements were being bettered, thanks to the watchful, production-conscious eye of Sylvia Anderson: '… the leading men were always good looking, but I made sure they were always different,' she recalls in 2001. 'Steve Zodiac was blond in contrast to the hero of the previous show *Supercar*, where Mike Mercury was dark-haired.'[90]

Where Gerry is often credited with striking up the hardware aspect of the series, Sylvia's contributions to characterisations and ensuring quality control in production design where possible remains equally vital. Whilst it's easy to see with the benefit of hindsight how other productions left *Fireball XL5* in the dust when it came to that sense quality control, Gerry and Sylvia maintaining their individualistic yet complimentary roles early on ensured that that evolution happened in the first place, whilst also demonstrating Sylvia's often underappreciated influence on Supermarionation.

Aquatic and International Rescues

This was clearly a style of wonder that was catching the eyes and minds of AP Films as much as the young audiences they were making these productions for. Shifting from the global regions of *Supercar* to the vast void of deep space, the special effects, models, miniatures and marionettes became more elaborate as planets, star systems, space stations and alien creatures filled the television screen as *Fireball XL5* met with tremendous

---

[90] Lewis, J. Anderson, S. (2001) 'Lady Penelope Speaks: Interview With Sylvia Anderson' *Action TV* (ed Richardson, M). No. 4, p. 9.

success for Lew Grade's television empire. Inevitably though, *Fireball XL5* cannot help but appear trapped in a trashy, unsubstantial identity compared to the more refined and sophisticated minds and eyes that produced future Supermarionation productions.

That handling of quality control becomes more controlled and more assured with 1964's *Stingray*. Essentially *Fireball XL5* Mk. II in its premise, the similarities are fortunately only surface level, as we explored in **Stand By For Stardust**, as *Stingray* elevates *Fireball XL5*'s concepts by diving into the deepest depths of the world's most unknown oceans. Every chapter in Supermarionation is an essential one, but few chapters bridge the gap between two eras like *Stingray* does. *Stingray* is the aquatic link between the monochromatic, pioneering days of *Fireball XL5*, *Supercar* and *Four Feather Falls* and the glory days of *Thunderbirds*, *Captain Scarlet*, and *Joe 90*. In the minds of audiences, it's *Joe 90* that's better remembered than *Stingray*, despite the holy trinity being found in those three.

Stingray couples the light-heartedness of Supermarionation's early days with the scale and consistency of its later winning streak. With the added advantage of being the first Supermarionation series to be filmed in colour, the aquatic landscapes which the intrepid *Stingray* crew traverse appear more convincing in their otherworldly qualities than just about anything seen in *Fireball XL5*. *Stingray* remains a benchmark of Supermarionation's narrative and thematic qualities, a series where humour, adventure and characters met on equal standing, where neither element outshines the other and all interlink *Zero-X*-like to create an impressive, witty and watchable tour-de-force of how decent Supermarionation can be when each department has the same sharp eye for focused creative success.

In true Supermarionation fashion, the next series would therefore raise those foundations to even higher levels of visual stimulant. For many, 1965's *Thunderbirds* marks the point where Supermarionation had its wings clipped, for the simple reason that nothing that came after *Thunderbirds* could be considered as exhilarating. The key to *Thunderbirds*' appeal makes perfect sense when you examine the scenarios Supermarionation blasted off from prior. Given that AP Films had enjoyed international success with adventure series set on Earth, outside the Earth and underneath the Earth, then surely a series that combined all of those base elements would amplify the company's success. *Thunderbirds*' blend of riveting adventure and far-reaching story-telling is, on the surface, nothing new to what had been filmed in Supermarionation before, but it's all a case of how it's executed. Initially produced under the working title of International Rescue and with its episodes filmed in the traditional half-hour format, it was Lew Grade's infamous reception to watching the half-hour cut of 'Trapped in the Sky', where he declared *Thunderbirds* to be not a television series but a feature film, that enabled *Thunderbirds* to blast off to even higher peaks.

No colossal disaster is beyond the realms of possibility for *Thunderbirds*. The threat of being consumed by the Sun or a passenger jet unable to land due to having a bomb strapped to its undercarriage is unexpectedly countered by scenarios involving exploding dog food and enemy spies hijacking fashion shows. We've previously explored how *Thunderbirds'* focus on riveting techno-disaster gives the series much of its narrative thrust, but the series also demonstrated a curious and underplayed sense of humour that makes sense when viewed in the context of the other Supermariontion works that surrounds *Thunderbirds* and how humour, whether through unpredictable emergency scenarios or character synergy, is a unifying theme throughout many of these works.

This is The Voice of Supermarionation

Thunderbirds' ascension for Century 21 Productions, as AP Films was now known as, was short-lived for all concerned. Having become comfortable in the belief that *Thunderbirds'* immediate success would mean that he and his team would simply stick to producing adventures for International Rescue for the foreseeable future, Gerry must have been understandably dispirited to see his greatest creation crash-land. Lew Grade's cutting off of the series' financial umbilical cord owing to the Stateside sale of *Thunderbirds* going rather pear-shaped necessitated the need for fresh product to shift. What would fill the gap left by *Thunderbirds* feels like a manifestation of the collective mood Century 21 must surely have been experiencing at the time.

From the even greater style of puppetry than before to the almost clinical approach in model design and its morose premise, *Captain Scarlet and the Mysterons* stands as the exact opposite of *Thunderbirds*. Intergalactic warfare, grotesque body horror and a fierce tearing away of the sense of humour that had made the likes of *Supercar* and *Stingray* so buoyant makes *Captain Scarlet* one of Supermarionation's most stand-out eras. The death-ridden adventures of Captain Scarlet and the other members of Spectrum as they battle the methodical invasion of the invisible, omnipotent Mysterons clashes greatly with the life-saving heroics of *Thunderbirds*. As well as pushing the narrative tropes of Supermarionation to bloody extremes, *Captain Scarlet and the Mysterons* pushed the production values to their most precise format. Having introduced better proportioned bodies in *Thunderbirds Are Go*, but retaining their caricatured looks, *Captain Scarlet* takes the plunge to fashion the marionettes used in this series, and every Supermarionation TV production afterwards, to a correctly proportioned, hyper-humanised style.

The end result continues to polarise to this day. Fans, critics and even those who worked on these shows deriding the lack of warmth these freakishly ultra-human marionettes gave off, whilst others praise the next stage in the evolution of the art form. In the context of *Captain Scarlet*, it's difficult to imagine the previous form of marionettes being able to convincingly pull off the series' regularly serious and grim storylines, which made little room for humour and character development, a sign that Gerry and Sylvia in particular were having their minds focused elsewhere in Century 21, developing their film division after *Thunderbirds Are Go* failed to be the hit all had presumed it would easily be.

As the 1960s drew to a close, Gerry and Sylvia's influence in the day-to-day running of their puppet empire slipped away more noticeably as *Thunderbird 6* and *Doppelgänger* commanded their efforts. *Joe 90* may have proved that the newly proportioned marionettes are capable of humour and charm, but the series was met by a low-key deliverance on ATV's part, as the series wasn't screened as nationally as past efforts were. Nevertheless, *Joe 90* exhibited a perverse sense of humour in its premise of boy hero psychologically experimented upon by his immediate elders to save the world on a regular basis. The fact that *Joe 90* hangs together at all is rather a miracle, but *The Secret Service* takes this attitude to ludicrous heights, with the result being that only 13 episodes were ever made. From both Gerry and Sylvia's perspective, it was less of a missed opportunity to make more episodes and more of a mercy killing. '*Joe 90* wasn't as successful as *Captain Scarlet* but by that time I was drowning in my own product,' is Gerry's succinct summary of his career at that point (1991). 'My shows were being shown all over the world and I guess I had just done too well for my own good; why buy *Joe 90* when they had access to hundreds of episodes of my shows already.' It's worth noting that *The Secret Service* isn't even mentioned in the interview the above quote is taken from.[91]

Sylvia (1991) recalls this era of matters winding down with more thoughtfulness: 'We went for charm in *Joe 90*. Then we did *The Secret Service*. I don't know exactly why it failed. Once again, we weren't "hands on" producers. Gerry and I were setting up *UFO*. That meant you were leaving very talented people to make it, but without your supervision. We weren't there to say no to anything and change it. If we had been we'd probably have done something drastic half way though to liven it up, but by that time I was bored of puppets anyway … We lost interest in *The Secret Service* very early on.'[92] It's telling that Sylvia speaks of having little regret with the way *The Secret Service* was handled, not because of how it was produced, but simply because hers and Gerry's minds were onto bigger and, as they saw it, better things.

---

[91] Drake, C. Pixley, A. Anderson, G. (1991) 'Twenty-First Century Man' *Time Screen* (ed McKay, A). No. 17, p. 17.

[92] Russell, G. Anderson, S. (1991) 'The Power Behind the Rolls' *TV Zone* (ed Vincent-Rudzki, J). No. 20, p. 12.

Sylvia's comments are also striking in that despite her apparent acceptance of how unserviceable *The Secret Service* was as a concept, she gives the impression that she overlooks how she co-created the series. Whatever *The Secret Service* was trying to be, it didn't last long enough for folks to figure it out. Part quaint espionage caper, part jarring experimentation with marionettes and live-action in more deliberate and diabolical manners than past Supermarionation efforts, if Philip Larkin or John Betjeman had produced a Supermarionation series, it would have looked like this. Country vicar Father Stanley Unwin masquerading as a member of the clergy, but in reality an undercover operative for B.I.S.H.O.P. and armed with the ability to miniaturize himself, was never going to appeal to young audiences the same way that *Thunderbirds* had. This perceived low quality of *The Secret Service* is pinpointed as the reason for its downfall, but as Stephen La Riviere notes (2009), many other reasons can be considered. These include how 'the whole of APF / Century 21's back catalogue was on a loop throughout the 1960s ...', '... the puppets (were) no longer generating significant revenue ...', and how Lew Grade 'may have had doubts about who exactly *The Secret Service* was aimed at.'[93] If *Doppelgänger*, then in production at the same time, had given Century 21 their first tentative steps towards realising how their well-worn and dependable science fiction concepts would function in a live-action context, then surely *The Secret Service* can also be seen as a very tactical form of self-inflicted harm on the Andersons' part to convince Grade that it was time to throw the puppets in the skip.

Supermarionation's first era drew to an end not in a fireball of explosive action, but on a mixture of quiet reflection and feverish activity as work on *The Secret Service* was completed throughout January 1969. Whilst many in Gerry and Sylvia's care were excited to be going up in the world to work on *UFO*, those who had served Gerry and Sylvia so nobly in the early, monochrome days felt that they were abandoning the marionette wonders that had given them fame and creative success. What was slowly forged as a pioneering and incredibly unique medium that enabled some of the most imaginative and exciting science fiction ever told was being tossed aside without a second thought from its masters. Gerry and Sylvia had used Supermarionation to do exactly what they needed and wanted it to – making live-action productions. Flourishes of the art form would remain in *UFO*, *Space: 1999* and the single episode TV drama *Into Infinity* via a continued expansion of practical effects and model sets, but the sheer uniqueness of Supermarionation, it seemed, had served its purpose.

Supermarionation began as an accident and it ended as an afterthought.

---

[93] La Riviere, S. (2009) 'A Case for the Bishop' *Filmed in Supermarionation: A History of the Future.* p. 195. Hermes Press. 1st edition.

An unceremonious dumping when something bigger was within reach. For the next 50 years, Supermarionation would succumb to an extensive period of hibernation, often parodied and replicated, but rarely equalled or bettered. An extensive passage of time, during which numerous demographics of Anderson fandom would help to maintain popularity of Gerry and Sylvia's works, would enable a resurgence of the art form to commence.

21st Century Supermarionation

Throughout the years after *The Secret Service*, time has allowed Supermarionation to be thought of in several perspectives. It's applauded for its substantial production techniques, whilst some dismiss it as having only a novelty value, that it's something that should be pointed and laughed at. Both perspectives are united in their assumption that Supermarionation was something relegated to the past, that it had no future. Echoes to Supermarionation's past have been made in the Supermacromation stylings of *Terrahawks* and the Hypermarionation techniques of *New Captain Scarlet*. However, these methods aren't as labour intensive, structurally complicated or idiosyncratic as Supermarionation.

The efforts of Anderson Entertainment and Century 21 Films have done much to dissuade that mentality. Numerous new marionette-based Anderson productions are making valiant strides to bring Supermarionation, of sorts, to a contemporary audience; Anderson Entertainment's *Firestorm* and Century 21 Films' continuing output of retro-minded work, the highlight so far being *Nebula-75* and *Thunderbirds: The Anniversary Episodes*. Where *Firestorm* makes use of a more advanced and modern form of puppetry, the continuing projects of Century 21 Films are a determined effort to celebrate and maintain the art of Supermarionation and remind audiences that the art form remains valid in its entertainment value and that there's demand for it.

Firestorm and *Thunderbirds: 1965*, as it was then known, turned to Kickstarter to raise funds, with *Firestorm* beginning its campaign in December of 2014 and eventually raising enough funds to produce an eight-minute pilot minisode, the sort of thing produced to entice further potential financial backers rather than be seen by a wide audience. Prior to adopting the name Century 21 Films, Pod 4 Films succeeded in convincing ITV that a unique way of celebrating *Thunderbirds'* 50th anniversary in September 2015 would be to actually produce new, official episodes of the series itself, adapted from original 1960s audio dramas. Spearheaded by Supermarionation historian Stephen La Riviere, the Kickstarter campaign commenced in July of 2015 and went on to raise nearly a quarter of a million pounds, resulting in the campaign achieving huge success and raising enough funds for all three proposed adaptations to be made. The joint brand recognition of *Thunderbirds* and Supermarionation clearly commands staying power.

Supermarionation in its purest, unfiltered form is the realised achievement of the *Thunderbirds'* anniversary episodes. Practical effects, explosive models and well-performed puppetry bring these half-forgotten supplementary audio stories to energetic life. The attention to detail throughout these episodes feels as if it's there for two distinct reasons: the most obvious being that we're meant to feel like we're watching a trio of previously lost episodes of *Thunderbirds*, freshly discovered. The other reason is that Supermarionation is a complex medium that naturally demands that attention to detail.

Equally arresting in detail yet with a shifted set of goal posts is *Firestorm*. It's a production that's endured long and troubled period of gestation. The series has its origins around the early 2000s when Gerry and his then-business partner John Needham developed the Firestorm concept, only for their original vision to be scuppered when the series was purchased by Japanese studio Enoki Films and produced as an anime series. The series swiftly vanished from sight following its broadcast and is barely more than a footnote in most history books. Anderson Entertainment has since chosen to rebirth the concept, but in a form that's futuristic in style whilst remaining recognisable. Whilst Century 21 Films mine past techniques for their continuing ventures, Anderson Entertainment are keen to embrace new technologies. *Firestorm* blends practical effects with digital trickery. Rod-operated puppets allow for greater body movements, along with enhanced facial features to allow a greater range of emotion than Supermarionation's interchangeable heads.

Firestorm's premise is in unintentional synergy with the current new Cold War emerging between America, Russia and China's various efforts in 21st century militarised space exploration. In the year 2202, the terrorist organisation Black Orchid necessitates the creation of Storm Force, a highly advanced security organisation, who proceed with Operation Firestorm to bring down Black Orchid. The first minisode hints at treachery within Storm Force itself, whilst the Kickstarter campaign teases a much larger threat at play behind the scenes. At the time of this book's publication, the series remains in development, with the assurance that a full series going into production remains an achievable target. How exactly Ultramarionation may be carried out remains to be seen, but the fact that there is a future at all for this highly cutting-edge reinvention of Supermarionation remains a hugely exciting prospect.

Whilst work on *Firestorm* progresses behind the scenes, more open to audiences are the extraordinary lengths that Century 21 Films is going to in order to preserve Supermarionation. Alongside other officially licensed works involving *Thunderbirds*, Century 21 Films' most valiant effort to keep the Supermarionation flames flickering has been *Nebula-75*. Whilst *Thunderbirds: The Anniversary Episodes* is an undisputed peak of Century 21 Films' output, it's likely that *Nebula-75* is the series that strives to be the most successful and has the brightest future. At the time of this book's publication, *Nebula-75* isn't an artefact, but an ongoing creation, a hopeful signal that this 'lost' Supermarionation series is forging and maintaining a new thirst for the retrofuture medium of space-age entertainment.

The financial capital raised during the Kickstarter campaigns for *Firestorm* and the anniversary episodes of *Thunderbirds*, along with *Nebula-75* scoring over half a million views of its episodes across social media platforms, confirm that there remains an unquenchable thirst for Supermarionation product. The story of Supermarionation now has a renewed course as new, forthcoming adventures are to be enjoyed. It no longer has an ending. Its artistic value has always been obviously apparent, but it's perhaps taken half a century for Supermarionation to be taken seriously. Supermarionation is often utilised to imagine far-flung, technologically-enhanced futures where optimism for a unified world prevailed. The future of Supermarionation itself is appearing just as positive, for the simple reason that there are people ensuring that there is a future for the art form at all.

PUBLISHING HISTORY

The Posthuman Heart of *Captain Scarlet and the Mysterons***:** First published on wearethemutants.com in August, 2019.

Marine Morals: *Stingray*'s **Aquatic Antagonists:** First published in *Andersonic* issue #24.

Supersonic Fantasies: Celebrating the Mecha of Supermarionation: First published on wearethemutants.com in January, 2020.

ABOUT THE AUTHOR

Fred McNamara is an atomic-powered writer, author and comic book editor who is based in the not-so-atomic rural landscapes of Lincolnshire. After being exposed to *Thunderbirds* and *Captain Scarlet* during their reruns on BBC Two in the early 2000s, he was never the same again. He thrills in overthinking the thematic aspects of vintage and obscure science fiction and other genre media. He's previously written for *We Are Cult*, *Starburst Magazine*, *Andersonic* and *Comic Scene*, amongst others. Between 2014 and 2020, Fred was the senior editor for the superhero/indie comic book website *A Place To Hang Your Cape*. His debut book, *Spectrum is Indestructible: An Unofficial Captain Scarlet Celebration*, was published in February 2020. He's permanently chipping away at more book-length projects whilst dipping his editorial toes into new comics. In his spare time, he wonders why he has so little spare time. He's probably the only person who thinks *Terrahawks* is as good as *Space: 1999*.